GOOD WITH THEIR HANDS

GOOD WITH THEIR HANDS

BOXERS, BLUESMEN, AND OTHER
CHARACTERS FROM THE RUST BELT

CARLO ROTELLA

UNIVERSITY OF CALIFORNIA PRESS

Berkeley / Los Angeles / London

University of California Press
Berkeley and Los Angeles, California

University of California Press, Ltd.
London, England

Portions of chapter 1 were published in substantially different form in
Critical Inquiry 25, no. 3 (spring 1999) and *Boston College Magazine*
(winter 2002). They are reprinted here by permission.

Library of Congress Cataloging-in-Publication Data

Rotella, Carlo, 1964–.
    Good with their hands : boxers, bluesmen, and other characters from the
rust belt / Carlo Rotella.
        p.   cm.
Includes bibliographical references and index.
    ISBN 0–520–22562–7 (alk. paper).
    1. United States—Social life and customs—1971–   2. United States—
Social conditions—1980–   3. United States—Intellectual life.   4. City
and town life—United States.   5. Deindustrialization—Social aspects—
United States—Case studies.   6. Work—Social aspects—United States—
Case studies.   7. Social change—United States—Case studies.
8. Creative ability—United States—Case studies.   9. Blue collar
workers—United States—Biography.   I. Title.
    E169.04 .R68 2001
    306'.0973—dc21   2001007086

Manufactured in the United States of America
10   09   08   07   06   05   04   03   02
10   9   8   7   6   5   4   3   2   1

The paper used in this publication meets the minimum requirements
of ANSI/NISO Z39.48–1992 (R 1997) (Permanence of Paper).

FOR TINA KLEIN

CONTENTS

ILLUSTRATIONS

TRUTH AND BEAUTY
IN THE RUST BELT

Remember the Key Word is 'WORK'

Sign on the wall at Goody
Petronelli's gym in Brockton

"HE HAD A GOOD PAIR of hands," said Frank Marcotrigiano about his
son Matthew, who was killed in a traffic accident on the Long Island Expressway twenty minutes before midnight on New Year's Eve 1998. The
son, a twenty-one-year-old student at Suffolk Community College, also
worked with his father, a plumber. "He was a good guy," added the
father, "just starting to come into his own in life." Matthew Marcotrigiano was more than a pair of hands, in other words, but the way in
which he was good with his hands expressed possibilities extending before and behind him: forward to the promise of a working future as a
skilled tradesman (or, should his education guide him to other employment, at least the promise of lifelong handiness around the house), but
also backward to the ground of values and virtues that undergirded his
father's worldview. "A good pair of hands" implied a thick tangle of
connections to the world, suddenly severed.[1]

"A pair of strong hands are not what they used to be," said former
senator and former professional basketball player Bill Bradley when he
was battling Al Gore for the Democratic presidential nomination in
1999. "Now those hands have to be able to use a keyboard." Bradley,
who was trying to win the support of unions away from Gore, had come
to Peterborough, New Hampshire, to talk about improving community

colleges, one of several ways that government could help Americans adjust to the demands of what he called "the new global economy." Bradley contrasted the "Norman Rockwell" world of his youth in a Missouri town to the social climate created by a high-pressure employment market that increasingly requires college-level training and obliges both parents to work. "The new global economy just doesn't care about 6:30 dinner," he said. "It doesn't care that you don't know how to use a computer. The global economy isn't worrying about you at all." America's increasingly postindustrial portion of the increasingly integrated global economy does not care if you are good with your hands, he was saying, and it does not care about ways of life that strong hands might have built. As husband and father in a two-career household, Bradley claimed to know something about what it takes to make one's way in a changed world. He had prepared his share of frozen dinners for his daughter, and, he added, returning to the image of hands, "When I took the oath of office, I raised my right hand high, but in my left hand I held Theresa Anne," his daughter.[2]

Being good with your hands is a deceptively unsimple virtue. It involves technical skill and finesse, craft mated with strength—in handling tools or machinery or raw materials or bodies in motion, in making or fixing or disassembling things, in labor or art or self-defense—but it implies much more.[3]

The hands express a larger competence. Bradley used "a pair of strong hands" to refer to skills traditionally required to make steel or assemble goods in a factory—the kind of work that has become more scarce in America's older manufacturing centers and has been thrown into unsettling new contexts during the postindustrial economy's maturation over the past forty years. Similarly, to describe a boxer as good with his or her hands encompasses the rest of the body—head movement, footwork, conditioning—but also the boxer's understanding of how to fight. So the phrase encompasses not only the strategy but also the physiology and psychology of fighting, everything from a feel for leverage to familiarity with pain. Or, as former light-heavyweight champion Bobby Czyz put it, "Good is your ability to give a beating; tough is your ability to take a beating."

But the good in "good hands," like the strength in "strong hands," means more than just competence. Frank Marcotrigiano understood his son's good hands to be connected to the fact that his son was a good guy with a good future before him. The three different nuances of good—skill, character, way of life—become aspects of one another in this portrait of a life interrupted. The power of Bill Bradley's speech, and the import of his self-portrait as the ex-ball-playing senator making dinner for his daughter, similarly resided in listeners' belief that strong hands doing skilled work had built particular ways of life infused with value. A late-night car crash upended the Marcotrigianos' world all at once; Bradley argued that economic change was doing it less dramatically, but perhaps more comprehensively, to many other people. His mention of "6:30 dinner," for instance, meant a balance between making a living and family cohesion enabled by the eight-hour workday; and, at least to some listeners, "6:30 dinner" also meant a conventional division of labor in which men who earned a family wage outside the home supported women who worked in the home and assumed the burden of child care. Technology-driven economic change had destabilized not only that frame of arrangements, he was saying, but also the larger structure of assumptions resting on it—assumptions about how to be a man or a woman, the value and meaning of work, the importance of education, the boundaries between home and job, how to identify one's place in the world.

Bradley appealed to his listeners' investment in that larger structure of assumptions, which still commands a certain normative status as the architecture of the good life. If that particular edifice of the good life as it was constructed in previous generations seems to be falling down or even in ruins these days, overthrown by forces too large for regular folks to reckon with, it still persists as a golden-age ideal that Bradley could conjure with his audience.

This is a book about some people who are good with their hands and the meaning we can find in their handiwork. I encountered them all in industrial cities that have become more or less postindustrial. How I came to these people and their work says something about the rooting of culture in a changing landscape.

Growing up on the South Side of Chicago, I came early to the Chicago blues played by master guitarist Buddy Guy (the subject of chapter 2); also to the crime movies of the 1970s, especially *The French Connection*, on which a pair of hardhanded cops-turned-moviemakers named Sonny Grosso and Eddie Egan left their fingerprints (chapter 3). I came to blues and crime movies early enough that I find it difficult now to reconstruct the paths I took to reach them. Even though both Guy's torrent-of-notes sound and *The French Connection*'s documentary feel were actually recent innovations in the 1970s, they seemed at the time to be natural elements of the aesthetic atmosphere I breathed. Happy to have stumbled upon them at an impressionable age, I assumed they had always been there. Back when I was in high school, I did not think of spending an evening at Guy's Checkerboard Lounge or watching *The French Connection* as research for a book I would write someday. I thought of that music and that movie as what I liked, in part because they fairly reeked of a certain kind of city life I recognized as familiar yet strange without knowing exactly why.

I came to boxing as a serious interest later, when I lived in Easton, Pennsylvania, a small former mill city in which former heavyweight champion Larry Holmes figures prominently. I found my way to women's boxing on an afternoon in 1996 when I went to a card of Golden Gloves bouts in nearby Bethlehem, where I happened to see a hard-hitting lefty named Liz McGonigal (the subject of chapter 1). Her fight and the uproar it inspired in the crowd probably caused the idea for this book to begin germinating in my mind, thereby proving the point made by a retired middleweight named Skeeter McClure when he told me, "Geography is destiny": seeing the Golden Gloves was one of the several but not limitlessly various things to do in the Lehigh Valley, so I went. Geography is destiny, too, in that moving from Pennsylvania to Boston in 1997 helped me find my way to nearby Brockton, Massachusetts, and its cult of Rocky Marciano—to the work of sculptor–turned–landscape artist Patricia Johanson, to the lonely crusade of a handy custodian named Mark Casieri who wanted to restore the old Marciano house, to the intertwined struggles over Marciano and the city's transformation in which they participated (chapter 4).

So, besides engaging my interest and reaffirming the power of both urban serendipity and McClure's Law of Geographical Destiny, what do boxing, urban blues, crime stories, and the refashioning of cityscapes have to do with each other? Ultimately, the answer addresses how creative people negotiate tradition and innovation in making culture, but it begins with a shared grounding in the history of work and the Rust Belt.

Like anybody else, the makers of culture I consider do not create from scratch; they have improvised within the conditions of city life in the latter part of the twentieth century. Those conditions include the particular styles—of fighting or making music, to take two relevant examples—available to them and the institutions in which novices encounter those styles and master them. Boxing styles take shape in gyms and in bouts; blues styles in bands, at clubs, at record companies.

Styles and institutions, then, provide vessels into which individuals pour their inspirations, producing distinctive forms of culture. The availability and character of work suffuse every aspect of that process—often, work is the main reason that makers of culture and their audiences live where and how they do, allowing them to come together in a critical mass of producers and consumers. Work also shapes the affinities and aptitudes of practitioners, the materials they use, the tastes and resources of their audiences, and the flow of money that allows institutions and their house styles to exist at all.

Everything, at least in this book, proceeds from and returns to work. The sure-handed characters who inhabit its pages make culture, a form of work in itself. The artifacts they make are not always transparently "about" work—a hook to the ribs or a guitar solo may not be about anything at all—but one of my main purposes is to show how a whole way of life, including the character of the labor on which it is founded, can move in the arc of a well-crafted punch or in a sequence of notes.

All of the forms of culture I consider have histories intertwined with the history of body work—by which I mean labor that may well engage the intellect but turns on physical adeptness and strength. Because they are significantly city-based, their histories intertwine in particular with the history of body work in factories, or industrial work. Boxing, blues, crime stories, and landscape design were all shaped by the three-headed process of industrialization, immigration, and urbanization that dominated American city life between the mid–nineteenth and the mid–twentieth centuries. This was the high period of industrial urbanism, by which I mean ways of living in cities organized around the manufacturing economy and its work: extracting and processing raw materials, turning them into finished goods in factories, circulating them to buyers, and maintaining the massive infrastructure this system required. Especially when seen in hindsight, which is increasingly the case, industrial work was quintessential urban body work. A nineteenth-century artisan might well have scoffed at the idea that factory workers toiling on the line were good with their hands, but a twenty-first-century customer service representative probably would not.

This is also a book about the Rust Belt. None of the forms of culture I consider is exclusively native to the old manufacturing cities of the Midwest and Northeast, but all have flourished there with special vigor. I think of "Rust Belt" as a heroic and perhaps even poetic term rather than a pejorative one. Like other "Belt" usages, it probably owes its derivation to "Bible Belt," which may have originated as a term of Menckenian contempt but becomes something else when used by those whose region and way of life it describes. To my ear, "Rust Belt" has the right ring of machined metal and weather. It resonates with hard use, also disuse and reuse. It sounds like the right name for a region in which you can always find your way to the railroad tracks or the old working waterfront. Somewhere in town there will be a district of large, solid brick buildings that once gave conventional form to the principles of labor and capital, and somewhere nearby will be stretches of workers' housing arranged tightly and neatly as if packed for a long voyage. You know where you are, whether you are in a midsize mill city like Erie or Brockton, in the once-paradigmatic industrial city of Chicago, or even in New York—which, let us not forget, was and in some ways still is a great manufacturing center. You know where you are even though—or because—the landscape has changed over time. The factory buildings and warehouses may have been shuttered or converted into loft apartments or offices. Perhaps a brew pub has moved in: "We *need* one of those," Mayor Jack Yunits of Brockton told me, speaking of his depressed downtown. The workers' housing, too, may have been gut-rehabbed or just gutted, made to age with more or less grace.

The aging of industrial urbanism in the Rust Belt, its partial collapse into history and its partial supersession by other kinds of city life, forms the general backdrop of all the local stories I tell in this book. After the midpoint of the twentieth century, the reputations of many older economic and cultural capitals of the Midwest and Northeast swung from good to tough as they registered the effects of deindustrialization, globalization, the expansion of service work, the rise of the information economy, the suburbanization of capital and population, and other processes summed up by Bill Bradley as the arrival of a "new global economy." This gradual but profound change in the form and function of cities, already under way by the Great Depression, became increasingly evident after World War II. The big—if still and perhaps forever incomplete—story readable in the landscapes and cultures of Rust Belt cities was the passing of the nineteenth-century industrial city and the emergence of the postindustrial metropolis.

In the decades after World War II, interlocking flows of people, capital, power, and ideas remade the urban landscape. Starting in the 1940s, period-defining folk migrations flowed into midcentury America's two promised lands: black southerners to the northern inner city, predominantly white urbanites to the suburbs. At the same time, public and private capital flowed from city to suburbs, from Rust Belt to Sun Belt, and, crucially, from manufacturing to the service sector. Cities that had been organized primarily around the processing of raw materials into finished goods in factories were significantly reorganized around the provision of services and handling of information. Progrowth coalitions of business and government built highways, airports, convention centers, high-rise office buildings and residences, and other vital elements of the postindustrial city. To make room they labeled as "blight" and cleared what had been vital elements of the industrial city—railroad tracks, factory districts, and especially the industrial neighborhood orders typified by densely packed low-rise workers' housing.[4]

The major urban news stories of the past thirty or forty years have added chapters to this account of the layering-under of industrial urbanism. The urban crisis of the late 1960s, with its spectacular riots and apocalyptic talk of cities at the edge of disaster, gave way to fiscal emergencies and the final collapse of important city-based heavy industries in the 1970s. Sensational news of crack plagues and conflicts over gentrification in the 1980s gave way to stories of an urban boom and a widening gap between the urban rich and poor in the 1990s. That boom was driven by all sorts of forces, including prosperity and new immigration, but in particular by suburbanites' return to remodeled cities and by the increasing sophistication of culture-based economic development in entertainment and historic districts. The changes brought on by both crises and recoveries often came especially hard to urban villages and mill cities, places that had been thoroughly organized around the skilled labor of industrial workers. As familiar arrangements of work and play broke up, as familiar neighborhoods underwent disorienting adjustments, people felt themselves pulled up or down or otherwise out of the lives and communities they knew. And, once again, money proved to be more fluidly responsive to technological change and other macroeconomic processes than did place-based ways of life.

These transformations directly and indirectly affected cultural orders that had flourished in industrial cities. In Erie, as we will see, the waning of industrial urbanism destabilized the edifice of masculinity built on the principle of being good with one's hands at work and in the ring. That created an opportunity for Liz McGonigal, a female psychologist-in-training who was not even from Erie, to become a local hero by upholding the city's honor with her fists. In Chicago, the blues world made possible by industrial work began to fall apart in the 1960s, but the postindustrial city's emergence helped make possible a new blues synthesis that replaced it. That created an opportunity for Buddy Guy to find a new audience for his changing music, and to make some money. In New York, the layering-under of the urban village by the postindustrial inner city demanded and made possible a new order of American crime movies. That created an opportunity for Sonny Grosso and Eddie Egan, streetwise neighborhood guys, to help craft a revised cinematic style suited to exploring the revised social landscape. In Brockton, planning elites and citizens confronted the problem of what to do with the physical plant and cultural legacies of industrial urbanism when the mills cease to mill. That created an opportunity for both the internationally prominent artist Patricia Johanson and the highly motivated regular guy Mark Casieri to take a hand in shaping the city's history and future.

The protagonists of this book, makers of culture, have worked in these changing urban conditions, fashioning new things from the resources and opportunities made available to them by city life in the Rust Belt. They are all, in some sense, pioneers, and not only as stylistic innovators. They have incited disputes by testing the color and gender and class lines we draw to keep culture tidy. Often, they pursue their motivations against the grain, forcing their way into situations in which convention dictates they do not belong. Liz McGonigal's entry into the male preserve of boxing may be the most dramatic example, and Patricia Johanson's stormy cameo in the long-running local soap opera about Brockton's toughness may be the most melodramatic, but all have made similarly bold moves against the grain. Their work incites disputes, too, over the durability, flexibility, and portability of local traditions and materials bearing the marks of industrial urbanism. Because their pioneering often takes the form of salvaging usable parts from the ruins of risen-and-fallen cultural arrangements, the tangs of both atavism and heresy adhere to their handiwork. Forward-looking and backward-reaching, laying claim to a traditional sense of place but also helping to transform that sense of place, their careers and creations attest to the layered, overlapping quality of city life.

The "post" in "postindustrial" does not amount to a claim that "America doesn't make things anymore," as Mayor Yunits of Brockton put it. The "post" suggests, rather, that subsequent layers of economic and social arrangements have at least partially succeeded factory-based manufacturing as a defining condition of American life. Reacting to the aging of industrial urbanism and especially to the departure of factory jobs from the Rust Belt in the latter part of the twentieth century, trend spotters have been perhaps overly quick to attach a nostalgic aura to good hands and body work. Advertisers, Internet zealots, and advocates of historical tourism, among others, have encouraged Americans to regard the industrial working class—and its signature places, like the urban village and the mill city—as native to an elapsed age rapidly receding into misty antiquity. The term "blue-collar," increasingly detached from any reference to work done by the industrial working class, is often used today to describe any style distinguished by skillful diligence rather than flashy inspiration—hence the notion of unshifty running backs or unhandsome political candidates as blue-collar stylists. Separating the virtue from the work to which it inheres, this use of "blue-collar" eulogizes actual blue-collar labor in such a way as to end up prematurely dismissing it as an anachronism. Millions of people who leave their jobs bone tired and sore could tell you that it is plain wrong to say that nobody does body work in America anymore, or that we all do brain work and face work in a service- and information-dominated economy.

But it is more and more true, as Bill Bradley asserted in his appeal to unionized voters, that body work no longer occupies the center-stage position in the material and imaginative lives of Americans that it did until the latter part of the twentieth century. Especially in cities, it has increasingly become an object of historical memory. Stripped of the prickly details of historical particularity—plants do not just close, their owners close them over employees' protests—some forms of body work and associated aspects of industrial urbanism have acquired myth-historical status. Steelworkers serve as golden-age figures of manly productivity in the marketing of clothes or trucks. Trolley cars, or buses designed to resemble them, indicate the presence of History in a neighborhood officially designated as interesting. Boxing, blues, and other work-suffused cultural forms serve to mark a certain kind of old-school authenticity, which might explain the tendency of advertisers to draw upon them: both Burger King and Pizza Hut, for instance, have run ad campaigns that take a belt-and-suspenders approach to authenticity by using *both* blues and boxing. Like the vanishing Indians in *Dances with Wolves,* who obligingly pause while being shuffled off the Western stage to deed the authentic essence of their culture to Kevin Costner, these embodiments of the old ways are made to give up the ghost with a kind of untroubled fatalism. The history and legacy of industrial urbanism deserve more humane, more open-ended stories.

"How much history can be transmitted by pressure on a guitar string?" When Robert Palmer posed this rhetorical question at the end of *Deep Blues,* he had in mind not only a universal tale known by "any human being who's ever felt the blues come down like showers of rain" but also a particular, well-known account of black history that culminates in migration from rural South to urban North.[5] When you are done reading chapter 2 of this book, I want you to hear other stories moving within and around Buddy Guy's guitar playing. The yoked transformations of Chicago and Chicago blues include two *other* great migrations: the movement of the blues business from the black South Side to the white North Side and the shift of musical emphasis from voice to guitar. Similarly, I want your reading of the book's other chapters to inspire a reckoning with the multiple and, I hope, equally familiar and unfamiliar stories within and around a women's boxing match, an early 1970s crime movie, a partially restored two-family house on a quiet street in a shoemaking city that has largely ceased to make shoes.

But I do not want to reduce these artifacts or the makers of culture who create them to merely functional conduits of period and place. I feel obliged to regard aspects of the makers' gifts or characters as irrecoverably personal, beyond my ability to explain. I would insist on it. I do not wish to explain away everything about Buddy Guy's distinctive musical diction. I would not presume to account for his taste for noise or his desire to please an audience. The same goes for, say, Eddie Egan's theatrical flair or Mark Casieri's persistence. But the effect of even the most deeply personal impulses can be located in history; and, vice versa, the shaping flows of history can be located even in artifacts that owe much to their makers' irretrievably personal impulses. I do that by locating makers of culture and their handiwork in relation to overlapping shifts over time in cultural styles, institutions, audiences, ways of life, and the landscape of the Rust Belt in which they all have worked.

I would be less than honest if I did not add that my own family's story helps to charge my subjects with meaning, at least for me, because it replicates in miniature some of the history and principles taken up in the following pages.

My grandparents were good with their hands. On my father's side were artisans: a carpenter and a seamstress who moved from a small town in Sicily to Asmara, in Eritrea, and eventually to New York. For Italian immigrants to America, they arrived late and from an odd direction, Africa, but they followed the classic formula. When their ship passed the Statue of Liberty to make port on the day after Christmas in 1951, relatives waited at dockside to help them set up a home in Queens and find work. On my mother's side were artists: a pianist-conductor-composer and a violinist, Catalans well embedded in the musical culture of Barcelona. They did not emigrate to America; their daughter came by herself in 1958, under the auspices of the Sisters of Mercy and then the University of Chicago. All four grandparents made things of beauty—furniture, dresses, music—and all of them made a living at it, which occasioned plenty of scrambling during wars and depressions. All were good with their hands in ways that expressed a larger competence: an understanding of wood and metal, of fabrics and bodies, of harmony and melody. And, at least as I know their legacies, their expertise figured prominently in the construction of ways of life that still matter to their descendants. They have handed down attitudes toward work and play, a sense of the interconnectedness of art and commerce. They have handed down, also, a respect for the priorities of genre and local cultures—*this* is how they make it *here, this* is how they play it *there*. Those and other influences obtain in this book and in descendants' lives that do not resemble my grandparents' lives in many details.

My naturalized American parents, both of them academics, and their American children—a reporter, a professor, a lawyer—handle information and deal in words. None of us makes a living with his or her hands and body in the ways my grandparents did, or in the ways that industrial urbanism once made obligatory for arriving immigrants and their children. I grew up in South Shore, on the South Side of Chicago, which used to be America's industrial city of the future—Hog Butcher, Freight Handler, you know the old song and dance of the Big Shoulders. The two houses in which I grew up are both about a block from the old Illinois Central tracks that lead to the nearby East Side, once one of the world's great concentrations of steel mills and other heavy industry. I have lived in or near most of the old manufacturing centers I write about in this book; I have, in fact, lived all my life in midwestern and northeastern cities, large and small, with significant industrial pedigrees—the first eighteen years in Chicago, the next twenty in Middletown (Connecticut), West New York (New Jersey), Brooklyn, New Haven, Easton (Pennsylvania), and Boston. But all my expectations and aptitudes for making a living are postindustrial: the first working instinct drilled into me by experience and a late-twentieth-century education has always been to go get some information and start kneading it.

The first urban instinct drilled into me by the South Side, and reinforced by the other cities in which I have lived and poked around, has always been that both landscapes and cultures accrue in layers. You can

make your way along the railroad tracks—or along the stylistic con-
tours of a fight, a song, a movie, a public debate, a life story—to the
persistent past and the formative future. And, while cataloging first in-
stincts and training, I should also admit that the cities in which I have
lived also inhabit me in return: I am not impartial, especially when it
comes to Rust Belt history and aesthetics. Navigating in this book
through layers of landscape and culture, I want us to make our way to
truth and beauty as I have found them in places that matter to me.

Competences and perhaps virtues have been lost and gained, but my
family's story is not one of decline or of ascent (except, generationally,
in class status); it, like the stories told in this book, is an account of layering. On the desk where I work at home is a formal photograph of my
Sicilian grandmother taken in the 1920s, when she was in her late teens
or early twenties, with her parents and two of her siblings. The parents
sit; their son and two daughters stand behind them. The fashionable
young seamstress smiles a bit, leaning an elbow playfully on her brother's shoulder, but the others pose stiffly in their Sunday best, glowering
at the camera in the standard Sicilian manner of that (or any) period.
The fiercely mustached father, my great-grandfather, dangles one rock-
like hand in his lap and clutches a pair of dress gloves in the other. He
looks as if he would be a lot more comfortable using his bare hands and
feet to bend semipliable stalks into baskets, which is what he did for a
living. Next to the picture, buried where I can find it under papers and
books, is one of my grandmother's thimbles, worn smooth with use.
Get to work, the picture and thimble say, and make it good.

1

THE CULTURE OF THE HANDS

Things change. Now . . . we have women boxers. Look, I know it's not politically correct to say this, but I'm against women boxing. I've got no problem with women as referees or judges. But women are too precious to get banged up. I see women as a minority, just like black folks, and recognize that they're discriminated against. I'm sympathetic to them. Fact is, I don't like to see women driving big tractors or fighting with guns in a war. I like to see women doing things that aren't hazardous to their health.

Larry Holmes, former heavyweight champion

They say that men box to get out of the ghetto. I joke that boxing was my way into *the ghetto.*

Kate Sekules, author, travel editor of *Food & Wine*, boxer

I FIRST SAW Liz McGonigal fight at the Golden Gloves competition held in Bethlehem, Pennsylvania, in April 1996. Young amateur fighters and their retinues of trainers, parents, broken-nosed uncles, and advice-shouting friends had gathered from all over the state in the big gymnasium at Liberty High School to contest the state novice-class championships. Success in the novice class allows a fighter to move up through what is left of the fight network's strata—into the open amateur class, where more experienced opponents await, and perhaps eventually into the local professional circuit, the regional, the national. In Bethlehem that evening the most polished boxers, narrow-waisted and black, came from Philadelphia. For the most part they managed their rougher-edged opponents like toreadors coaxing performances from tank-town bulls. The biggest hitters came from Pittsburgh, blocky white guys throwing bombs with both hands. Most of the fighters came not from these metropolitan bookends of Pennsylvania but from the small cities and big towns that lie between and around them, places whose names still bear the resonance of heavy industry long past the time when fac tory work was the principal livelihood available to their residents: Bethlehem, Allentown, Easton, Erie, Lancaster, Harrisburg, Scranton, Hanover, York, Altoona, Mechanicsburg. These Pennsylvania mill cities, and others like them, were a cradle of the American Industrial Revolution in the nineteenth century and a heartland of manufacturing well into the twentieth. But on this April evening, Bethlehem's last rolling mill and blast furnace had been cold for six months. For the first time since before the Civil War, no steel was being made in town, and the Bethlehem Steel Company, which had played such an important role in building America's cities and military, had cut its local workforce to a mere twelve hundred employees, down from a high of thirty-one thousand in the 1940s.[1] The fighters climbed through the ropes at an uncertain moment when many people in town, and no doubt many people at the fights, were wondering what the city's next organizing principle would be: the Christmas City? Affordable housing for transient service professionals within commuting distance of the office parks of suburban New Jersey? Historical tourism built around oddly paired nostalgias for the Moravians' progressive moral rectitude and the heroic productivity of Big Steel?

The emotional peaks of the event came early. Angel Nales, a local high school hero who trained at the Larry Holmes Training Center in nearby Easton, won his 112-pound bout against Ernie Bizzarro, one of the fighting Bizzarros of Erie. It was the first bout of the card, an undistinguished affair in which both kids threw plenty of punches, most of which did not conform to the textbook definitions of jab, cross, hook, and uppercut. Bizzarro might have been the more accomplished boxer, but he lost the initiative and forgot his craft. The judges' decision in favor of Nales seemed fair, but the Bizzarro corner erupted when it was announced. Even before the crowd was settled in its seats, there were paunchy men in sweat clothes shouting and passionately restraining one another while guards rushed to ringside to calm everybody down. After the Bizzarro Boxing Club faction stormed off, the audience settled in happily, like fighters who have broken a sweat and are ready to get to work.

After a few more bouts, though, they were beginning to fidget again, since three-round amateur scuffles between novices tend to resemble one another and do not often feature spectacular knockdowns. The crowd's attention was reclaimed before intermission, though, by the evening's one bout between women: Liz McGonigal of Erie's Lower East Side Boxing Club versus Sarah Kump of the Hanover Boxing Club. Kump was a head taller and at least twenty pounds heavier, an advantage so enormous that the tournament's organizers behaved unethically in offering the matchup to the fighters' trainers. The first time Kump whacked McGonigal with a right, the smaller woman was lifted up and thrown back a step as if by a strong wind. Kump, however, was the greenest of beginners, and McGonigal, though still a novice, was not. McGonigal looked at home in the ring: surefooted and quick-handed, nicely balanced in her southpaw fighting crouch; always in motion seeking a line of attack; light on her feet, heavy with her punches. She clearly knew how to box, but after tasting her opponent's advantage in power and reach, she dispensed with fistic nuance and went for a quick knockout. The two women spent most of the first round exchanging murderous blows like granite-jawed movie heroes. Kump loaded up big right hands, which usually missed; when she did land one, it knocked McGonigal back on her heels. McGonigal, for her part, punched more crisply and with either hand, navigating past Kump's long arms to land left-right-left combinations to the head. Between rounds, McGonigal's cornerman reminded her to keep moving from side to side as she bored in, thus neutralizing Kump's ponderous right leads. McGonigal, embarrassed at having let herself be drawn into so unlovely a brawl, weaved contritely on her stool to show she understood and would do better. She returned to work with greater precision, and by the middle of the second round Kump was almost finished—beat-up, arm-weary, and winded. The referee stopped McGonigal's battering of Kump along the ropes to administer a standing eight-count, at the end of which he asked Kump if she wished to continue. Her ambiguous answer—it looked like she said, "I can't breathe"—obliged him to stop the fight.

The paying audience responded to the bout with the curious mix of prurient hysteria and sporting fervor that female boxers excite in fight crowds, which are overwhelmingly male. Most of the men in the Liberty High School gym were sports fans rather than boxing fans, and most of them were Lehigh Valley sports fans who reserve their appreciation of technique for high school wrestling and professional auto racing; so they were not particularly interested in pugilistic niceties. Like most people at the fights, who want to see rolling heads rather than accomplished footwork, they were happy to see lots of punching and drama. But they were especially moved by a fight between women. They may have enjoyed it for the same reasons they enjoy offense-heavy slugfests between stalwart men, but they also responded to the action as if it were a kind of advanced Jell-O wrestling or striptease, with damage replacing flesh as the dirty female thing to be revealed. When Kump began to break down under the smaller woman's assault, her head snapping back with the punches and her face reddening, they whooped and howled like conventioneers at a strip joint. This wild electric climate, part sex and part violence, was only partially tamed by protestations of more conventional sporting admiration—"those young ladies are really scrapping, buddy"—offered most earnestly by men who were there with wives or children and therefore felt obliged to reel in their tongues off the floor. Both reactions, the prurient and the sporting, were about girls and about boxing and about women boxing—three different things—at the same time.

The contrast between the fighters and the ring girls further complicated the crowd's responses. In the last twenty years there has been a significant increase in the number of female noncombatants one might see at the fights—seconds, judges, referees, ring physicians, lawyers. But until the upsurge in women's boxing in the 1990s, the only women one could count on seeing in the ring during a fight were the ring girls, who, uniformed in swimwear and high heels, climb through the ropes between rounds with a signature bend-and-wriggle motion and sashay around the inside perimeter of the ropes with a card indicating the number of the next round. The traditional division of labor in pugilistic spectacle has men fighting while ring girls do a different kind of public body work more closely related to sex work than to manual labor. The ring girls at the Golden Gloves in Bethlehem had the long legs, prominent breasts, and glossy hair expected of them, they had obviously spent time working out in the gym to tone their bodies, and they had more flesh on display than did the female fighters (since the fighters wore shorts and sleeveless T-shirts), but compared with the fighters, they looked unsavory, even sickly. Kump, bigger and darker than McGonigal, was strong and well built, with a tattoo of Superman's S insignia high on one shoulder blade. McGonigal was compact and graceful, in fine fighting trim, with a smart, sharp-featured face and a thick blond braid swinging down her back in rhythmic counterpoint to the movements of her boxing style. On her shoulder blade she wore a tattoo of the Tasmanian Devil, the perpetual-motion cartoon character who rips insatiably through trees and everything else in his path. Stalking and planting to throw punches, the fighters made the ring girls' shapely calves and buttocks, tensed by high heels, seem like side effects of some unhealthy hobbling practice akin to foot binding.

Some of the more demonstrative men in the crowd had hooted and called out perceptive remarks the first few times the ring girls made their rounds, but after a while the novelty began to wear off for all but the most dedicated poltroons. The women's bout, though, touched off a more general surge of wolfish behaviors that felt like an extension of the ring girls' reception. Something about potent, capable women in the ring caused even men who had been silent before to throw off their reserve and howl not just for female flesh but for women's blood (at least the kind that emerges north of the waistline). Evidently, it was stirring to see these women fight, and it was important to see at least one of them hurt. In the second round, when McGonigal was nailing Kump with solid punches and the referee was getting ready to step between them to wave off the fight, it sounded as if a hotly contested high school basketball game and a giant stag party were being held at the same time in the old gym.

When it was over, with the crowd abuzz and Kump sitting blearily on her stool in the corner, McGonigal stood in the center of the ring amid the usual postfight chaos of seconds and officials. Her trainer had taken off her headgear and gloves and jammed a billed Everlast cap on her head. As she made her way to her corner to descend from the raised ring, a photographer rushed up an aisle to the ring apron and called out to her. She turned to give him a traditional dukes-up pose: hands still taped, chin tucked in, eyes meeting the camera, a cool smile that both disdained this regrettably necessary game of publicity and promised another butt-whipping to whoever messed with her next. I followed the line of her gaze through the cameraman and into the crowd, where it transfixed a guy one row ahead of me and a few seats over. He had come to my attention earlier because he knew two tricks he thought worth repeating over and over: one was holding up a dollar bill and yelling, "Come get your money, baby" when the loveliest ring girl did her turn with the round card; the other was loudly heckling another ring girl whom he found insufficiently appealing. Now he was standing, openmouthed but silent, looking up at McGonigal. It was hard to tell from my vantage point—or perhaps from any—whether the look on his face was one of awe or rage.

This little triangular encounter, occurring at the junction of many tangled lines of social force and historical circumstance that linked the young fighters and their audience to the mill cities of Pennsylvania, made me wonder how it came to pass that women in the ring had moved the crowd so powerfully on that April evening in Bethlehem. I wanted to find out how a woman becomes a fighter and pursues her craft in places where skilled labor and rough sport—two ways of being good with one's hands—have been traditionally yoked as manly body work. A *New York Times* reporter, writing an elegiac piece about "life after steel" in Bethlehem, captured the conventional wisdom about factory work and manhood in a nutshell when he observed that the steel industry and other heavy manufacturing work have traditionally provided jobs that not only pay well but also have special added value in the calculus of American masculinity: "It is also gloriously proud and male work." This calculus is especially ingrained in regional culture: "Bethlehem and steel have long been intertwined, much as Kentucky and bourbon, Wisconsin and cheese, Winston-Salem and cigarettes," and one can extend the local relationship between Bethlehem and steel to embrace Pennsylvania and heavy industry in general.[2] The contraction of heavy industrial work and the expansion of service work in the latter part of this century—the complex, layered process condensed into the word "postindustrial"—have been intertwined with changes in what it means for men and women to work and play. Boxing is the sport farthest from play and closest to work, especially body work. Women in the ring, good with their hands, inspire in fight crowds powerful reactions that seem to be both about the isolated sphere of boxing and about a set of related matters—among them the character of work, the value of skilled aggression, definitions of manhood and womanhood—that frame boxing within a larger social world. I wanted to understand the encounter of female fighters and their audience within the specialized confines of the fight world, which has grown increasingly alien to Americans as boxing has taken on the air of an esoteric throwback practice. But I also wanted to understand female fighters, their audiences, and the fight world in relation to a social landscape that was changing around them.

ERIE

I went to Erie to see where Liz McGonigal came from. It takes six hours to drive from Easton (where I lived) to Erie on the interstates, straight west almost all the way across Pennsylvania and then up to the lakeshore. If you cut a corner by departing the westbound interstate early and taking smaller roads to go north, you pass through brick-and-wood towns like Clarion and Oil City, up through Titusville to Centerville and Union City. In this part of the world, the winding two-lane road runs between heavily wooded hillsides, briefly becomes a main street as it passes through a town, then curves out the other side of town, where the trees crowd down to the shoulder once more. Between towns there are hunting lodges, motels, antique shops. In the fall, bearded men in bulky camouflage jackets with cased rifles stand around smoking next to pickups parked on the shoulder. Erie boosters make a habit of deploying tables of comparative weather data to prove that Erie is not as cold and snowy as one might imagine (Fewer cloudy days than Pittsburgh! Less average annual snowfall than Buffalo!), but my sense of approaching the place—having made the trip the first time in November—is of gradually sharpening cold air, windblown eddies of snow skeining on the road surface, and wet, black branches and trunks making strong lines against white hillsides.

Erie is a foursquare little city surrounded by suburbs and malls and bolted onto the southern shore of Lake Erie. State Street runs south from the lakefront through the downtown and up a gently rising slope to the South Side, where Mercyhurst College, the Veterans Administration hospital, and some of the city's most prosperous neighborhoods are located. Bisecting the city's rectangular layout, State Street divides the East Side from the West. Some people in town consider the East Side, where the giant General Electric plant is located, to be the "grittier" (by which it is meant both the more blue collar and the poorer) part of town; some consider the West Side, with higher land and housing values and a higher proportion of tidy residential blocks, to be more respectable (or less suffused with character) than the East Side. A pleasing collection of midsize prewar buildings dominates the downtown, and more recent architecture has been mixed into that older urban texture with less ground-clearing urgency than is evident in other Rust Belt cities. Erie's principal historical attractions, a bicentennial tower and the Flagship Niagara museum that exploits the American victory over the British at the Battle of Lake Erie in 1813, are sited on the central axis just north of downtown where State Street meets the lakefront. The Presque Isle peninsula, joined to the mainland just west of the city and curving out offshore to enclose a bay, forms the backbone of a lively Rust Belt riviera during the summer—which seems like a long time ago when winter ice storms buffet the motels and beachfront facilities. On one return visit to Erie in

March, I had one of only four or five occupied rooms at a downtown motel: the sound of wind-driven ice particles hitting the north-facing metal door of my room was so insistent that I turned off the television and the lights, opened the curtains, wrapped myself in musty quilts off the bed, and spent most of the night in an armchair by the window watching lonely cars in the parking lot rocking in the gusts.

I was in town that time to see the Golden Gloves competition of 1997, which was hosted at Headliners, a West Side nightclub, by the Lower East Side Boxing Club. The crowd at Headliners was full of thick-shouldered, helmet-haired men and women in black T-shirts or shiny windbreakers. The sound of countless plastic beer cups being drained and crushed underfoot approximated that of a spirited exchange of musketry, and nonstop smokers created hanging blue clouds that limited our already obscured view of the feebly lit ring. I sat in front of a large bloc of GE employees, who cheered lustily for the East Siders in their struggles against devious outlanders from abodes of effeteness like Pittsburgh, Altoona, and the West Side. The GE crew vigilantly studied the fighters for signs of flashiness, retrograde movement, or other indicators of questionable virtue. On those rare occasions when a young amateur blocked or slipped a punch or otherwise showed signs of passing familiarity with the manly art of self-defense, voices from behind me would yell, "Showboat! Get to work!" The East Siders were therefore displeased when Lou Bizzarro Jr., the talented standard-bearer for the next generation of fighting Bizzarros (who are West Siders), took the decision in the evening's big local grudge match by outboxing Jose Otero. The latter, an intense-looking guy with dark hair parted in the middle and frightening basket-weave stomach muscles (also parted in the middle), represented the Lower East Side Boxing Club. Bizzarro, expertly neutralizing the endlessly game Otero's rushes and sticking him with hard counterpunches and combinations, had very evidently won every round, so the crowd could not complain that Otero was robbed, but there were rumblings nonetheless. A greasy-bearded biker type seated near me turned to his pals and said, "If they're giving points for moving around and punching, that's one thing. But what about taking it to the other guy?" Everyone nodded and drank beer glumly, considering the dark implications of the thought.

The East Siders were reassured, though, by local darling Liz McGonigal's fight. Once again matched out of her weight class, this time against a Pittsburgh beanpole who was six inches taller and (no matter what the program claimed) about twenty pounds heavier than she,

Liz McGonigal works the speed bag. Photo: Vince Moskalczyk, *Erie Times-News*. Reprinted with permission of Times Publishing Company, Erie, Pa., © 2002.

McGonigal upheld the Lower East Side Boxing Club's honor. She bored in against long jabs, taking her punishment and giving some back, and won a questionable decision on the strength of her indomitable advance rather than her considerable boxing skills, which were largely negated by her opponent's advantage in reach. Prurience did not audibly animate the crowd's reaction to the women's fight as it had in Bethlehem, where McGonigal was a blond stranger. In Erie she was local and widely respected as a scrapper, and she had many friends in the crowd—plus, this time her opponent was not a babe. The hometown fans (and, apparently, the judges) wanted to see a local boy or girl wade into an opponent, absorbing punishment in order to dish it out, and gradually wear down that opponent by relentless application of the local virtues: gumption, elbow grease, strength, resilience. They wanted to see the local heroes impose their will on their own and the other fighters' bodies—which one might see as recalcitrant pieces of machinery or raw material, depending on how one wishes to cast the industrial metaphor. The blows absorbed and sweat expended by the local fighter in persevering were of primary importance; the hero had to labor spectacularly as an earnest of his or her representativeness. Without such suffering, the victory was too cheap and smacked of white-collar work, a puling matter of loophole exploiting and rule bending.

The GE line workers who supported Liz McGonigal so devoutly are the standard-bearers of industrial Erie's social order and cultural traditions. Erie is still recognizably the city it became during the high-industrial period between the Civil War and the Great Depression. Its physical form still tells the story of a place shaped by the processes of gathering raw materials (ore, grain, coal, rubber, wood), turning them into products (locomotives, machine tools, building hardware, hospital supplies, castings), and circulating them (Erie was an important railroad city, lake port, and canal nexus). Postindustrial expressways and poured-concrete buildings are contained within the older frame made by the port, railroad tracks, brick factory buildings lining the Twelfth Street corridor, the GE locomotive works that dominates the East Side, and rows of workers' housing flanking what were once immigrants' parish churches. Erie's demography also bears the imprint of migrations that supplied the growing city with factory workers in the late nineteenth and early twentieth centuries: people of German descent form the largest ethnic group, followed by Poles, blacks, Italians, the Irish, Yankees who drifted west, and Hispanics who found their way north. That mix is typical of the inland Rust Belt, so typical that test marketers often use Erie as a guinea pig for commercial and political campaign strategies. The industrial-era infrastructure and demography are not just of historical interest: Erie is still a manufacturing city. In the last fifty years, the percentage of American workers employed in manufacturing has been contracting (to about 12 percent of total employment in the nation, a bit more in the state) and the service sector has been expanding, but about 25 percent of Erie's working residents still make things in the city's diverse and often homegrown factory enterprises. Of course, as is the case elsewhere in the Rust Belt, technological advances have allowed the manufacturing sector to get more productivity out of fewer and fewer workers. GE may still be the city's largest employer, and there are other industrial firms on the list of the city's most important employers, but the list is dominated by hospitals, schools, an insurance company, government, supermarkets, and fast-food outlets. The GE plant may be the city's most imposing structure, but the giant mall in suburban Millcreek functions as the region's central business place, attracting shoppers from northwest Pennsylvania, Ohio, New York, and Canada.[3] The city's industrial sector and the cultural and social traditions that grew up with it may no longer be dominant, but they enjoy the special cachet of tradition because they trail long roots in local senses of past and place.

The history of boxing in Erie intertwines with the city's industrial history. Erie was never a particularly important fight town and certainly is not one today, but like almost all Rust Belt cities, it was a thriving outpost of the fight world between the late nineteenth century and World War II. A sampling of local heroes from this period makes a map of the city's immigrant ethnic–dominated industrial working class: Nonnie Kane, Bing Welsch, Leo Finneran, Billy Purdy, Kid Gleason, Derby Giles, Jerry Cole, Young Frank (an Italian), Kid Xeny (Xenophon Kakouras), Jimmy Dean (a popular black fighter), Tommy Freeman, Heavy Andrews, Maxie Strub, Frankie Bojarski.[4] In that period, the golden age of boxing as an American institution, there flourished in Erie a network of gyms and clubs, amateur organizations, and professionals across the range from local club fighters to creditable national figures. This network, and the national network of which it was a part, sustained itself because it attracted paying audiences and because it provided niches for men of various skills and at every stage of a fighter's life. From amateur novice to retired professional, fight people within the network met one another's demands for opponents, sparring partners, trainers, managers, students, referees, and so on. As a boxing city, Erie served as the central place of a minor region comprising the mill towns of northwest Pennsylvania, each with its own local network, and was in turn a satellite of Cleveland, Pittsburgh, Detroit, and other capitals of the fight world. Scores, perhaps hundreds, of practicing boxers lived in the city and surrounding towns, and a large audience followed boxing. If most of those fans went to the fights to see blood and guts, a minority of connoisseurs cultivated some appreciation of boxing skill and supported fighters who demonstrated it, and in any case both kinds of fans went to the fights regularly.

The industrial working class produced most of the fighters and most of their audience. Many Erie fighters and fight fans worked in local factories, and one can see a further intertwining of industrial work and boxing in GE's sponsorship of amateur boxing in the 1930s.[5] The GE plant was a kind of town within the city, with its own busy civic life, a newspaper, cultural and social organizations, and athletic leagues. Jim Donnelly, an employee at the East Line Assembly that made flat-top refrigerators, had been a professional boxer and had trained, managed, and promoted local professionals before becoming GE's in-house fight promoter and trainer in 1932. In 1936 he had thirty-two men, all of them GE employees or affiliates, in training at the company gym six days a week for amateur bouts against opponents in Erie, surrounding towns like Meadville and Titusville, and cities as far away as Syracuse and Rochester. Many of those opponents also represented industrial employers. Retired Erie fighters served as referees and judges on Friday evenings at GE Field, where for fifteen cents one could watch a card of bouts as well as a baseball game, all featuring GE athletes. "Interest in the Friday night bouts this year is more enthusiastic than ever before," reported the always boosterish company paper in 1936, "and as the crowds increase, better boxers will appear—the worth of the talent depending on the size of the patronage."[6] Both management and shop-floor workers were invested in the fight world, and their patronage, measured not just by financial backing or size of crowds but also by the extent and integration of the region's boxing network, produced skilled boxers. The institutional arrangements of industrial labor and boxing—two forms of skilled body work—fit together like hand and glove, and the precipitous contraction of the fight network in the industrial heartland has paralleled the contraction of factory work in the last fifty years.

Erie's fight network and industrial sector may be much reduced in comparison to those of the century's early decades, but they persist, and there continues to be a vital connection between them. In 1997, when Liz McGonigal had a chance to go down to Georgia to compete for the women's national amateur title in the 112-pound class, GE workers donated the $2,500 she needed to make the trip. "They had a party at a bar with a five-dollar cover and a raffle," she told me, "and people came up with five or ten dollars or whatever they could. The GE people, the East Siders, who don't always have a lot of money, they always support me." It was a reminder that boxing, as a form of rough, work-related play, still retains its cachet in what the sociologist Kathryn Dudley calls "the culture of the hands," the system of values and meaning that evolved around the sweat and shopfloor cooperation of industrial body work. Dudley contrasts the culture of the hands with a competing worldview associated with service-professional work, the "culture of the mind" built around intellectual credentials and individual self-improvement.[7] The GE hands cared that a hardworking local girl who was good with her hands—even one who, as we shall see, was also deeply invested in the culture of the mind—had a chance to make good. They pooled their limited resources to put their money behind their convictions.

McGonigal fought out of the Lower East Side Boxing Club, a fragmentary revival of the old fight world network during its postindustrial contraction. GE workers, this time with no significant help from management, have been instrumental in rebuilding what is now regarded as an esoteric institution—the local boxing gym—that their grandfathers and even their fathers would have taken for granted as part of the fabric of the old neighborhood. After the city's remaining gyms closed in the 1960s and 1970s, a group of men started the Lower East Side Boxing Club in the late 1970s, not to save boxing in Erie but to give East Side kids a place to go. "It started out as a place for kids to go who didn't have anything," said Matt DeForce, the dedicated, patient, reddish-blond-bearded man who runs the club and trains its fighters. "A bunch of friends started it who were basically the tough guys in town. We had poorer backgrounds, working-class backgrounds. We had ironworkers, bricklayers, painters, and five or six GE guys." DeForce was one of the GE guys, a rigger-millwright who set up and maintained machinery at the plant. (He retired in 2000.) The kids who have come into the club over the years make up a motley bunch: white and black and Hispanic, male and (lately) female, curious athletes and dead-end kids, young people headed variously for the shopfloor or college or nothing much at all. Most of them dabble, do it for the exercise and fighter's confidence, and drift away; some do well as amateurs, a few turn pro and win some fights.

In the 1970s the mayor gave the club an abandoned turn-of-the-century firehouse on the depressed eastern fringe of downtown, but, DeForce said, the city later threw them out when the block went upscale during a resurgence of historical renovation. It turned out that the owners of a new restaurant coveted the picturesque site. The restaurant, named the Pufferbelly after a nickname given to steam pumpers and engines of the late nineteenth century, is a classic postindustrial reuse of an atmospheric industrial-era brick building. I went there for dinner once. Everything on the menu was spuriously presented as the product of exacting workmanship mixed with healthy good sense, as if old-time craftspeople with a New Age horror of saturated fats were in the back doing the cooking. Flipping past the menu's pages of char-grilled, hand-tossed, and apricot-glazed selections, I encountered a history of the Erie Fire Department's early days, an account of the building's construction, and an invitation to prove the vaunted synergy of historical tourism dollars by visiting the nearby Firefighters Historical Museum, Inc. A capsule account of twentieth-century urbanism lurks in the displacement of the boxing club by the restaurant, which sells as atmosphere the history of high-industrial-era masculinity embodied once upon a time by mustachioed firefighters and now by the restaurant's period decor.

Since being evicted, the Lower East Side Boxing Club has moved several times—"*always* on the East Side," insisted DeForce. When I began visiting it in 1996, the club occupied a sort of garage down an alley. It was hard for me to believe that the Lower East Side Fighting Eagles (as they are called) had only been training in this garage for a few years. The fantastically cramped, weathered interior of the gym made it easy to imagine that guys named Mushy and Skids were heaving medicine balls at each other in there in 1926. Branching lines of tarry black glop filled chinks in the cinderblock walls; poolroom-style fluorescents hung down from a wooden ceiling reinforced with metal brackets; ropes, chains, and wires trailed down to punching bags, lights, and fuse boxes. DeForce and his associates had managed to wedge three heavy bags, two speed bags, three bob bags, some free weights, a couple of exercise bikes, moldy rug remnants, and an undersized sparring ring into a space the size of a two-bay car repair joint, and at times it appeared that the fighters in training came dangerously close to blindsiding one another while they worked. Training in these close quarters, the Fighting Eagles filled the room with a thunder of gloves on bags, huffing and puffing, and stamping feet, all counterpointed by a loud warning buzzer and a quieter bell that divided the training session into round-sized segments. DeForce had given generously of himself to a shoestring operation—hustling to put together fight cards at a local parish or bar, finding suitable opponents, driving fighters long distances to out-of-town bouts, training his charges and working their corners during fights—and he dreamed of somehow getting his hands on the resources to buy a building for the Lower East Side Boxing Club, turning it into a permanent institution he could pass on to successors.[8]

The Bizzarros, his crosstown rivals, had money and owned property. The elder Bizzarros sold cars, ran bars, had their own gym, and employed their offspring in the family businesses. They exuded an air of comfort that made a strong contrast with the scrappy Dead End Kids atmosphere of the Lower East Side Boxing Club. Lou Bizzarro Sr., father of Lou Jr. (an up-and-coming amateur in the late 1990s, now a professional) and the veteran professional welterweight Johnny Bizzarro, had a good lightweight career. Lou Sr. fought for the title in 1976 against the great Roberto Duran, who knocked him out in the fourteenth. Lou Sr. has since acquired the ring in which they fought and had it installed in the Ringside, one of his bars. John, his brother and business partner (until his death in 1998), was also a very good lightweight, earning two title shots: Flash Elorde beat him by decision in 1963, and Carlos Ortiz stopped him in 1966. Other brothers—Angelo, Paul, Ralph—all fought, and Ernie, one brother who did not, now has a son who does: young Ernie Jr., who lost the close fight to Angel Nales in Bethlehem in 1996. As Lou Sr. tells it, the original Bizzarro in the Erie region was his grandfather, an Italian who settled in Meadville; that man's son, father of Lou Sr. and his many fighting brothers, worked at Bucyrus Erie making cranes. When Lou Sr. was coming up, the choice of livelihoods he faced was still the traditional industrial one: "It was fighting or factory work," he said. But the fight world of the 1960s in which he was formed was already much reduced from its prewar extent. "There was the one real gym in town, but it wasn't like it used to be. To get really good you have to spar with pros, and there weren't that many decent fighters around anymore." In 1997 his son Lou Jr., the family's best amateur prospect, had a distinctly postindustrial and middle-class choice to make: turn pro or go to college, or try to do both at once. Lou Sr. thought his son was ready for the pros; he was certainly smart and confident enough in the ring. On the other hand, a young man with his background needs a college degree and not just property to establish credentials that enable an upward-curving class trajectory, so perhaps the best thing might have been for him to hit the books, not the bags, with everything he had.

Not all gyms have a house style, but many do. Bizzarro fighters stress technique and defense, while Lower East Side Boxing Club fighters always press their opponents, advancing with bad intentions. "Matt trains all his guys to be straight ahead, put your hands up, and go at the other guy," said Lower East Side stalwart Jose Otero. "Because I studied karate first, I'm probably the slickest amateur fighter in there," he added, laughing at the thought of himself as a paragon of finesse by default. "They've got heart, but they just walk in and swing," young Lou Bizzarro Jr. said of the Lower East Siders, shaking his head. DeForce saw it differently: "Mostly, the kids from the Bizzarro gym don't fight worth shit. They run, then complain. My kids *fight*." DeForce told me he never boxed, but he does seem to know something about fighting. He starts slowly with his protégés, first teaching them to place their feet right and manage their balance, then slowly builds their punching skills and conditioning. Defense does not enjoy a place of honor in the curriculum. When a dejected Jose Otero, having abandoned any pretense of slickness and rabidly pursued Lou Bizzarro Jr. from bell to bell every round but lost the fight anyway, turned to his trainer for a word of wisdom, DeForce said, "You got to throw more punches." Even DeForce's most skilled boxers—like Liz McGonigal, and Otero, who is better than he looked against Lou Bizzarro Jr.—treat defense as a matter of neutralizing an opponent's punches as they advance to land their own blows. The Bizzarros are more polished boxers, in part because they are connected to the remaining fight world through an older generation who fought professionally and learned from good teachers. Their house style includes side-to-side movement to create advantageous angles, clever escapes when cornered, and counterpunches against an advancing opponent. But, especially in a time when boxing is an esoteric rather than a common interest, fight crowds are less impressed than ever by such fetches of style, and too many people in Erie with an opinion on the subject are inclined to believe that the Fighting Eagles (male and female) fight like men and the Bizzarros (senior and junior) run like women.

Most of the Lower East Side Boxing Club fighters have at best rudimentary skills, but they win many fights on the strength of unremitting aggression, which impresses crowds and judges and opponents, especially at the amateur level. DeForce is not an old boxing hand, and he cannot call upon the deep store of boxing knowledge that more traditional trainers accrue as they pass through the fight world network, so he has wisely taught his charges what he knows best—how to win a fight. Every boxing match is also a fight, but the two things are not identical. Although Lou Bizzarro Jr. outmaneuvered Jose Otero and kept their boxing match from turning into a street fight, Lower East Siders have won many bouts by inducing opponents to abandon boxing technique and maul with them. DeForce told me that his fighters have won most of their bouts with Bizzarro fighters, a plausible claim because good boxers take much longer to develop than hearty brawlers. Even though a seasoned technician who can fight will almost always pick apart a brawler of similar experience, at the lower amateur levels a well-developed aggressive impulse can often overwhelm a nascent boxing style. DeForce and his friends built a boxing institution, but they could not rebuild the whole boxing network and high-industrial milieu in which such institutions thrived. In the absence of most of the old network, and in the absence of the professional teachers and good sparring partners it provided, his rough-and-ready fighters charge ahead and prosper because they have heart, not because they are expert boxers.

AN ENIGMA TO THE SPORT

When I began poking around Erie in 1996 and 1997, I was mildly surprised to discover that many people considered Liz McGonigal—a
woman, a relatively inexperienced fighter already in her early twenties, an
aspiring psychologist whose education was more important to her than
her boxing career—to be the most promising ring prospect in town.
Mike Acri, a promoter based in Erie, thought the Bizzarros should "take
it slow" in developing Lou Jr., but in 1997 he already wanted to rush Mc-
Gonigal into turning pro so she could appear on the undercard of a pay-
per-view fight between Macho Camacho and Sugar Ray Leonard.
Women's boxing appeared to be the next big thing, and Acri wanted to
get in on it. He knew McGonigal's Irish name and banty blond good
looks would add to her appeal, but, he said, "The main thing is she can
fight." If McGonigal had all the fighter's heart and verve that character-
ize the Lower East Side Boxing Club house style, she was also a more
complete boxer than most of the maulers she trained with. Asked to eval-
uate her strengths, Matt DeForce said, "She's got good technique. She's
real smart, she can take punches real well, she's got good defense. And
she's a tremendous puncher. For a girl her size, 112 pounds, she hits girls,
she hurts them."[9] She *can* fight; how did she get to be that way, and what
might it mean?

As is the case with many gifted pugilists, some of McGonigal's talent
is inexplicable enough to fall under the category of "natural": some
people have a knack for imposing their will on others, or a feel for nuances of movement, force, and damage. But, with the help of teachers,
she has also worked diligently at her craft. "Sooner or later," said De-
Force, "I was going to get a girl." Other women have trained at the
Lower East Side Boxing Club since McGonigal started there, but she
was the first. She came to DeForce through Jose Otero, whose karate
student she had been for years. Otero had his own East Side karate
school, the Otero Goshin Jutsu, but he also trained at the Lower East
Side Boxing Club. "I followed my sensei to the gym," McGonigal said,
because she was curious and because she had grown impatient with the
restraint and stop-start character of karate. "With karate I was fighting
and winning," she explained, "but after a while I wasn't making any
progress. It was like tag. I found boxing harder, faster, more continuous, more strength-to-strength." The black belt did assist her development as a boxer, though. "When you fight, any kind of fighting, you
have to keep control of your center. Martial arts was great for that, and

for doing it in front of an audience. Most people when they get hit in that situation they just freeze, but I'm used to it." And it helped that her stepfather had taught her the rudiments of boxing when she was very young. "He would put the gloves on me and my sister when we were fighting, to settle our fights. He trained boxers in college, and he didn't have any sons of his own, so he worked with me on basics and combinations. It's just like he did with a football, throwing it at me and teaching me how to tackle." DeForce showed her how to train with bags and jump rope and sparring partners, and she watched professionals fight on television. "I try to watch good fights," she said, "so I can pick up something and use it when I spar." Her voice is soft and very clear, with a hint of iron in it when she wants to underscore a point: she has good form in that, too.

After three months of training, McGonigal asked DeForce if he could get her a fight. He did, and she won it, breaking her opponent's nose and winning by knockout, despite being matched against a larger woman. Her increasingly fearsome reputation in the region and her size—"She's so damn little" at 5′2″ and 112 pounds, said DeForce—made it hard to find willing, qualified opponents in her weight class in the still-formative world of women's amateur boxing. DeForce always had to balance the need to build up McGonigal's ring experience against the danger of putting her in with women she should not be fighting. One of the principal deficiencies in her style, punching to the head too much and to the body too little, can be traced to the unsuitability of her opponents. "When I'm in against somebody much bigger," she said, "I know that one punch can put me on my butt. So I try to get them out of there quick with a knockout. That means I go for more shots to the head and can't work the body as much." Even though she had won the Pennsylvania Golden Gloves championships in both novice (1996) and open (1997) classes—which is supposed to mean she had met and beaten the state's best female amateurs in her weight class—she had rarely fought a woman her own size until she fought for a national amateur title. In July 1997, funded by the GE workers' $2,500, she added to her list of accomplishments the 112-pound title at USA Boxing's National Women's Boxing Championships in Augusta, Georgia, by dispatching opponents from New York City and Boston in the eighth and ninth bouts of her career.

That a woman can be a national amateur champion or have an amateur boxing career at all, and that she can have prospects for pursuing that career in legitimate professional circles, is a recent development that

Liz McGonigal hits her trainer, Matt DeForce, in the body. Photo: Greg Wohlford, *Erie Times-News*. Reprinted with permission of Times Publishing Company, Erie, Pa., © 2002.

points to significant changes not only in boxing but also in the sexual division of work and play. There was a much commented-upon upsurge of women's boxing and related practices in the 1990s, part of a larger post-industrial boom in strenuous exercise. Many women come to, or toward, boxing through fitness training and body sculpting. "Boxerobics" and similar exercise fads that appropriate elements of a boxer's training routine draw inspiration from the fact that fighters tend to be in superb shape. Their broad-shouldered and narrow-waisted bodies, armored with flat bands of muscle, radiate supple competence and easy power. Next to fighters, serious weight lifters often appear to be blown up into showpieces—like the ring girls—rather than trained down into fighting machines. Liz McGonigal is one of millions of women, especially students and service-professional types, who lift weights, although women do it in smaller numbers than men and with less imperative to develop massive muscular bulk. A special impulse to get big informs the weight lifting of male brain and face workers, who, working out during time set aside for play, effect a compromise between the neck-up quality of their jobs (which build up their phone-cradling and smiling muscles rather than their chests or legs) and the persistent demands of an older tradition of masculinity rooted in body work that thickened the male physique. Convention still often labels such thickness in women as unlovely, freakish, or grossly mannish. Women with money to spend on fitness regimes, women who must deal with pumped-up male associates fondling their own muscles and cracking their backs all day in the surrounding cubicles, have found that boxing and boxing-related exercise produces a streamlined sort of fitness, as well as the tangible air of confidence that goes with learning how to throw an old-fashioned punch. Women in health clubs mime a boxer's training to get in shape, and more and more women have found their way to boxing gyms to do the real thing. Most of this latter group go to boxing gyms just to get in shape (also true of men) rather than to work up to amateur or professional bouts, but a significant number of women mean to get in the ring and fight somebody. Among this latter group of serious practitioners, especially among achievers looking for progressively stiffer tests of their mettle, many women with martial arts training (again, like McGonigal) consider boxing to be the logical next step.

The individual and ad hoc character of boxing, with a core of serious practitioners and many more who are semiserious or just in it for the workout, makes it difficult to determine how many women box. Frank Globuschutz, president of the International Women's Boxing Federation and proprietor of the Academy of Boxing for Women (an all-women's gym on Long Island), estimated in 1999 that there were perhaps two thousand licensed female professionals in the United States and perhaps a thousand amateurs, each group constituting no more than a third of the worldwide total. More were arriving in gyms all the time.

Among the several social and cultural frames one might place around this phenomenon—and its high visibility in a recent round of movies, books, news features, and advertisements—is the larger movement of women into traditional proving grounds of manhood. The generation of women currently integrating boxing, contact sports, the big-time corporate stratum of professional team sports, hunting, and the military combat arms (not to mention the action movies that sublimate these sources into bang-bang mythology) has grown up in a time of remarkable fluidity in the sexual division of work and play. In particular, the assumption of a male monopoly on skilled, socially valued aggression has been seriously undermined, and not only by the feminist impulse.[10]

The movement of women into previously off-limits areas of work—and areas of sport connected to them—has also been driven by the final collapse of the family wage system that theoretically allowed a working man's salary to support his wife and children, and by a complementary movement of men into service jobs that resemble what used to be called "women's work." Postindustrial transformation also drives this process. Deindustrialization and the expansion of service work have helped to throw off the traditional calculus of masculinity based on body work and associated rough play, on being good with one's hands.

Enterprising women, exploring the evocative ruins of that partially collapsed tradition, have salvaged usable parts for their own purposes. Women pushing for access to the fight world have been part of a larger push, in both work and play, to claim once-"manly" virtues that boxing is supposed to nurture and embody: autonomy, physical competence, and discipline, all wrapped up with productive aggression.

There have also been institutional changes in the arrangement of athletic resources that help women find their way into the ring. Most broadly, the Title IX legislation of 1972 enabled the boom in women's sports of the last quarter century; more specifically, in the 1990s, women's amateur and professional boxing organizations were established to meet the demand of female boxers for a network in which to develop. Women have been boxing, usually on the fringes of the business, since the emergence of modern pugilism—prizefights between women were held in England and America throughout the bare-knuckle era[11]—but the arrival of legitimate women's boxing in the 1990s is significant not only for the numbers involved but also because it has at least the rudiments of an institutional base. The new sanctioning bodies, amateur tournaments, and other institutions of women's boxing form the outline of a self-contained system, but they also draw strength from links to the promoters, managers, and especially the training grounds of the formerly all-male fight network. As women's boxing flows into and from men's boxing, the fight network may yet find itself reinvigorated as a result. Old hands who hang around gyms looking for fighters to train have found that female novices are seeking them out. Many of these old hands dismiss women's boxing as a freak show or a steep comedown from men's boxing, but others are happy to have eager fighters to train. Often the same guy will have both reactions. Some mangled codgers in a Boston gym introduced two of their number to me as "Hansel and Gretel, the guys who handle the girls," and they all laughed, including the two who train the women, but half an hour later "Gretel" was all business, hanging over the ropes to urge one of his female charges to hook to the body of the man she was sparring with.

The recent growth in women's boxing and signs of intermittent, grudging acceptance of it by male fight people should not lead one to conclude that the current state of women's boxing will do. Many women who satisfy the public's and promoters' demands for female action are just not good enough boxers to merit a place on a professional card, but they are game enough to wade in swinging, which always sells. Euphemistic talk of women's boxing as "more honest" than men's boxing, "more action-packed," "tougher," and "fresher," draws a veil of marketing-speak over the plain fact that green female scrappers, fighting shorter two-minute rounds that encourage bell-to-bell punching (men fight three-minute rounds), often beat the hell out of one another with less regard for defense and technique than more seasoned men display. Women's boxing often pleases crowds because it looks, paradoxically, both conventionally manlier than men's boxing and more womanly. It looks more like the way men pretend to fight in movies, more like the way Superman and the Tasmanian Devil and other cartoon icons of male aggression dish it out and take it, yet at the same time those women's bouts that collapse into unskilled pummeling call to mind certain forms of pornography premised on the principle of the catfight (of which more shortly). In addition to overplaying this drawing card by showcasing female brawlers and comely incompetents with no defensive skills, managers and promoters also engage in plenty of skullduggery leading to awful mismatches. The proportion of bad bouts remains far too high. One should bear in mind, though, that all of these failings are manifest—to a lesser degree, usually—in the male fight world. Women's boxing is still an institutional fledgling. Like female hockey players, deer hunters, and foot soldiers, female boxers in America have not had many chances to work on their violent craft, but it appears that they will.

Liz McGonigal seriously considered turning pro in the spring of 1997, but she did not, and therein lies a distinctly contemporary boxing story. Part of her reasoning did indeed have to do with the grim state of professional matchmaking. "I've been fighting girls who are a lot bigger than me, twenty or thirty pounds" she told me before she went to Georgia and won her national amateur title. "I think that there would be the chance for the same kind of thing to happen to me if I went pro, and there would be more pressure on me because of contracts and promoters to go ahead and take a really badly mismatched fight. It happens all the time. When Deirdre Gogarty fought Christy Martin, they said she was within ten pounds of Martin, but it looked like fifteen or more. They just aren't as strict with women fighters." But the most important factor in her decision to remain an amateur had nothing to do with mismatches or promoters. She was in her senior year of college, at Edinboro University outside Erie, and she worried that her grades would suffer if she had to take too many out-of-town fights. She was on the dean's list, and if she finished well, she could win a fellowship that would enable her to enter the graduate program in clinical psychology. "The most important thing is education," she said. "No doubt about it, education comes first," agreed Matt DeForce, who has seen enough kids pass through his gym into the job market to know that good futures are founded on training that college and graduate school can provide. Liz McGonigal remained an amateur, got the fellowship, and started in the master's degree program in the fall of 1997. She was planning to get her degree first, doing her master's research on how athletes respond to serious injury, while staying in training to defend her national amateur title in the spring. ("I hope my professors understand I'll need to take a week off to go down there and fight," she told me.) She hoped that women's boxing would become an Olympic sport soon enough that she might have a chance to fight for her country while she was still of boxing age. With an M.A. in clinical psychology in hand by 1999, she would face the next round of decisions: Turn pro or hold out for the chance that women's boxing would be an Olympic sport by 2004? Pursue a doctorate? Fight full-time for a while and then go back to school? If she decided to become, say, a sports psychologist, the experiential credential of a successful boxing career would make an impressive addition to her résumé, balancing book learning with hard knocks and perhaps a world title. "I love boxing, but I know I can't box for the rest of my life," she said. "A lot of people put all their stock in it, but I don't have to. If I win, I win; if I lose, I go back to my studies."

As it turned out, a chronic injury to her left wrist forced McGonigal to get out of boxing in 1998, shortly after she suffered her first defeat when she returned to the amateur nationals to defend her 112-pound title. Between the demands of graduate school and the reluctance of other women to fight her, she had gone an entire year without a bout since her victory at the 1997 nationals. She won her first match at the 1998 nationals but then lost to Jamie McGrath, of New York, who frustrated McGonigal by tying up her punches (which involved questionable holding tactics) and landed some telling blows of her own. As a result of the

loss, McGonigal failed to qualify for the first-ever women's national amateur boxing team's international competitions. But, she told me, she
could not have participated anyway. "I injured my wrist in '96 or '97,"
she said, "but I kept training, and it got worse." The remarkable force
with which she hit bags and opponents had always been her calling card,
but every time she used her left hand, she further damaged the bones in
her wrist. "I would do a boxing workout," she said, "and I wouldn't be
able to write for a week. Finally, in 1998, I had surgery, and the doctors
told me to stop. I thought about going back and training anyway, but
they were probably right." She added that her master's research on injury
gave her a good idea of what she would go through and how to handle
it. Still, it bothers her that her last fight was also her one and only loss.
"Not a good way to go out," she said in 2001, "but I feel I accomplished
a lot in boxing; it was the most exciting thing I ever did. Anyway, I'll always have my black belt; you can do karate your whole life." She was already looking forward to the next challenge: joining the air force as a research scientist specializing in the human-machine interface, opening up
a future choice between a military career and a doctorate in psychology.

The story of a good amateur who does not turn pro, choosing
instead a more promising or reliable future outside the ring, has been
told before; what makes McGonigal's a distinctly contemporary story is
that a female graduate student had legitimate prospects as an amateur
or professional boxing champion. Women's boxing, still in an institu-
tionalizing phase that resembles men's boxing a century ago, has plenty
of room for female versions of the "gentleman" boxer—people who
present solid middle-class credentials of education and property and
who would risk flattening or even reversing their class trajectory by seriously pursuing a long-term boxing career. At the national amateur
championships in 1997, for instance, McGonigal, with a freshly minted
magna cum laude B.A. in psychology, won her title by decisioning
Laura Schere, a Georgetown graduate pursuing a Ph.D. in cultural studies at the University of Minnesota, and then overwhelming Raphaelle
Johnson, a graphic designer (who also led "cardioboxing" classes) with
a degree from the Art Institute of Boston. Among the sixty-five participants in the tournament, there were professionals, high-end service
workers, and graduate students (including other women with training
in psychology, a traditional college major for female jocks), as well as
women with high school educations and low-end service jobs. Jimmy
Finn, a leading proponent of women's boxing and cofounder of the
Women's International Boxing Federation, explained to an interviewer

that "most of the women [who box] are educated professionals" who come to it "primarily as an exciting hobby. Many come from martial art disciplines such as kick boxing." [12] Bruce Silverglade, owner of Gleason's Gym, the Brooklyn fight mecca, concurred: "They're real tough competitors who are highly educated, who have these power jobs." [13] In 2000 there were 116 women training at Gleason's—seven professionals, sixteen amateurs, the rest in it for the workouts and expertise—constituting about 15 percent of the gym's membership. [14]

These women do not want to be industrial workers; they want command of body skills and associated character traits traditionally identified with industrial work and with masculinity, both of which are root components of boxing's heroic appeal. Some middle-class women turn out to be good boxers and have successful careers. But, except in the case of Christy Martin (who allied herself with Old Scratch himself, Don King) and a handful of others, even a successful career will not enable a woman to support herself with boxing alone. "They're not in it for the money," said Finn, "because, right now, there's no money to be made." [15] McGonigal agreed: "At the moment, there's so little money in boxing for women that you can only do it for love, or because it requires total dedication and you value that. Maybe, once there's money in it, the poorer and hungrier fighters will push people like me out who have less to lose, but right now we've got a great heterogeneous mix of people doing it with similar drives that come from different sources."

McGonigal offered a persuasive reading of this fledgling moment in women's boxing. Only a few men can support themselves by boxing, but enough of them do so that other men aspire to it—or at least these others can tell themselves they aspire to riches, legitimating their less quantifiable reasons for boxing. If women's boxing develops to that point, then one can expect to see the "gentlewoman" boxers pushed to the margin of the profession by working-class women who commit themselves utterly to boxing when they are adolescents and who regard boxing as a better career—in terms of money and status, not just athletic and psychic satisfactions—than whatever else they can envision for themselves. Already, said Frank Globuschutz in 1999, "we're beginning to see athletes from eighteen to twenty-two going straight into boxing as a career. They're pushing out some of the more educated women in their late twenties and early thirties who dominated six or seven years ago." If women's boxing becomes an even marginally viable profession, people with less to lose will dominate it. There are many individual exceptions, but as a general rule people who have or expect to get advanced degrees and undertake careers in professions requiring those degrees are more likely to regard the risk of brain injury, facial damage, and unreliable paydays as unacceptable than are people whose alternative to the ring is working in a sweatshop or cleaning toilets. If ambitious teenage women of limited means throw themselves into the boxing business full-time, women in their twenties and thirties with other careers who can only devote themselves to boxing part-time will be obliged to divert more resources to it to keep up. Many of these "gentlewomen" will then drop out of serious competition.

Right now, though, the "gentlewomen" are still in the business in force, especially in the amateur ranks where the sport's future develops. Many of them are winning amateur and professional fights. Some have taken advantage of their experience to analyze the fight world from within, contributing with authority to a significant new fight literature that has commanded a relatively high cultural profile. Rene Denfeld (*Kill the Body, the Head Will Fall*), Kate Sekules (*The Boxer's Heart*), Lynn Snowden Picket (*Looking for a Fight*), and others have written about their entry into the ring. Karyn Kusama (*Girlfight*), Katya Bankowsky (*Shadow Boxers*), and other filmmakers with boxing experience have done much to make the female fighter a figure in the visual landscape, as have documentaries like *On the Ropes* and melodramas like *Knockout*. The books and movies have helped to move women's boxing in from the far margin of freakishness. The much-publicized entry of Laila Ali, Jacqui Frazier-Lyde, and Freeda Foreman into the ring, renewing their fathers' heavyweight rivalries of the 1970s, has in some ways pushed women's boxing back toward that margin—especially to the extent that none of the three could box well enough to merit the attention they received. But one might also see a further mainstreaming of violent female aggression in the fact that most people in the general public and the sports business had no problem accepting the notion that daughters would want to defend the family honor in the ring.

By 1999, I no longer felt, as I did in 1996 when I first started investigating women's boxing, that I had found my way into an obscure back corner of the fight world. Women's boxing was suddenly turning up in TV shows, editorials, features, and advertisements; friends sent me dozens of clippings and reported sightings all over the mediascape. For months, I kept encountering a giant billboard picture of a woman with wrapped hands in an approximation of punching position, showing how Noxzema kept one's skin healthy and supple. The satirical newspaper *The Onion*, which tends to take up a subject only after it has generated a field of clichés to play with, published a mock survey in 1999 that sought to explain "the increased interest in women's boxing." The answers included: "Nation finally coming around to idea of sweaty, underdressed young women," "Fans enjoy nicknames like Tanya 'The Good Listener' Smith," and "Women can do anything men can do, no matter how fucking stupid it is."[16]

The sudden prominence of women's boxing proceeded at least in part from the cultural confusion it caused. "Liz McGonigal is an enigma to the sport," said Matt DeForce. He meant that in some ways she fits his notion of a typical, even a traditional, Erie fighter—of German-Irish-Italian ancestry, fighting out of the East Side, in love with hard work, connected through the Lower East Side Boxing Club to the GE pugilists of old. Yet she does not have the traditional fighter's background or future prospects. DeForce's comment describes not just a female boxer, an enigmatic figure to many people inside and outside the fight world, but a woman who is going both with and against the grain of history. McGonigal goes with the grain in that, after growing up in factory towns in upstate New York and arriving in Erie with her family as a high school senior, she plugged herself into what is left of the fight network rooted in the industrial past. Several traditional elements are in place: early instruction within the family and then in a neighborhood gym, support from industrial workers who sustain local boxing institutions, gradual movement from the local fight network into regional and national circles, a local promoter who wants her to turn pro. And yet when she entered the ring, she also moved against the grain of history, against the traditional identity between boxing and industrial work. Her family's class trajectory has been working to middle: away from the factory, the immigrant-ethnic inner-city neighborhood, the ring, and other features of industrial America's signature landscape. Her father, mother, and stepfather worked in factories (her mother as a secretary), but her stepfather moved from the shopfloor to management as an executive of a machine company. Liz McGonigal and her five siblings have extended the trajectory via college and military service (two sisters in the marines, two brothers in the navy, and Liz herself in the air force). Those in the workforce have moved into a variety of jobs, principally midrange service work like accounting and retail sales. Her family home in Erie was not on the East Side in the shadow of GE but in subdivided suburban Millcreek, where the mills are only a memory and the giant regional mall squats amid ramifying highways and subsidiary business strips. She came to boxing through karate and fitness, not neighborhood life, street life, prison, or shopfloor culture. She went well out of her way in seeking out the East Side's cult of blue-collar toughness and the single remaining gate to the fight network it keeps open. She did not grow up in a world where a variety of well-beaten paths would naturally lead her to the ring.

And, of course, every time Liz McGonigal climbed into the ring, she went with the grain of women's concerted advance into legitimate boxing but against the deeper grain of powerful, resilient traditions in the public display of male and female bodies. Women's boxing is hounded by a widely held assumption that the female body plus violent aggression always equals pornography. One might argue that men's boxing also has a sexual subtext, and there are plenty of fans who watch it just to see near-naked men hurt one another (a group overrepresented among Mike Tyson enthusiasts, I suspect), but that subtext typically has to coexist with other kinds of meaning: spectators do value men's boxing as sport, craft, or tribal drama. Women's boxing, though, has to contend with the fact that many men (and women), set in their ways of thinking about work and play, can understand women's boxing *only* as a sex show. Advocates of women's boxing sometimes call this "the foxy boxing problem."

Foxy boxing shows are sex work. These alternately choreographed and chaotic affairs, in which women put on oversize gloves and little else and whale away inexpertly at one another in the ring, form part of a constellation of live, taped, and still-photo pornographic practices that burlesque boxing. Generic cousins of foxy boxing include catfights, gloveless exhibitions with lots of bitchy screaming and hair pulling; "apartment wrestling," a curious variant of catfights employing a domestic setting; boxing-themed pornography, in which mock boxing matches between women serve as foreplay or main event; "mixed boxing," in which women pummel men or vice versa and then do or do not have sex; boxing-themed "dominance," which looks like what it sounds like; and so on down or up some roughly delineated scale to weapons and elaborate restraints. The Internet is a contrived and misshapen index of cultural logic, but a search using the keywords "women" and "boxing" can be revealing. Besides the usual avalanche of useless noise, it will turn up home pages and discussion groups genuinely devoted to women's boxing, material on men's boxing that mentions women peripherally, and a sampling of the pornographic cosmos mapped here. All this falls under the rubric of "women and boxing," so even when such a search leads to useful information on women's pugilism, one is always a couple of mouse clicks away from foxy boxing. Legitimate women's boxing pages have registered that proximity by posting messages instructing those in search of pornography that they have taken a wrong turn.

Pornography has shadowed women's boxing for a long time. One typical advertisement for a prizefight between women in eighteenth-century England started with jibes and counterjibes from the combatants but ended with descriptions of what they would and would not be wearing. The ad, published in a British newspaper in 1726, announced an upcoming fight between women to be held "at the Request of several English and Irish Gentlemen." It led off with the challenger's statement: "Whereas I Mary Welch, from the Kingdom of Ireland, being taught, and knowing the Noble Science of Defence, and thought to be the only Female of this Kind in Europe, understanding here is one in this Kingdom . . . I do hereby invite her to meet me." The English Championess responded: "I Elizabeth Stokes, of the famous City of London, being well known by the Name of the Invincible City Championess for my Abilities and Judgment in the abovesaid Science . . . shall make no Apology for accepting the challenge of this Irish Heroine." The statements attributed to the fighters emphasized experience, technical accomplishments, and identification with a constituency that would help turn the bout into a nationalist grudge match. The ad, though, struck a very different note in closing: "N.B. They Fight in close Jackets, short Petticoats, coming just below the Knee, Holland Drawers, white Stockings, and Pumps."[17] Women at the close of the twentieth century also insist that spectators watching their fights should be thinking about skill, heart, and tribal affiliations, but fight crowds and fight world insiders frustrate them by concentrating on sex roles. Female fighters are too womanly or not womanly enough, too manly or not manly enough, desirable or undesirable, appropriate or inappropriate—everything except boxers.

The Onion nailed this contradiction with typical accuracy. Other reasons it cited for the popularity of women's boxing included "Taps into U.S. sports fans' love of violence against women" and "Now that outmoded sexist paradigms of female subjugation and powerlessness have been subverted in the traditionally male-dominated arena of boxing, you can see some major titty-bouncing." This is the core logic of the foxy boxing problem, and it plays out inside the fight world and beyond it. In the late 1990s, *Boxing Digest* (formerly *International Boxing Digest*) introduced both a new section reporting on women's boxing in the back of the magazine and a photo spread of the near-naked Round

Card Beauty of the Month near the front of the magazine. The round card beauties persist, but the women's boxing update did not last more than a few issues (although the magazine's ringside correspondents do include the results of women's bouts, and often comment on their high action quotient, in their capsule summaries of fight cards around the world). Female fighters themselves, sometimes because they wish to attract fans by exploiting the link to pornography, have also helped to muddy the distinction between foxy and legitimate boxing. A well-known professional named Mia St. John—not much of a fighter, but easy on the eyes—posed on the cover of *Playboy* with her gloved hands covering her naked breasts. A couple of the women who fought in the 1997 amateur nationals in Georgia listed beauty pageants among their credentials (McGonigal dismissed them as "West Coast" dabblers), and more than one buffed "exotic dancer" has entered the legitimate ring, usually to be slaughtered by a woman who means business.

Jimmy Finn, who became a full-time promoter and manager after being squeezed out of the Women's International Boxing Federation, had in mind this mess of competing meanings stirred up every time women fight when he said, "There's sexism, homophobia and the threat to the world's most exclusive men's club. If I brought a group of prostitutes into the ring, I'd be more accepted."[18] When I talked to him, I was struck by how even his conversational style expressed the encounter of traditional and emergent boxing cultures occasioned by the arrival of women in the ring. In his lovely brogue, he switched easily from the usual complaints about the business ("Aah, these roaches all around me, these roaches are fucking me") to a discussion of men who in his estimation fight like girls (like Henry Akinwande, disqualified in a title fight for excessive holding, who "was like a little girl in there, trying to hug and kiss Lennox Lewis") to explaining how female boxers pose "a threat to patriarchy—we're talking about patriarchy and male privilege here, don't you know?"

Liz McGonigal had to negotiate these tricky currents of meaning, too. Although anything but delicate, her fine features excited spectators' anxiety for her looks. She told me, "People always ask me, 'But you've got such a pretty face,' or whatever, 'Why do you want to mess it up?' I don't look at myself as a physical object; the most important thing is my mind." Having started out boldly to refute the premises of the prettiness question, she laughed and reversed field to engage the question on its own conventional terms. "Anyway, I've already got a big nose, and there's a lump on the side of it, and it's off-center already. I've been kicked in the nose a few times, it's pretty beat up." The drama surrounding her narrow, breakable-looking (but unbroken) nose always did seem to engage a crowd; a matronly Hispanic woman in Bethlehem shouting for McGonigal to keep her hands up may be the only spectator I have ever witnessed rooting for good defense at a fight in Pennsylvania. But it was McGonigal's relentless Lower East Side offense that broke down opponents, whipping crowds into a frenzy that made her think twice about the spectacle she participated in. McGonigal told me that she usually paid no attention to the crowd because she was concentrating on her opponent, but sometimes she wondered about what men got out of her fights. "Sometimes I can hear them yelling 'Hit that bitch' or something that makes me think about it. After a fight some people will come up and say 'You fought well' or 'You had good technique,' but other guys will say 'You messed her up' or 'You broke her nose.' That's when I ask if this is really ethical. That gives me kind of a conflict because I'm doing it for the skill. I respect women, and I don't want to hurt anybody, and outside the ring I would never do anything like that."

Headliners, the Erie club where McGonigal won the 1997 Golden Gloves open-class title, appended a pornographic shadow to her victory by putting on a foxy boxing show a couple of weeks before it. "They called it 'Babes in Bikinis Boxing,' or something like that," she told me. "My stepfather came into my room with the newspaper ad, and he wanted me to pull out of my fight. They had these women in little bikinis with humungous boxing gloves on. I felt like I've worked really hard"—at boxing, that is—"and this ad was awful; just these women as objects. If they had tried to advertise the Golden Gloves in any way like this, I would have pulled out."

Even when foxy boxers are nowhere in evidence, at every fight the ring girls remind the crowd of its investment in the link between female body work and sex work. When women box, argued McGonigal, "There's two totally different things going on with them and the ring girls. There's women's bodies on display, as objects, and then there's women fighting in the ring with skill." In her view, the fighters are *doing* something— skilled work—while the ring girls remain passive as things to be viewed. She suggested eliminating the semiotic signal jamming that the ring girls produce at women's fights: "They ought to have men up there walking around carrying the cards." I ran her proposal by three ring girls next to whom I found myself seated one night at the fights in Boston. They were for it. "Put the guys in *boxer shorts*," said one, "it could be like a theme thing." And, we agreed, certainly there are literally millions of men in the working-out class who have been preparing themselves for such display with weight-lifting regimens, removal of body hair, and other such practices designed to turn their bodies into beefcake sculptures suitable for ogling. A trio of veteran referees—Messrs. Flaherty, Fitzgerald, and Ryan—were seated on the other side of me, so I asked them what they thought of this inspired idea. They had no opinion.

McGonigal's and the Boston ring girls' wish came true in January 1998, when a 6′1″, 258-pound "round card guy" in a "skin-tight, zebra-striped one-piece leotard with shoulder straps" worked a card of eight women's bouts in Atlantic City. The Associated Press account reported a positive reception. "Women wolf-whistled. Men cheered. 'Meet Larry,' said ring announcer Ed Derian wryly, pausing for effect. 'Isn't he just divine?'"[19]

BODY WORK

The identity between boxing and work has always been right there on the surface of the fights. In the labor-obsessed language of the fight world, fighters work the body, outwork an opponent, impress the judges with a good work rate, display good work habits in the ring. The identity between boxing and work also persists in the bodies of fighters and the traditional training regimens that produced them. Fighters in training do exercises that still betray origins in precise, repetitive labor. Once upon a time, fighters got into shape by systematically hewing wood and drawing water—and some still do today when they feel it is time to get back to basics. When word got around in 2001 that Oscar De La Hoya was up in the mountains chopping wood, fight people began to assure each other that the Golden Boy had put his recording career and other distractions behind him and was ready to get back to work in earnest. Work and the materials of work also find their way into fighters' ring names (Christy "The Coal Miner's Daughter" Martin, Iron Mike Tyson), a practice that was more common among British bare-knuckle heroes like Bill Stevens the Nailer and Big Ben the Collier—and also among early female prizefighters like The Fighting Ass-Driver from Stoke Newington, A Female Boxing Blacksmith, and The Vendor of Sprats.[20] Now *those* are ring names.

The identity between boxing and work can be found as well in the biographies and backgrounds of the combatants, the deep structure of historical and social situation that remains largely invisible to us when we watch two fighters moving in the blank space of the ring. Sociologists have unsurprisingly observed from time to time that, as S. Kirson Weinberg and Henry Arond put it in their definitive 1952 study, boxers "are recruited from among the youth of the lower socioeconomic levels. Their changing ethnic composition reflects the ethnic shifts in the urban lower socioeconomic levels."[21] A French participant-observer named Loïc Wacquant, revisiting the Chicago fight scene that Weinberg and Arond studied, recently reiterated and elaborated upon their finding. Copious interviewing, sparring, and hanging around, combined with an impressive command of the sociological and theoretical literature, equipped Wacquant to conclude that "boxing is a working-class occupation," a fact "reflected not only in the physical nature of the activity but also in the social recruitment of its practitioners and in their continuing dependence on blue-collar or unskilled service jobs to support their career in the ring." Wacquant also pointed out that fighters are not in it simply for the money. They treat their bodies as capital to be accrued through labor, and the rewards of their investment extend beyond the financial into the realm of labor-related satisfaction. They are not pushed unwillingly into the esoteric practice of boxing by poverty so much as pulled into "a form of physical work that boxers seek out because it grants them a high degree of *control over the labor process and unparalleled independence*," especially when compared with "factory jobs."[22]

Until the parallel contraction of industrial work and the fight network in the decades after World War II, most men who aspired to a boxing career faced the classic choice between the ring and body work. For a very good, lucky, or well-connected few, boxing might bring riches. For others it was a widely respected career path that, while youth and vigor allowed, both diverged from and paralleled the one on which a fighter's peers trudged, lunch pail in hand. For some it was a route toward work and away from crime or dissipation, for others the reverse. For the legion of part-time boxers it was something rewarding one could do—for money, for recreation, for the satisfaction of doing it well or hurting somebody—with a body hardened by regular, strenuous work. Members of the fight world intelligentsia have remarked repeatedly on the link between manual labor and pugilism; by the mid–twentieth century, Cassandras like Nat Fleischer and A. J. Liebling were already warning that postindustrial transformation posed a threat to boxing as they knew it. The contraction of heavy industry and the breakup of industrial neighborhood orders, the expansion of secondary and college education and their sporting cultures, the postwar expansion of the middle class, and the rise of television (which helped to kill local boxing clubs)—all these processes, warned the Cassandras, threatened to strain the life-giving link between the manly art and the industrial milieu in which it grew to maturity.[23]

The sociologists and Cassandras share the habit of thinking about boxing as heroically productive men's work on the industrial model, but that traditional understanding has been under pressure since the passing of the high-industrial moment when America's heavy manufacturing sector and fight network rose in tandem to worldwide dominance. Postindustrial static has at least partially obscured the connection between body work in the ring and in the factory. In a labor market and culture dominated at Weinberg and Arond's "urban lower socioeconomic level" by low-end service jobs rather than manufacturing, the traditional body work of boxing may eventually be dismissed even by working-class men as painful, overly demanding, barbarously anachronistic drudgery. Of course, it is possible that those same throwback qualities, combined with the reversal of postwar conditions like the expansion of the middle class, will help boxing to persist or even be revived as an avenue back to traditional manhood. Loïc Wacquant emphasizes the importance of boxing as such an avenue, "a self-enclosed moral, emotional, and sensual cosmos in which skillful and fateful engagement of the trained body offers a 'space of forgetting' from restricted everyday lives and a scaffolding for the public erection of a heroic hypermasculine self."[24] This talk of erection and hypermasculinity adds up to the notion that, within the fight world's special atmosphere, even men with little power or capital outside the gym can make something of their own—literally making something of themselves and thus reclaiming the heroic, productive virtue associated with manhood since the Industrial Revolution. Certainly that might help to explain the continuing popularity of the fights on television. Americans shell out for pay-per-view fights to see muscles, action, pain, and violent parables of class and race (all of which they can get cheaper at movie theaters or on "free" television), but they also pay through the nose for that whiff of traditional manhood that lingers around bodies doing the work of fighting, an aura that usually does not attach to pneumatic thespians cavorting with bazookas or to athletic bodies playing with a ball.

Liz McGonigal and others like her complicate the conventional wisdom about boxing, which both does and does not account for her. On the one hand, exploring her career and Erie, I found various connections to the social and cultural order of industrial America that shaped her engagement with the fight world. Those connections help explain what she was doing in the ring and what it might mean to her and to spectators. On the other hand, I found that the standard models do not make much room for a fighter who is not a man, not in pursuit of "hypermasculinity," not strictly working class (and upwardly mobile, through means other than boxing, to boot), not black or Hispanic (Jimmy Finn estimated that in boxing, white women outnumber non-whites about three to one), not feeling especially alienated from her labor or threatened by postindustrial society, not cut off from other avenues to satisfying work and play. The contradictions multiply. McGonigal was drawn to boxing by tradition, especially its durable commitment to self-fashioning through hard work, but also by the prospects for breaking with tradition by pioneering the movement of women into what used to be a men's preserve. She is a proud apotheosis of Kathryn Dudley's "culture of the hands," ratified in that role by the GE hands who pitched in hard-earned dollars to send her to Georgia, but she also lives by the fundamental principles of the "culture of the mind": individual success through credentialing (in her case, by advanced academic study of the mind itself), progressive personal development through the clearing of obstacles, a belief that her mind is "the most important thing." Fighting in the ring, she offered a spectacle with contradictory resonances, reinforcing some people's tendency to see any conjunction of women and aggression as pornography but also, by fighting *well*, doing something to help break that cultural habit. She is, in short, a postindustrial fighter who came to the ring through a mixed and changing landscape and culture. The way things used to be both enables and constrains what comes next, even though what comes next may well help to destroy the way things used to be.

It is worth reminding ourselves that, for complicated reasons connected to the cultures of both hands and mind, McGonigal loves the art, craft, challenge, and excitement of being a boxer. She smiled happily at the thought of good times to come when she told me, "I lift weights for strength and bulk, but when I know I have fights coming up, I start to train down." Boxers are not simply made by "situations" and "conditions"; almost nobody becomes a boxer against his or her will. Individuals have to choose the ring and choose to stay with it, and very few of them do. The argument that working people are pushed into the ring to serve as gladiators who amuse the middle and upper classes tends to ignore not only the fact of boxing's traditional working-class audience (and the fact that boxers do not come exclusively from the working class) but also the extent to which boxers are consenting adults attracted to the satisfactions of an esoteric and difficult practice. The gladiator thesis finds slightly better, though still shaky, ground when it comes to football and basketball, which have had an incalculably more significant effect on the futures, imaginations, and bodies of people of modest means than boxing ever did or will. (The gladiator thesis might be on still better ground in helping to explain the production of fashion models and gangster rappers, but that is a different argument.) The notion of a consenting adult has its limits, but it is vital to understanding that one must work hard and significantly depart the path of least resistance to even find the entrances to the fight world anymore. Women, on the move into once-male territory, are seeking out those entrances in greater numbers and with better prospects than before.

Boxing may be highly visible on television from time to time, but the entrances to the boxing world are often out-of-the-way, dingy places wedged into a city's gray areas—between the railroad tracks and the expressway, between the past and the present. It is much easier to find one's way to a basketball court, a weight room, the mall, or a television. The gym was once a very accessible part of a chain of institutions that shaped the industrial city's landscapes of neighborhood and manhood. "I grew up in blue-collar America in the years after the Second World War," wrote Pete Hamill in his introduction to a book of photos of the now-closed Times Square Gym. "There were institutions where I lived: the factory, the church, the police station, the saloon, and the gym. I have lived long enough to see them slip into the irretrievable past. The factory was the first to go, and that was the crucial blow."[25] Hamill, an old hand at elegizing industrial urbanism and its native forms of masculinity, looks back to the last days of an urban world bracketed by factory and gym. The now-deceased cultural historian Frank Sinatra backed him up: "In my particular neighborhood in New Jersey, when I was a kid, boys became boxers or they worked in factories; and then the remaining group that I went around with were smitten by singing."[26] Taking a break from the heavy bag, sweat soaking through his clothes and forming a puddle beneath him on the gym mat, the former heavyweight champion Larry Holmes offered a postindustrial variation on Hamill and Sinatra's theme in explaining his decision to fight on into his late forties: "What am I gonna do instead? Drive a truck? That business closed *up*. Work in a motherfuckin' factory in Bethlehem? That business shut *down*." All three of them exaggerate, of course, in putting the gym on a par with the factory as a principal element of the American landscape—and the thrifty, prosperous Holmes, whose brief working stints in Lehigh Valley steel mills and as a truck driver for Strongwear Pants are decades behind him, exaggerates by implying that he might still be obliged to do blue-collar work to pay the bills. But they exaggerate, rather than fabricate, to make a point.

A. J. Liebling, the dean of American boxing writers and a believer in the gospel of conventional masculinity circa 1926 (he pretended to be more ironic about it than he was), would have been floored by the boom in women's boxing. Liebling, who by the 1950s was already lamenting the lost golden age of boxing, preceded Hamill in identifying the gym as a place that embodies not only pugilistic tradition but also a way of life, a broader set of time-tested orthodoxies that included his sense of manhood. He saw fighters' bodies themselves as similarly embodying tradition, a view captured neatly in his observation that "the Sweet Science of boxing is joined onto the past like a man's arm to his shoulder."[27] He meant a *man's* shoulder. "The presence of women, chaperoned or not, is contra-indicated in a training camp."[28] Traditionally, women in the gym meant spectators, either girlfriends or wives, and were signs of a male fighter's dangerously divided attention. Times have changed. If crowds still often react to women's boxing matches as pornography, in the gym—where boxing renews itself and where women willing to work hard at their craft are increasingly accepted—fight people tend to stick to business. Male fighters busy themselves with their own training, and the hard core of gym regulars not in training want to spend their afternoons standing around, arms folded, watching fighters apply themselves and get better. For that, women fighters will do just as well as men. The sweet science, still joined to the past like a man's arm to his shoulder, can only sustain itself if it remains joined to its traditions and accumulated lore. But boxing may also find itself joined to the present, and the future, like a woman's arm to her shoulder.

I was sitting in a corner of the Lower East Side Boxing Club one afternoon in 1997 when the fighters started coming in to train. Outside it was a cold and overcast November day, a Pennsylvania specialty, with rain coming down at an angle and the old brick structures of the East Side looking built to last through this and whatever else you got. Inside the gym it was hot and close. The fighters' movements and the sounds they raised in that confined space made a kind of rondo, with each fighter entering in turn, stripping off layers of outdoor clothes, wrapping hands, getting loose, shadowboxing, moving to one bag and then another. The buzzer and bell went off in sequence every three minutes to mark time. The first to come in was a big, light-skinned black guy, who nodded to me and set to work. By the time he was hitting the heavy bag, two high school girls, one dark-haired and one fair, had arrived and were getting warm. By the time those two were working on the speed bags, Jose Otero had arrived and started stretching. Then Liz McGonigal came in, dropped her jacket, twisted her curtain of long, blond hair into a braid, wrapped her hands, limbered up a bit, and started shadowboxing. She had on a sleeveless blue Cleveland Indians T-shirt and gray sweatpants. From her southpaw crouch she was throwing a right jab and then following it with a short left cross. She did this carefully, over and over, turning her shoulder just so and watching her form in a wide mirror that was propped on a ledge along one wall. She was working a staple of the fistic armament—the old one-two—into a personal instrument, ingraining an old move and a young woman's body into one another. It looked like she knew what she was doing.

2

TOO MANY NOTES

Chicago blues is the music of an industrial city, and it has an industrial sense about it. It's also a cold city, and Chicago blues has a sense of fighting the cold, and it's an angry city, and the Chicago blues has Chicago's anger in it.

Bruce Iglauer, founder of Alligator Records, on
"the toughest, hardest, rawest form of electric blues"

And, to get to the bottom of it, everything I sing I haven't experienced it. You know, people look at a blues player sing, "I worked five long years in a steel mill." I never been in a steel mill. But they look at me and they say, "Wow, man, you must have been catching hell in that steel mill. . . ."

Buddy Guy on authenticity

BUDDY GUY WAS PLAYING slow blues at the Trump Marina casino in Atlantic City. The second song in a Buddy Guy set is almost always a slow blues. This time he was doing one of the core tunes of his repertoire, Eddie Boyd's "Five Long Years," which begins, "If you ever been mistreated, well you know just what I'm talking about." This early in the set, before guitar-induced brain fatigue had set in, the crowd responded vigorously to every line and guitar fill. The majority of those present, casino patrons with no particular investment in Guy, seemed to regard his performance as a choice service provided by The Donald. Many of them had been comped for tickets by the casino. They had not been away from the gambling tables and machines for very long yet, and they were in an expansive mood. They did not even seem to mind that the first verse's kicker—"I worked five long years for one woman, and

she had the nerve to put me out"—committed the double gaucherie of
mentioning hard work and domestic troubles at the Trump Marina.
The distractive poetics of casino gambling is supposed to erase such
prosaic matters from one's consciousness. Mixed in with casino tourists
and committed gamblers on break were people who were there primarily to hear Guy, blues fans who had penetrated layers of Trumpismo to
get to the music. They were pleased to find their man in fine voice and
playing in New Jersey, near their suburban homes, rather than in New
York or Philadelphia. Everybody was in a good mood, Guy included. It
was late July 1998: he was almost sixty-two years old, trim and prosperous; he had a new CD, *Heavy Love,* on the shelves and a long-term
recording deal with Silvertone; and he owned Buddy Guy's Legends, a
thriving blues club in downtown Chicago. He wore crisp denim over-
alls (with a certain cosmopolitan irony) and played a customized black
Buddy Guy model Fender Stratocaster guitar with white polka dots all
over it.

    "Five Long Years" is a great song, one of many that came out of Chi-
cago during the blues boom years from the late 1940s to the early 1960s.
Nostalgia and recrimination intermingle and push against each other in
three short verses that manage to be at once sad and comic, wise and self-
deceiving, battle scarred and freshly wounded. Looking back at those five
years, the singer sees himself as a virtuous dupe. In the second verse he
tells us he got a job in a steel mill, dutifully bringing home his paycheck
every Friday in the naive conviction that he and the little woman were
pulling together for the long haul. He was good then, he wants to tell us,
young and strong and committed to being a steady provider, but he was
also green. It pains him to recall delivering his hard-earned pay to a
woman he had misjudged, who was figuring out how much she could get
out of him before showing him the door. Whatever really happened—
whether she was truly on the make from day one or they had a good thing
that later went bad, whether she cheated on him or they had a mutual falling out or *he* in fact mistreated *her* first and chooses not to mention that
inconvenient aspect of the story as he tells it (the song leaves room for all
of these possibilities)—he is resolved to play it smarter next time. "I
finally learned a lesson I should have known a long time ago," he tells
us in the third verse. "The next woman I marry, she's got to work and
bring me some dough." Depending on how Guy sings it, that final resolve can come off as a wiser man's hope for a better marriage next time
around, an embittered loser's woman-hating bluster, a paean to the
virtues of hard work, or an aspiring parasite's resolve to never again play

the working stiff. "Five Long Years" is about the way experience lives in us where we can get at it, for good and ill. It is about an adult form of heartbreak and also—or, perhaps, therefore—about the character and meaning of work. The two subjects collapse together with the trenchancy of good blues as spouse and employer become one in the phrase "I worked five long years for one woman." The specter of last-hired-and-first-fired haunts the song's account of domestic life; the specter of unrequited love haunts its account of the shopfloor. And "Five Long Years," like many blues songs, contains compressed within it a history and a landscape: one verbal gesture, "got a job in a steel mill, trucking steel like a slave," panoramically embraces southern slavery and the steel mills of the Rust Belt.[1]

The story of pianist Eddie Boyd, who composed the song, covers the blues territory in a long north-tending sweep. Born in Coahoma County, Mississippi, in 1914, he spent his childhood on Stovall's Plantation, a cotton-growing area usually identified as a cradle of the Delta blues style that became the basis of Chicago blues. Boyd went north in 1941, finding work in a Chicago defense plant during the gearing up for war that helped draw so many southern blacks to the North. Boyd said he was inspired to compose "Five Long Years" by the sound of machines in a Cicero steel mill in which he worked. "I never wrote down one word of that tune," he told an interviewer in the 1970s, "and the rhythm came from the sound of that power brake machine I was running. And I would sing that song, man, until it got to be one of those things like I used to listen to Roosevelt and them. It used to grow on me. So then I knew I was ready."[2] He knew he was ready when the song in his head he had built from life—from the parts made available by migration, industrial work, and domestic arrangements—began to resemble the music he heard in clubs and on records, especially the songs of established bluesman Roosevelt Sykes. Boyd first recorded "Five Long Years" in 1952, when it spent seven weeks at number one on the R & B charts. A series of unrewarding encounters with shifty or disorganized record companies—an occupational hazard, especially in the heyday of small blues labels—left Boyd disgruntled with the blues business in Chicago. He went to Europe in 1965 as part of the American Folk Blues Festival, a pioneering effort to encourage and exploit the period's revival of the taste for blues in nonblack audiences. Boyd liked Europe and eventually moved there for good, settling in Helsinki. He also recorded "Five Long Years" again in Europe. During his tour in 1965, he took time out to record a set of his songs in a Hamburg studio, this time with the young hotshot Buddy Guy playing subtle, swift guitar behind him.

Eddie Boyd, Finno-Mississippian bluesman, died in 1994, but Buddy Guy is taking good care of his song. Guy sings the hell out of "Five Long Years," making it the most powerful song of his set on the nights he performs it. He turns Boyd's tight midtempo tale into a showstopping slow blues, sometimes singing its three-verse narrative twice as he works through the song's shadings of sound and meaning. Guy has just the voice for singing "Five Long Years." His lower register has a dark pulse suited to brooding or threatening; in his midrange he eagerly bends and jumps notes as the spirit moves him; and when his voice sails into its piercing upper register, it acquires an unsettling conviction that manages to be both aggrieved and joyful at the same time. It is a voice that sounds like it started out to be churchy but got mixed up with a faster crowd.

He also plays guitar. Guy's playing, as instantly recognizable as his voice, can be shrewdly pent-up, but when he lets himself go—which is most of the time—it soars wildly over the top in a torrent of fast, loud, often distorted notes that regain their purity when sustained on a bent string pinned to the fingerboard. He has a strangler's touch, squeezing strings to produce vertiginous dissonances that resolve themselves and pass into dissonance again as he lets up and reapplies the tension. Especially in live performances, he favors a variety of staticky, clangorous tones that evoke a giant turbine's whine, a downed power line whipping back and forth in a thunderstorm, or a thousand horns played in loose unison through a bad long-distance telephone connection. Guy's playing often feels more than a little out of time and out of tune, but never unmusical; he does not rest easily within the confines of a song or a style, instead machining the music into his own jagged diction.

At the Trump Marina show, as he usually does, Guy played a couple of sweet, muted guitar choruses to open "Five Long Years." The audience, still recovering from the set opener, a full-bore rendition of Muddy Waters's "I Got My Mojo Working," had to listen hard to catch the bends and sustains. They actually shushed one another. Once Guy started singing, though, his guitar fills between sung lines became harsher and broader, and the drummer (Ray "Killer" Allison, Guy's principal abettor) kicked the band to keep up with the surge. By the time Guy had worked through the song's three verses, arriving at "and bring me some dough" in a highly exercised state, the band was crashing along behind him, and the moment was ripe for one of the night's episodes of high musical drama.

Guy's solo escalated rapidly from a few scattered notes into an un-broken fusillade. Furious runs up and down the guitar's neck, punctu-ated with the startlingly human-sounding groans he wrenched from the strings, produced a nearly solid, thickly textured block of music that ex-panded until it filled the room. Members of the audience—those who had known what to expect, as well as those who had been expecting ei-ther a younger Muddy Waters or a blacker Eric Clapton—were ex-changing glances: some shocked, some deeply satisfied, some suggest-ing a headache was on the way. It was as if they were realizing that the drinks were dosed. Some were going to enjoy the trip, some sensed a rough night ahead, everybody felt the strong medicine moving in us.

The set developed along lines that Guy has established in more than forty years of performing. At some point he took a meandering walk through the crowd, soloing frantically and carving a path with his gui-tar through the press of excited humans, while the band vamped duti-fully behind him. He did imitations and homages. He had the crowd sing along frequently, and he got the usual ovations by remarking he felt so good that he could play all night and by instructing his band to play it so funky they can smell it. He played some standards and a couple of new songs from his current CD. He let his rhythm guitar player, Scott Holt, take a couple of confident, accomplished solos and (somewhat more gingerly) sing a song. Guy's own solos grew longer and more par-oxysmal. As the evening progressed, he largely dispensed with the busi-ness of building to emotional peaks and tried instead to turn the whole experience into a single, impossibly extended emotional peak.

Although a few in attendance were put off by all this—and a silver-haired couple seated near me, casino habitués dressed in loose-fitting pastel athletic togs, slipped out halfway through—the vast majority of the crowd gave itself over to Guy's music with great enthusiasm. Guy was visibly, honestly, passionately grateful to them. As he has admitted over the years, he is anxious to please to a fault. Extraordinarily sensitive by nature and fixated on bringing joy to an audience at all costs, he fears his listeners will be put off, unmoved, or—to raise the bar higher—thrilled but not quite thrilled enough. He therefore regards a live show as a do-or-die matter of scaling to ecstasy, a more delicate operation than his penchant for exaggerated volumes and guitar-heroic grimaces might lead one to believe. Inevitably, he does not always manage to sus-tain the balance between establishing a structure and transcending it. Especially in recent years, since he succeeded in becoming a minor rock star in addition to being a major figure in the blues, he has tended to sacrifice structure in pursuit of transcendence. As the set develops, one can begin to feel bludgeoned, not so much by the impressive volume of guitar playing (measured in both decibels and notes to the bar) as by the sense that Guy's determination to take us all up one ecstatic peak after another becomes oppressive. He cannot reach the pinnacle every time—nobody can—and even a series of successful ascents begins to wear on a listener. Imagine boxing boiled down to a series of bone-cracking knockout punches, as it often is in highlight sequences: one begins to miss all the other business that gives boxing its thickness and complexity, not least the unfolding of a narrative proportioned by skill, strategy, and the pattern of action and rest.

If Guy feels obliged to give a crowd what he thinks it wants, he is also driven by a very personal sense of what music is; sometimes the two impulses move together, sometimes at cross-purposes. Peter Watrous has astutely labeled Guy an abstractionist.[3] Guy would have made a great free-jazz player, and I can imagine him entirely liberated (at least for a night) from the orthodox bluesman's role, sharing a stage with "out" players like John Zorn or the late Sonny Sharrock, happily blasting the eardrums of gaunt edge-music connoisseurs at the Knitting Factory. The pleasures of Guy's guitar playing have much to do with his tendency to overleap the barriers of any song, any genre, in his urge to ramble in the fields of abstract noise beyond. It can be exciting to follow him on such journeys, but by the middle of Guy's set I often find myself wishing for less abstraction, for more rigorous and nuanced attention to constructing blues songs. Guy's music works best and goes deepest when his will to travel up and out has genuinely interesting limits to press against and transcend, a better-defined musical ground to which he feels obliged to orient the solo flights that take off from it. I also find myself wishing to hear more of his voice. He plays more and sings less as the set proceeds, and the quality of articulate expression recedes from his increasingly superhuman-scale guitar playing. Because the guitar solo—thanks to rock—has become the industry standard when it comes to vehicles bearing us toward ecstasy, an audience at a Buddy Guy show hears as much guitar as it can take and then some.

Guy, who reads crowds attentively, is not unaware of the need for solid grounding occasioned by his flights into abstraction. At some point in almost every set, after he has done the slow blues and perhaps two or three other songs, he will gesture at establishing that ground by offering a thumbnail history of the blues in a series of imitations and homages. Guy initiates the set's midgame, bringing the crowd to heel, with a little speech about the importance of recognizing the leading lights of the blues, many of whom have passed and did not receive their due when they were alive. Then he offers a musical genealogy of his style—what he believes his audience knows and ought to know about his blues. When I first started going to hear him play live in the late 1970s, he would do Muddy Waters, John Lee Hooker, T-Bone Walker, Jimmy Reed, and perhaps a few notes of Cream's "Sunshine of Your Love" or a Hendrix riff to tease the rock fans in the audience. Then, dispensing with homage, he would abruptly cut off the band and call out in a stern voice, "Now this here is some Buddy Guy," launching into something neither traditional nor rock-inflected—an R & B workout, for instance, like the soul-blues standard "Chicken Heads." The double point of the exercise seemed to be to affirm his blues credentials and to take everybody else—orthodox bluesmen as well as classic rockers—down a peg. He would finish his Muddy Waters routine by exaggerating the old master's Delta diction until it became a parody, at which point Guy would pause and then add, "Ho ho ho." This twitting of the aging, portly king of the Chicago blues came abruptly to an end in 1983 when Muddy Waters died. Guy, having succeeded to the throne, assumed an attitude of pious respect toward his predecessor, trying to keep alive a sense of Muddy Waters's greatness in a new generation of blues fans. Since then, many of not only Muddy Waters's but also Guy's contemporaries in the blues have died, Guy has become as big a star as his primary identification with the blues will allow, and Guy's musical genealogy has changed.

At the Trump Marina, a typical late-1990s show, Guy did Muddy Waters and John Lee Hooker, but he also did Eric Clapton and Jimi Hendrix, and at the end of the show he explained to the crowd that he had forgotten to do Stevie Ray Vaughan, so he played "Cold Shot," too. Guy's place in the world had changed. When he was touring in the summer of 1998, his fifth Silvertone CD had recently arrived in stores, and he could reasonably expect to make some money from it, thanks in great part to the rock stars in his musical debt who had helped secure the Silvertone contract, boosting his career. A marketing push had cast Guy as a gray eminence stepping forward to claim long-overdue credit for fathering classic rock. Jonny Lang, a teenage blues-rock phenom whose first major CD had sold a million copies, toured with Guy as a co-headliner. The blues-rock synthesis was much in evidence. One could hear Guy's influence in Lang's playing and singing, and Guy demonstrated the reflexive influence on him of Lang's predecessors, a long train of rock guitar heroes who had worshipped and studied Guy in their youth. Guy was not, precisely speaking, doing any of them in the sense that a mimic does someone. Rather, he invoked them. He would call out a name from the pantheon, launch into a recognizable riff, and either perform the song as pure Buddy Guy or cut it off and move to the next one. The audience roared approval for each and all.

It was startling to hear Guy's initial speech about lost forefathers and founding influences of the blues segue into a tribute to the gods of rock guitar who had been his apprentices. "Now," he said, "in 1958, John Lee Hooker was doing like this," and then he played a taste of Hooker's "Boom Boom"; a minute later, he was explaining that "in the sixties, the Cream was doing like *this*," and then he played a good chunk (not just a dismissive snippet) of "Strange Brew," following up with Hendrix's "Voodoo Chile." Gone from the repertoire were T-Bone Walker and Jimmy Reed, whose names and music would not ring any bells for most of the audience (unless Guy were to do Reed's "Bright Lights, Big City," which might cause a few in attendance to recall the movie version of Jay McInerny's novel of postcollegiate angst in New York). Gone also was Guy's once-prickly reaction to a crowd that cheered his rock homages. In the 1970s and early 1980s, he would get mad when white patrons greeted the teasing partial riff from "Sunshine of Your Love" with the same cheers they had given to invocations of Muddy Waters et al. Back then it visibly bothered him that Clapton, Hendrix, and the like held high stations in blues fans' pantheon; it bothered him that his patrons, having cheered for Guy's mentors in the blues, cheered just as lustily for his apprentices who had outstripped him in fame. In the summer of 1998, though, Guy plunged enthusiastically into the classic rock grooves, turning them all into Buddy Guy tunes that produced the ecstatic response he craved. Guy's revised history of the blues sounded like the story of how people who listened to rock found their way to the blues—how the rock guitarists he had influenced had taken over the world and made it safe for the blues.

THE STATE OF THE BLUES

Buddy Guy, abstractionist guitar hero, is certainly not today's most classically orthodox exemplar of Chicago blues style—Morris Holt, a nononsense fellow who answers to the stage name Magic Slim, probably is—but Guy enjoys the highest commercial and artistic profile in Chicago blues. That disjunction has made his music a battleground in the public struggle over the state of the music. One side in the struggle, dominated by critics like Bill Dahl and a few musicians like Billy Branch, sees Chicago blues in steep artistic decline since its golden age in the 1950s. These prophets of decline see a once-vital genre reduced to a hot-licks subset of guitar rock, a new Dixieland (with "Sweet Home Chicago" in the role of "When the Saints Come Marching In") designed to satisfy tourists seeking the rock aesthetic's equivalent of the source of the Nile. Stasis, and then the genre's slow death, ensue: Dahl told me, "I think the writing of the Chicago scene's artistic obituary is not far down the road," and he has been publishing rough drafts of that obituary for years.[4] The other side, the boosters, a sort of Benetton universalist coalition led by successful blues players like Buddy Guy and entrepreneurial promoters like Lois Weisberg, Chicago's commissioner of cultural affairs, sees Chicago blues enjoying an era of unprecedented success. Celebrated as great art and party music around the world and especially on its home turf, Chicago blues has been thoroughly mainstreamed in everything from PBS documentaries to advertising to sports talk radio. It may be that only Buddy Guy and a handful of other blues musicians have prospered of late, but it is hard to deny that the music made by inheritors of Muddy Waters's legacy enjoys not only artistic respect but also revived commercial circulation.

Buddy Guy offers the decline faction and the boosters much about which to disagree. Increases over the last forty years in the density and frenzy of his guitar playing, accompanied by verbal and musical homage from rock-star acolytes like Jimi Hendrix, Eric Clapton, Jeff Beck, Jimmy Page, the Rolling Stones, Carlos Santana, Stevie Ray Vaughan, and most recently Jonny Lang, have turned Guy into an ur–guitar hero and also made him the decline faction's Exhibit A. Purists dismiss his mature guitar style with recurring, resonant phrases. They say that "he plays too many notes," which is shorthand for too much flash and not enough substance, and is usually applied to young white guitar wizards with weak blues sensibilities and no singing chops (the kind of whiz kids who usually list Guy among their influences). The phrase is *not* usually applied to people like Guy—black, southern-born, in his sixties, with first-rate blues credentials and a formidable singing voice. Decline-minded critics also call his music "white noise," a pejorative reference to what they hear as rock influences in his playing.

The "noisiness" of his playing—the ratio of sounds regarded by critics as extraneous or even antithetical to whatever orthodox blues signal they hear in his music—has become more pronounced, and more

Buddy Guy, guitar
hero, at the Chicago
Blues Festival in 1988.
All photos:
© Marc PoKempner.

lavishly recorded and circulated, since Guy achieved long-delayed commercial success in the 1990s. Finally, after a lifetime of striving in relative obscurity, he had a profitable club and a long-term recording contract with a label that could put some resources behind him; he began to turn up on rock radio, the David Letterman show, and *Saturday Night Live;* he appeared in a Gap ad; his likeness presided over the music sections of Borders stores; Amazon.com pushed his CDs; the city of Chicago began to feature him in its tourism campaigns; and both the city's convention bureau and its office of cultural affairs made a practice of steering business travelers, pleasure tourists, and visiting dignitaries to his club. According to extremists in the decline faction, the price of this success has been steep: Guy is not playing Chicago blues—or blues at all—anymore.

Seen from one angle, the opposing factions, both of them interracial coalitions, disagree about the relationship between race and aesthetics. The argument for decline comes close to saying, and sometimes flat-out says, that the problem is one of people not knowing their place: black musicians inauthentically playing in a "white" way to satisfy audience demand for the roots of rock, white musicians inauthentically trying and failing to "sound black," white audiences inauthentically "acting black" in the cheapest kind of Saturday night appropriation rituals—a mutually degrading round of bad-faith love and theft.[5] The boosters make a countervailing universalist argument about the declining musical significance of race: Chicago blues was invented by southern blacks but now belongs to everybody because it speaks to everybody. This "everybody gets the blues" argument (also made by a cast member of *Ain't Nothin' but the Blues* finessing the matter of roots authenticity on Broadway)[6] often has its heart in the right place, but it can perform curious contortions to avoid the possibility that the social and cultural history of race in America does indeed inflect how the music is made and received.

Seen from another angle, the battle over Chicago blues is about change over time in generic orthodoxy. How much can a cultural form adapt without becoming fundamentally something else? What is still "Chicago" about an eminently portable blues style circulated around the world, a style mutating in a million suburban basements and a thousand Blue Monday open-mike jams far from the South Side, a style whose primary financial supporters encounter it at theme-park chain clubs like the House of Blues or on car stereos as they tool from subdivision to office park?

These often ungenerous and tautologically deadlocked controversies over the relative whiteness, blackness, and Chicago-ness of Chicago blues are, among other things, conventional ways to grapple piecemeal with the transformation of not only a musical style but also the institutions and the city in which it developed. A step back to gain a fresh angle of approach might help. The blues is many things to many people—a foundational African American cultural tradition, a way of being in the world, a philosophical system—but it is also a skilled artistic trade, a *how* and a *what* of music making that needs to be learned and practiced, and it takes shape when poured into the vessels of business institutions like clubs and record companies. So the transformation of the blues industry in Chicago, and its product, partakes of a larger transformation of all kinds of businesses and the city itself. The story is as simple and as complicated as the explanation offered by Otis Rush, one of Guy's contemporaries, for why he began playing North Side clubs where the blues-rock constituency held sway: "It doesn't matter where I play as long as I got a good guitar and an amplifier. It was jobs up there, they called me, I went."

NORTH

George "Buddy" Guy grew up in Lettsworth, Louisiana, a small town near Baton Rouge, and came to Chicago in 1957 on the train called the City of New Orleans. He was part of the second and larger phase of the Great Migration, the movement of black southerners to the urban North in the years between the Great Depression and the urban crisis of the 1960s. Guy, a son of sharecroppers, did not come to Chicago to work in factories, but plenty of his blues-playing colleagues did—and, more generally, factory work made the larger movement possible. Chicago blues can be described as the product of an industrial migration.

This chapter of the story is familiar. The strongest pushes and pulls guiding black migration to the North included manufacturing booms and labor markets associated with the world wars—especially the second, and the boom in consumer goods that followed it. Add to that the mechanization of southern agriculture and the enabling function of railroads—the paradigmatic high-industrial transport technology, which still pervades the blues soundscape. These industrial pushes and pulls were essential to delivering a critical mass of southern blacks to Chicago by the 1950s, including the musicians, initial audience, and some of the businesspeople who shaped the Chicago style.

That critical mass produced the golden age of Chicago blues in the 1950s and early 1960s. Among the many blues styles in Chicago, rang-

ing from hokum to jump, the label "Chicago blues" became attached
to the adaptation of Mississippi Delta style effected in the 1950s by
codifiers, especially Muddy Waters and his circle, and the cohort of
immediate second-wave successors who extended their formulas, especially Otis Rush, Magic Sam, and Buddy Guy. These emblematic Chicago stylists made the most of electric amplification, a hard regulariza-
tion of an often irregular country beat, and the tension between
acrobatically lyrical lines of voice or guitar and a dense, grounded, driving ensemble sound. Of all the blues genres, Chicago style may grind
the hardest and soar the highest over that grind, producing a peculiarly
sharp dynamic of tension and release that generates terrific emotional
force. The makers of this style commanded the attention of an expanding black audience with music singularly expressive of the encounter
with industrial urbanism: expressive in lyrics, theme, and the juxtaposition of strong, southern-accented feeling with mechanized, routinized,
mass-produced—that is, industrialized—sound and experience. The
Chicago blues synthesis was most importantly based in Bronzeville, the
relatively self-contained Black Metropolis on the near South Side given
cohesion by the dynamics of migration and segregation. The near
South Side—and then the West Side, as the city's black population
overspilled Bronzeville's boundaries—housed not only inspired musicians and enthusiastic audiences but also institutions: the independent
record companies, record distributors and retailers, dance halls, and especially the blues clubs that nurtured and circulated the music.

The rhythms, character, and textures of industrial urbanism per-
vaded the Chicago blues synthesis. One can hear them, for example, in
songs like Eddie Boyd's "Five Long Years," even when Buddy Guy sings
it now, far from the milieu that originally shaped the song—at his club
in the loft conversion area of the South Loop, at festivals, on TV, in European resort towns, at the Trump Marina. The song's industrial pedigree still registers in the lyrics, and in the groove Boyd derived from the
machines he operated. Perhaps, too, that pedigree registers in the ma-
chine-tool bite of Guy's guitar sound—more like an El train rounding
a corner overhead than a freight train heard in the distance on a rural
night—and in his stylistic gestures at Chicago orthodoxy circa 1952
when he performs it. "Five Long Years" is among the most traditionally
voice-centered, least rock-flavored tunes in his repertoire; performing it,
he often extends his momentary renunciation of guitar heroics so far as
to let Scott Holt or his keyboardist take the main solo.

The manufacturing economy was also worked into the fabric of blues
institutions. To take one of many possible examples, on Tuesday nights

in the late 1950s, if you had a quarter, you could get into Pepper's Lounge on Forty-third Street to see Otis Rush, perhaps the finest singer among the Chicago stylists. Johnny Pepper opened the club with $500 he borrowed from the credit union of the Ford Motor Company, for which he worked (supplementing other, perhaps less legitimate, sources of income). Rush, at the height of his musical powers, still worked day jobs in machine shops, packinghouses, and a steel mill to make ends meet.[7] The manufacturing economy brought together artist and entrepreneur, assembled an interested audience, and provided the minimal but necessary capital for equipment, subsistence, and institution-building, conditions allowing an inspired artist to produce superb Chicago blues.

More generally on the subject of blues and work, although I will not even begin to taxonomize the various blues styles here, it bears saying that any such account must go hand in hand with the history of work. That identity goes back to the root: to the unfree labor of slavery and to the work songs that were one of the principal sources for the modern blues that appeared in the late nineteenth century; also to the timber camps and other work-based communities in which early blues took form. As a subject, also, work has been on the short list of major blues themes, on a par with bad news, ecstatic experience, place, travel, and sex. The historical rhythms of labor that have shaped the development of blues forms range in scale from the cadences of body work and machines to long-wave, work-related folk migrations that made possible various blues syntheses. We might broadly periodize blues via work in three overlapping phases: an agrarian-to-industrial phase reaching from the late nineteenth century well into the twentieth; a high-industrial phase with strong agrarian undercurrents, typified by Chicago style, that rose to dominance in the decades spanning midcentury; and a postindustrial phase, initiated in the 1960s and maturing in the 1980s and 1990s, that has partially layered over the industrial and agrarian. And, of course, playing the blues is itself a form of work in an industry connected to more general economic and social conditions.

Although Guy had won some local notoriety as an up-and-coming bluesman in Louisiana, he has said he "felt like a ball in high weeds" when he got to Chicago in 1957.[8] After a period of scuffling and doing manual work, he entered and began to rise in the blues hierarchy by plugging himself into existing institutional structures: the South Side and West Side club circuits, where he was discovered, then the Muddy Waters band, Chess Records, Cobra, and other independent labels. Accounts of Guy's career tend to dwell on an epic cutting contest held at the Blue Flame Club in 1958, a clash of young titans in which Guy did much to make his name by besting Otis Rush and Magic Sam. That night probably did not make Guy's fortune all by itself, but it renders in shorthand the larger, more diffuse process of finding his way into a richly developed blues scene.

In the late 1950s, Rush and Magic Sam were, like Guy, southern transplants in their early twenties, but they were already established on the Chicago scene as accomplished young bluesmen. Possessed of big, supple, gospel-style voices and strong musical personas, they made an exemplary pair of second-wave Chicago bluesmen. Trained in the Delta tradition but guiding it toward renegotiations with the larger field of R & B subgenres, they drew new sounds from within Chicago blues that developed its seemingly bottomless potential as a generative style. Rush was already a master of chilling slow blues in a minor key. He squeezed strings with the best of them, bending single notes into affecting microtones and running them down into jazzy, pianistic chords. Everything Magic Sam played, even songs with mournful lyrics, had an infectious good-times quality; his propulsive, meaty picking style made people want to dance. Guy had the good sense to be scared of confronting them in the Blue Flame's competitive atmosphere before a crowd that may have included (depending on who tells the story) Chicago blues kingpins like Muddy Waters and Howling Wolf, world-class guitar virtuoso Earl Hooker, and Guy's future partner Junior Wells. Even the rhythm section reportedly backing the contestants that night was a Chicago blues dream team, including three men—Otis Spann, Fred Below, and Little Walter—generally deemed to occupy the first rank among pianists, drummers, and harmonica players, respectively. Hungry for recognition and painfully eager to please, Guy was still very green, not only as an urbanite but also as a musician. As Willie Dixon, who was always handy with faint praise for those who threatened to eclipse him, once said in recalling Guy's arrival on the Chicago scene, "His timing wasn't up to par, but he was trying so hard."[9]

All versions of the Blue Flame story emphasize that Guy, fueled by strong drink, went crazy. The details of his performance that night, establishing the pattern for decades of future performances, have taken on a stations-of-the-cross quality in frequent retellings. A long-cord gimmick allowed Guy to make his entrance, already playing, out of the bathroom and to exit the front door of the club, still playing, and head down the block in the snow. He played "Sweet Little Angel," a slow blues in the second-tune slot, during which he threw his guitar on the floor and stomped it, as well as hung it from the rafters and played it there. He parodied both Rush's and Magic Sam's guitar styles, running them through the blender of distortion effects until it all sounded like Buddy Guy. The crowd was agog; Guy was declared the winner. Rush, who did not go in for such hotdogging, and Magic Sam, who was by all reports an easygoing guy, did not dispute the verdict—although they took the liberty of drinking the bottle of whiskey awarded as first prize. Guy got the empty bottle, anyway, and the satisfaction of knowing he was launched.[10]

Lost in this stock portrait of the artist as a young maniac is the fact that Buddy Guy was an inspired, if raw, musician addressing an eager, knowledgeable audience. The fetches of showmanship caught the crowd's attention—and getting attention was hard to do in a city full of daunting musical craftspeople, especially guitar players—but what mattered most was that Guy made urgently compelling music. The notes, more than the histrionics, fairly forced the crowd to respond to a young Buddy Guy hellbent on getting to them one way or another. A freshly arrived country boy from back home, "green as a pool table and twice as square" (as he often says) but equipped with formidably southern cultural tools, he insisted that they ascend out of the ordinary in his company. Audiences responded to Guy's offer of ecstasy in large musical doses; black southerners in the urban North, as a transplanted people logically would, responded with special sensitivity to an ambitious newcomer's manifest and burning need to make it—in Chicago blues and, more broadly, in Chicago—or use himself up trying.

But the scene as he found it, the scene epitomized by that night at the Blue Flame, would not last. By the 1960s, as Guy came into his own, the institutional structure of clubs and record labels was losing coherence as an enabling framework for the industrial blues synthesis. That process, manifested as weak sales for traditional Chicago blues, loosened up the field of musical possibility but also deprived Guy of a straight-and-narrow generic path. Chicago blues passed through a period of overlap and adjustment in the late 1960s and 1970s until it stabilized in postindustrial form in the 1980s and 1990s.

What happened to the blues business in the 1960s? The answer has several parts. In the record industry, corporate consolidation put the squeeze on independents like Chess, while at the same time major labels attracted by the successes of various R & B forms moved into the independents' former territory. Rock and soul, both pitched to the teenage consumer who emerged from the 1950s as the hegemonic force shaping popular dance music, drew freely upon blues and largely supplanted it among young people. Blues, with its adult point of view and "country" associations, did not address itself as successfully to that decisive segment of the market. (And the so-called blues revival of the 1960s among white audiences tended to valorize precisely the market-unfriendly qualities of blues, relegating it to the idealized role of a precommercial and therefore authentic folk tradition, rather than a product of urban business enterprises.)[11] Among black audiences, the shock of the encounter with industrial urbanism began to wane, and the postmigrant generation began to turn from down-home ways—a domestic, African American version of the second-generation cultural crisis familiar among immigrants. As South-to-North migration slowed, stopped, and eventually reversed, the transplanted southerners who had invented and supported Chicago blues began to age out in earnest. Finally, and crucially, the social landscape of the inner city in which Chicago blues was rooted was in violent motion. Already under a variety of pressures, the institutions that housed Chicago blues were cut loose from their social underpinnings during the city's transformation.

If the Great Migration was an industrial folk migration, the migrants arrived in an increasingly postindustrial city. Already in the 1950s, sensitive urbanites felt tectonic shifts beneath the surface of the postwar boom. Especially in the case of black migrants, cities in transition like Chicago increasingly failed to provide the same structure of opportunity they had provided during their high-industrial periods. That transformation of opportunity was increasingly evident after 1970—especially after the urban crisis, dramatic plant closings, and a number of social scientific studies underscored the relationship between deindustrialization and inner-city poverty.[12] But even earlier, even as southern blacks poured into Chicago during the 1950s and early 1960s, capital was already in motion toward the service sector, the suburbs, the Sun Belt, the redeveloped downtown core, and the gentrified lakefront. The urban villages and factory belts of the inner city, the heartland of industrial urbanism, suffered the consequences.

Two elements of this story have special importance for Chicago blues because they contributed to the dismantling of the industrial blues synthesis and the emergence of a postindustrial blues synthesis. One is the breakup of the Black Metropolis and the formation of the second ghetto on the South Side and West Side. Capital flight, the partial departure of the black middle class, bulldozing of neighborhoods, siting of highrise housing projects, and subsequent depopulation all contributed to the destruction of Bronzeville's small business sector. That included blues clubs, dance halls, stores that sold records, and independent record labels—which were also reeling from all the other shocks associated with changes in popular music and the record business.

The other principal element of the story is the growth, especially on the North Side lakefront, of redeveloped districts that housed the city's growing numbers of information handlers, symbolic analysts, professionals, and higher-end service workers. They invested in a new set of cultural and economic institutions, including not only places to buy arugula but also the clubs and record labels that now constitute the institutional home of Chicago blues. Most of these new supporters were—and are—white.

It may be oversimplifying to say that starting in the 1960s younger blacks turned away from Chicago blues and whites replaced them, but the oversimplification addresses a significant truth. Alligator Records, the most important independent blues label over the last thirty years, and *Living Blues,* the most important blues magazine, were founded in Chicago in 1971 and 1970, respectively. Their customer surveys over the years have found that they serve essentially the same population: male, for the most part educated, middle-class, and overwhelmingly white baby boomers. In 1998, Bruce Iglauer, who founded and still runs Alligator, told me, "We'd love to have more black consumers, but our audience is well over 95 percent white." David Nelson, who was then editor of *Living Blues,* told me much the same thing. Iglauer added, "I started a record label to sell records to people very much like myself. I knew those people very well because I went to college with them, I grew up with them; I was born right in the cusp of the baby boom, July 1947. There were a lot of people born in 1947, and a lot of them graduated from college in 1969. A lot of them went through the civil rights movement, the British Invasion, the folk music scare." Most of his customers come to blues through folk music, through what is now known as classic rock (Eric Clapton or the Rolling Stones, usually), or, later, through Stevie Ray Vaughan. For at least a generation, this cohort has dominated the urban blues audience, especially in the case of the increasingly rock-identified, guitar-centered Chicago style (as opposed to its polar opposite, the voice- and groove-centered soul-blues style invisible to most rock fans: the music of Z. Z. Hill, Denise LaSalle, Marvin Sease, Tyrone Davis, and a host of Malaco recording artists popular with black audiences of all ages in the South and a mostly older crowd in the North).

Fans at a Buddy Guy show at B.L.U.E.S., a North Side club, in 1986. Photo:
© Marc PoKempner.

Black people do listen to Chicago blues, but the local, national, and
international CD-buying and festival-going audience is overwhelmingly
white, and for two decades most of Chicago's clubs have been on the
North Side and filled with white people. At century's end, most of
the South Side and West Side clubs had shut down or staged live music
only on weekends (and relied on white audiences to stay in business),
few blues headliners played regularly on the South Side or West Side,
and the increasingly important tourist audience—composed largely of
white midwesterners and Europeans—was concentrated downtown
and on the North Side.

"Wasn't for the whites, we wouldn't have survived," Ben Hampton,
manager of the Checkerboard Lounge, told me in 1998. A broad-
beamed, deliberate man of advanced middle years from Greenwood,
Mississippi, Hampton was wearing a magnificently broken-in specimen
of the three-quarter-length leather car coat favored by Chicago's black
and Eastern European tough guys, regardless of fashion or weather,
since the 1960s. We were huddled over drinks in a corner of the
Checkerboard, Bronzeville's last surviving flagship club, situated just off
the intersection of King Drive and a stretch of East Forty-third Street

renamed in honor of Muddy Waters. Outside, it was a raw early spring evening, streetlights coming on in the gloom. Forty-third Street, which in the 1950s had been a thriving commercial strip with several blues clubs, now looked like a second-ghetto cliché: lined with abandoned and ruined buildings, punctuated by vacant lots and the usual storefront churches, liquor stores, check-cashing joints, and government- and charity-run social service offices. Hand-lettered signs wired to street-lights advertised handyman services and slightly used tires. In the late 1950s and 1960s, urban renewal had flowed over the area, wiping out the business sector and leaving the monumental Robert Taylor Homes and other projects as second-ghetto moraines.

Inside the Checkerboard, the generic South Side tavern bouquet of cigarettes, stale beer, and the Johnson Products Corporation's hair care goods thickened the atmosphere. The jukebox played songs by B. B. King and Z. Z. Hill, drowning out the usual run of crime reports on the local television news. A few regulars collected along the bar. They were mostly southern-born black Chicagoans, representatives of the group that had once been the backbone of the local blues audience. Almost all of them north of sixty, they formed a demographic rear guard. The mis-matched chairs that lined the long, narrow tables in front of the club's stage area were empty. If the Checkerboard made some money later that night, it would for the most part be money brought in by nonblack blues fans—tourists or North Siders venturing south, buffs from the nearby University of Chicago—who would fill those seats.

"I hate to say it," Hampton continued, "but black people don't sup-port blues here. Blacks are more into going to casinos—down to Indi ana, all up into Wisconsin. Our customers are, I'd say, 60–40 white. A lot more than that on the weekend. They're the ones remember guys long gone, like Lefty Dizz or Sammy Lawhorn, been dead for years. They remember them better than the blacks do. Come in here asking about 'em." Hampton said the Checkerboard's daytime and early eve-ning clientele was almost exclusively black, "80 percent southern, and getting older. Those that are left. A lot of people I know have gone back south." Still, between the remaining southern-born blacks, the few northern-born blacks who take an interest in Chicago-style blues, and the whites who might show up later that night, he was not giving up on the business. "We don't have live music every night anymore," Hamp-ton said, "and we changed up the music a little. We moved away some from the low-down dirty blues, upped the beat. But the main thing don't change. People still have a good time and the music still sound better here." He was not saying that the Checkerboard books the most famous artists or has a superlative sound system. He meant that musicians playing blues in its traditional home on the South Side imparted a special force and meaning to the music that North Side clubs could never hope to match. The club's big weekend draw was Vance Kelly, who can play the Delta-derived, guitar-driven Chicago style (which is what Hampton meant by "low-down and dirty") to which white blues and rock fans are accustomed, but he also plays R & B and soul blues (what Hampton meant by "upped the beat"), which older blacks often prefer. Kelly was known at the time as the best young bluesman in Chicago without a recording contract.

When I talked with Ben Hampton in 1998, Bronzeville was girding for an economic comeback. Members of the black middle class—many of them the children and grandchildren of southern migrants—were staging a return to the Black Metropolis, which, although still semi-depopulated and intermittently ruinous and rough, was also a zone of affordable housing within a few minutes' ride of the Loop and the lake. Parts of the area, especially those closer to the lake, had already entered the early stages of a redevelopment boom. The city was preparing to knock down the high-rise projects along the lakefront, with the inland Robert Taylor Homes slated to follow soon after. City planners and developers were again talking, as they had been talking off and on for years, about turning Forty-third Street into a revived blues strip, the kind of cultural-historical tourism scheme pursued by many deindustrializing Rust Belt cities, as well as southern music capitals like New Orleans and Memphis. There was also talk of siting the blues strip—and moving the Checkerboard to anchor it—four blocks south on Forty-seventh Street, even if that meant uprooting extant businesses in that area. Neighborhood veterans argued that the stretch of Forty-seventh Street in question had been home to big-band jazz rather than blues in its midcentury heyday, but the location is closer to the middle-class university enclave of Hyde Park, a situation that, it was thought, might encourage potential patrons of blues clubs to feel that they were not venturing into the middle of the ghetto.

Even with versions of the blues strip on the planners' drawing boards, and even with condo gut-rehabs planned for buildings across the street, Hampton was not counting on big money flowing back into the ghetto for good anytime soon. For the moment, he planned to hold on to the Checkerboard's small and mixed market share. He thought the business would get by—if blacks and whites from the South Side kept coming, if North Side blues clubs and downtown hotels stopped scaring off customers who also wanted to visit the South Side, if the "Ay-rab taxi drivers" got over their fear of Forty-third Street, if occasional busloads of Japanese tourists continued to provide windfalls, if city government would continue to promote South Side clubs at blues fests and in its cultural development plans. ("They got to *liaison* with us," Hampton said with feeling.) "The club, it support itself," he concluded, "but not like it used to. There's no live entertainment on Tuesday and Wednesday. We make our money on Thursday, Friday, and Saturday and hope for the best."

If you wanted blues seven nights a week, headliners playing in clubs within walking distance of one another, and an unfailingly lively scene, you had to go downtown or to the North Side—two districts that, although they have yet to be widely celebrated in song as such, now constitute the institutional home of the blues.

The northward migration of institutions proceeded in stages, roughly paralleling the formation of a new white blues audience, the aging of Chicago's black blues audience, and the gutting of the Black Metropolis. It began in the 1960s as a coffeehouse scene. By autumn of 1970, *Living Blues* listed four North Side places where one might expect to hear live blues. The scene grew fast. By 1974, *Living Blues* listed fifteen clubs that, even if they could not offer the texture of South Side meccas like Florence's or Theresa's, did feature some of the best talent in town.[13] Bruce Iglauer, who knows his clientele, said the North Side clubs and his North Side record company prospered because the blues converts of the 1960s settled down and started making money in the 1970s and 1980s. Iglauer himself, a dark-haired Jerry Garcia type, was a scruffy-bearded "hippie-looking cat" (as the Kinsey brothers described him in a song) in the 1970s, when he scuffled to keep Alligator alive. He has grown more prosperous and spruced himself up a bit since then. He calls his own transformation and that of his customers a "hippies-to-yuppies" process, which he roadmarks with the usual haircuts and compromises with the market.

The members of the new core blues audience encountered the music most often on college campuses where many of them were credentialing themselves to work with information, provide services, and enter the professions: they were in training to be postindustrial workers and managers. As they entered the high-consumption period of their lives, they invested in Chicago blues, an increasingly guitar-centered style that appealed to them not only because it is good music but also because it scratches an itch for authenticity. Chicago blues answers a demand for "roots" as an aesthetic quality rather than as a social reality. That demand derives special force from the tendency of self-consciously urban people inhabiting the postindustrial city's elite districts and suburbs to indulge themselves in feeling deracinated, even disembodied, as they move through a landscape of work and home life that sometimes strikes them as only superficially grafted onto the older cityscape it supplanted. Chicago blues evokes the folk roots of mass culture and the blues roots of rock, and compressed within the music is a complex set of associations with industrial urbanism and its agrarian sources—color-coded notions of work, play, mobility, history, and especially manhood and womanhood. Iglauer thinks that, especially during the 1960s, bluesmen appealed to young white men of the baby boom in two principal ways. "The old guys, the old Delta guys, kind of appealed to the folkie in you, a part of you that says that middle-class values and popular culture seem to be lacking something, they seem tepid and empty. The young guys appealed to that lack in a different way. They seemed more manly, hipper, more knowledgeable, you know, more full of themselves in terms of 'I'm a man and I know I'm a man.'" These notions of manhood and everything interwoven with it enjoy the status of tradition—especially in a place like Chicago, the male residents of which must finesse the dissonance between a definitive notion of a broad-shouldered past when men were men (which, for blues fans, usually entails selectively failing to remember the blueswomen who dominated the business before World War II) and a less comfortably idealized present. Chicago blues is a real Chicago thing that makes people feel they are getting way down into the texture of neighborhoods, the history of peoples and place, the logic of hard knocks, and powerfully felt experience.

The new core audience of northern-born, middle-class consumers can be deeply engaged with blues as roots music, concert music, party music, or exotica, but they are typically steeped in rock aesthetics. They are rarely trained in the southern-rooted, northern-adapted traditions of music, spiritual life, and work that animated the original Chicago blues synthesis. Most of these consumers are white, but the foregoing applies to blacks of that class as well. To a lesser but still significant extent, the same shift has also occurred in the ranks of new musicians entering the business, the necessary pool of apprentices willing to accept low pay, erratic working conditions, and the discipline of mentors in order to become bona fide practitioners of the Chicago style.

By 1980, the balance had swung, and apparently for good. That year's *Living Blues* guide listed twenty-three North Side clubs and another dozen-plus in the suburbs.[14] Although there were still many bars on the South Side and West Side that presented live music at least one night a week, the North Side clubs were clearly blues capitals. They had the deepest lineups of local and touring headliners, often paid higher salaries, usually had more professional business policies, and did not operate under the threat of violence that sometimes shadowed a South Side or West Side gig.

As the industrial blues synthesis and the Black Metropolis that housed it continued to break up in the 1970s, South Side and West Side blues clubs found it harder to compete with North Side clubs. They had been ground down by economic and cultural disinvestment. Public and private capital had ensured the continuing weakness of the black inner city by abandoning it, and the children and grandchildren of black southern migrants were gradually disinvesting from the blues. Fear of crime, usually exaggerated but sometimes justified, formed the sensational veneer on the deep obscurities of economic and cultural restructuring. Located in neighborhoods feared and shunned by the middle class (and sometimes by musicians, even neighborhood guys like Otis Rush, who has talked and sung about violent incidents that put him off playing on the South Side and West Side), these clubs also had trouble attracting sufficient numbers of blues consumers.

Johnny Pepper, who ran his celebrated club at 503 East Forty-third Street from 1956 to 1971, said that after the riots of 1968 the gradually worsening problem of crime and fear of crime finally got out of hand. Gangs extorted money from musicians and hassled patrons, making life impossible for club owners. Inside the clubs, the music was still strong and the atmosphere festive, but the clubs were increasingly isolated on streets without other viable businesses other than liquor stores and check-cashing joints, streets that were desolate and sometimes dangerous after dark. "Pepper's was all right," Pepper told an interviewer in 1971, "but gettin' in and out of Pepper's is what was bad." Other club owners had it as bad or worse. "The majority of 'em do," Pepper said. "Yes, indeed, the gangs follow where the biggest crowd is to get the biggest hassles. . . . The place over here at 39th and Oakwood Boulevard, those little gangs broke that up. That's all deserted over there now. This fellow had a lounge there, the Blue Flame. It's all busted out, look like a barn now."[15] Pepper, always resourceful, responded to the crisis by moving his business northward toward his clientele, which he estimated at already "75–25 white" by 1970—even on Forty-third Street, even in the riots' immediate aftermath. He sold the place on Forty-third and moved up to Thirteenth and Michigan, where he took over a supper club that had been owned by jazzman Ahmad Jamal. It was on the very near South Side, almost in the South Loop, in a kind of pleasantly seedy no-man's-land where both whites and blacks felt equally at home. Pepper's new club did not last, but two decades later, when the time was right, Buddy Guy would follow his lead in moving his business from Forty-third Street to the South Loop—this time with what appears to be lasting success.

THE BLUES BUSINESS

Buddy Guy was taking a break in a dark, cluttered upstairs room at Legends. This was in April 1998, before he began the summer's touring in support of *Heavy Love* that would bring him to the Trump Marina. As on almost every night that he is in Chicago, he had been downstairs at the bar, handling the usual stream of handshakes, praise, and requests from grinning, nodding patrons. The place was crowded, and the surprisingly large operation—he had forty-five employees—was running smoothly. The guys at the door were collecting twelve bucks a head as the large room filled up with out-of-towners staying at the gigantic Hilton across the street, as well as other tourists and business travelers, suburbanites, North Siders, and occasional South Siders and West Siders. The kitchen was producing artery-clogging Louisiana-style cuisine, the concession stand was selling T-shirts and CDs, copies of the latest edition of the Legends newsletter were stacked just inside the front door, the Web site floated seductively in cyberspace waiting to be hit on, and the music-publishing and promotional arms of Guy's business were respectively guarding his intellectual property and trumpeting its virtues. A crew of local stalwarts who had served in the late Muddy Waters's bands were playing standards in honor of the man Guy had succeeded as king of the Chicago blues. Some of the music, especially the bass line and Ray Allison's idiosyncratically aggressive drumming, came up through the floor and walls of the upstairs room. Guy slumped way down in a sprung chair, one leg over the other, knees as high as his chin. He had flown up to Minneapolis earlier in the day to do a photo session with Jonny Lang, whose guest shot on Guy's new CD was advertised by a prominent orange sticker on the disc's wrapper.

At sixty-one, Guy was close to four times Lang's age, although he did not look it. In fact, he looked less careworn that night than he did when I first encountered him in the late 1970s, a period in which he was frustrated by a stalled career and by owning and running a South Side club, the Checkerboard Lounge, that ate up his money. Now, well set up at Legends and with Silvertone, he was moneyed and celebrated enough to satisfy him. A lean, dark-skinned, well-made man, he has an expressively flexible face. Sometimes when he smiles, a deep, chuckling laugh works up from inside him. A quality of stern passion resides in the laugh—and in his face, too—and he summons it when the conversation warrants a little extra feeling. His voice plays across the same range between warmth and fire. Supple and full when he reminisces or speaks well of someone, it rises, acquiring bite, when he gets excited. He was in a mellow mood that night, though, perhaps feeling his years after a day of traveling.

We were talking about the blues business, specifically about the difference between owning Legends and owning the Checkerboard. One way to track Guy's place in the history of Chicago blues is to do as Deep Throat instructed Woodward and Bernstein: follow the money. In 1972, Guy bought the Checkerboard Lounge, which lost money from day one but became world-famous as *the* place to hear Chicago blues. During Guy's lean years, the 1970s and early 1980s, when he was a guitar prophet without a record contract in his own land, he had to tour vigorously to support the club. "It was just like being a fighter," he told me. "No matter what happens to you, you got to keep getting back in the ring."

Guy took great pride in owning the Checkerboard. He has long argued for the institutional importance of clubs as the vital training ground for blues talent. "I spent a lot of money to keep the blues there," he told me, "because that's where Muddy Waters fathered the [Chicago] blues, Forty-third and Forty-seventh Street. I didn't get the Checkerboard or this place [Legends] to get rich. You can't get rich off a bar, I don't think." It was important to him to remember that, when he came to Chicago in the late 1950s, "someone found me at the 708 Club, Pepper's Lounge, places like that. A club is for the young people to have a place to play, be seen, and be heard, be talked about, so record companies will come." Guy enjoyed the way that black and white blues fans rubbed elbows at the Checkerboard, and he was crazy about the way music sounded in the narrow, smoky room. But the Checkerboard also caused him a great deal of pain; it was hard to run a business on Forty-third Street.

"Yeah, I loved that place," he said, smiling at the thought of it, but then his face got harder. "But if they didn't break in there twice a week and rip me off everything I got—and the help I had, I never went in the Checkerboard and they told me, said, 'Well, you made some money, why don't you go buy a steak?' It was always when I went in there I had to go in my pocket. They'd say, 'Send out and get a hundred cases of beer,' or 'The rent ain't been paid since you been gone.'" Besides being ripped off from all sides, he had to protect his customers from neighborhood operators intent on robbing them. Guy said, "I used to have to stand out there at night like a security guard or something. All these people who was doing that was the neighbors who was glad I brought people around to mess with." Every once in a while in the late 1970s and 1980s, I would come out of the Checkerboard, and there would be a group of people standing around a car that had been stripped of its battery. Especially if the car's owners were white, they looked as if they were trying not to panic. Older black blues fans were afraid, too, Guy said. "All those that is not dead is at the point where they won't even come out at night, 'cause it's so bad. They're afraid to drive 'cause they get ripped off, they get stuck up or carjacked. When I opened that place, wasn't no such thing as carjacking." He exaggerated—it would be news to some of the Checkerboard's longtime and still-regular black customers that they are dead, and it is not clear that crime ever got significantly worse in the area than it was in the early 1970s—but he was right to point out that many people his age stopped going out to South Side clubs.

Discussing the problem of fear and crime, Americans' favorite reductive shorthand for complicated urban transformations, made Buddy Guy angry. "I don't like to lie," he said, his voice rising and finding two notes in the last word. "Those are my people who was doing that. I *don't* like to lie. They did *me* that. And I didn't want nobody white to think that they got ripped off because they was white. They was rippin' off *any*body. They got my car down there too. They broke in my joint all the time. *I* wasn't white." As he tells it, in the end, in 1985, he was robbed of the Checkerboard itself. He was on tour in Europe when trusted associates got together with his landlady to take over the club's lease. He said, "It was like—what do you call that in those countries? Yeah, a coup." (Ben Hampton, who was managing the Checkerboard for L. C. Thurmond, the current owner and the main force behind the transfer of ownership, described the episode to me as "a misunderstanding.") Guy, looking back from the vantage point of his downtown

Buddy Guy turns away a troublemaker at the Checkerboard Lounge in 1982.
Photo: © Marc PoKempner.

club on events already thirteen years in the past, sighed and let it go.
"It's a long story. But I didn't fight about it. I'm not ashamed to say
that, and I don't have anything to do with them anymore." He paused
and then put the matter to rest: "I wasn't making any money down
there, anyway."

Losing the Checkerboard freed Guy to follow the money and action
downtown. In 1989, after four years without a club, Guy opened Legends, a much larger and more profitable place in the South Loop, which
was once a light manufacturing and flophouse district but in the 1990s
became one of Chicago's fastest-growing loft conversion zones, a
classically postindustrial reuse of industrial building stock. Legends is
downtown, across the street from the Hilton and near the city's (and
the northern Midwest's) central highway nexus, perfectly positioned
where the full range of blues consumers can get to it. In the late 1990s,
with business booming, Guy was talking about opening another branch
of Legends in New Orleans, or in London, or in the Loews House of
Blues Hotel set to open soon just fifteen blocks away on the northern
edge of the Loop. Another landlord problem inspired him to direct his
energies in a different direction. By 2001, he was planning to build a

new, bigger Legends on property he owned a block north of the current location. He had become the Chicago blues scene's most powerful artist-businessman by positioning himself to circulate his music and prosper, making moves in the social and cultural landscapes to harness flows of people, capital, power, and ideas that remade the city and the blues business.

Guy has been especially shrewd and forward-looking in exploiting the growing symbiosis between Chicago blues and tourism. Having moved downtown and to the North Side, the blues business increasingly depends on and has a significant role in the city's increasingly important tourist economy. At the time we talked, the city's latest numbers showed that business travelers spent $5 billion in Chicago in 1997, and pleasure travelers spent another $2.8 billion—together generating 110,000 jobs.[16] Add to that the vital importance of the culture business to attracting and retaining taxpaying property owners and money-spending renters. As Lois Weisberg, the mayor's commissioner for cultural affairs, said, "First you make a city interesting to its own people; then the visitors will come." As a synergistic means to sell dinners, hotel rooms, transportation, and so on, the blues is a bow on the ribbon of the package Chicago sells to tourists, suburbanites, and its own citizens. Weisberg, pointing a lit cigarette at me as we sat in her office in the city's official Cultural Center, midway between Legends and the House of Blues, explained it like this: "Look, the first thing *everybody* says is 'Where are the blues?' Not 'Where's Michael Jordan?' or 'Where's the architecture?' Chicago is the nation's premier cultural tourism destination—more affordable than New York, easier to reach for many more people, and friendlier. Blues is part of the appeal." One might see the current marketing of postindustrial cities as a struggle to show that the attractions of "culture" trump the fear of inner cities cultivated by crime stories, racial anxiety, and all the other deep-rooted antiurban sentiments that wound into a still-tight knot of conventional wisdom during the urban crisis of the 1960s. (And one might see the rough urban consequences of the attacks on American cities of September 11, 2001, as a reminder that an all-out civic investment in entertainment and tourism makes a city particularly vulnerable to the combination of economic recession and physical fear that makes "culture" seem like a superfluous expense.)

Chicago continues to mature as a city that sells services, atmosphere, and experiences rather than locally manufactured goods or animal parts, and blues enjoys corresponding new importance in the packaging of Chicago-ness.[17] The most readily consumed packages condense

Chicago-ness into images and atmospheres with familiar associations: the view from the Michigan Avenue bridge; the historical charge of big shoulders and hog butchers; the nostalgic appeal of robber-baron swankiness and the salt-of-the-earth charm of the urban village; a smokestack city rising from the prairie grass, a city of skyscrapers and high-end chain stores rising from the ruins of the smokestack city; sports, lots of sports; ethnic foods and ethnic music. Urban blues serves as one of the most effective and recognizable packages, one of the best ways to brand black Chicago in particular and Chicago in general. As Jeff Huebner put it in an article in the *Reader* on plans for a revived Bronzeville blues strip, "In Chicago, as in other postindustrial cities, the gap between the real cityscape and the stage set is shrinking." One sign of that process, Huebner argued, has been the sustained effort of city government—through manipulation of the landscape, public art, zoning, and cultural policy—to encourage the Hellenizing of Greektown, Italianizing of Little Italy, Asianizing of Chinatown, and Hispanicizing of Little Village, Pilsen, and West Division Street. At the turn of the twenty-first century, the next big step was remaking Bronzeville. "Using Chinatown, Greektown, and the Mexican neighborhood of Little Village as models," according to a report by the city's Department of Planning, a public-private partnership would create an "African Village"–themed commercial district and an entertainment district anchored by a blues strip. Market analysts warned, though, that the planned entertainment district had to overcome widespread "perceptions of the South Side as being unsafe." [18]

Tourists, as a rule, stay away from the South Side, especially after dark. Some do take daytime bus tours of Bronzeville, a popular part of the city's neighborhood tours program, but North Side and downtown clubs—and the city's big outdoor blues festival, held downtown every summer—serve the tourist industry's need for live blues. With the advent of the downtown House of Blues in the 1990s and the opening of the adjoining House of Blues Hotel in 1998, an arrangement that formalized the informal relationship suggested by the proximity of Buddy Guy's Legends to the Hilton, the union of Chicago blues and tourism entered its Disney phase. Warner Hedrick III, who was then general manager of the Chicago House of Blues, might have been talking about the whole city when he told me, "Blues by itself doesn't pay the bills, but blues is a hook for the resell."

I paid Hedrick a visit at the House of Blues the day after I talked to Guy. We sat in a windowless office deep within a low, curvaceous building—which once housed a bowling alley and resembles nothing so much as a whale—sited between the two corncob-shaped high-rises of Marina City. The Marina City complex fronts the Chicago River where the Loop meets the city's showcase district, the Near North Side. One cannot call the House of Blues a club; it is a small theme park, with a state-of-the-art main music hall, a restaurant, bars, private party rooms, a gift shop that does brisk business, and (when we talked in April 1998) the House of Blues Hotel under construction next door. "It's an entertainment complex," said Hedrick. Youngish and tanned, outfitted in black clothes and a good haircut, fluent in business-speak, he was a poster boy for corporate hipness. "Ten, fifteen thousand people a week come through the doors. Our issues are hospitality issues. It's very similar to a hotel environment; hotels sell rooms, we sell entertainment. We have auxiliary venues in the building that service the guests, same as in a hotel where the rooms division brings in the folks and the restaurant and room service provide the resell. Initially, the sell here is the talent, that's what brings people in the door. Then if we make an impact at the individual level, they'll come back." I had to keep reminding myself that he and Ben Hampton were, at least some of the time, in the same business. The planned hotel—which opened later that year—would put the seal on a kind of hermetic consumer paradise in which customers moved from one pleasure station to the next, awash in a carefully composed stimulus package featuring music, hearty food, densely crafted decor, and a seasoning of prosocial goodwill.

In addition to serving as one of the city's most active, best-run midsize concert venues, the House of Blues participated in the packaging of urban experience for tourism that Weisberg's office promoted. "We're strongly driven by tourists," Hedrick noted, "as the city is, but we have a strong local segment that comes to our restaurant, and local people come to our shows." Business was good. Tourists from outside the metropolis and locals in tourist mode feel drawn to the kind of clean, safe environment (with parking nearby) the House of Blues offers, featuring near-perfect insulation from the messiness of public space and the public life it harbors. People who have learned to value the sense of consuming under the tightly controlled conditions they feel while watching television can find that state incarnated in Disney's venues, in casinos, or in the House of Blues club and adjoining hotel. "I think our success is that we create a whole different vibe," Hedrick said. "Being in this building, I don't think you're going to know in any way that you're in Chicago 'til you step outside the door. It's like you're stepping into a whole different environment." That different environment appeals to a range of customers—not only tourists and business lunchers but also the aging white boomers who come to see Robin Trower and the young people of all races who count on the House of Blues to present rap shows when other upscale clubs are afraid to.

The House of Blues company already operated venues in cities across the country (including, at this writing, clubs in the theme-park cities of Orlando, Anaheim, and Las Vegas), a record label, a radio division, and a national concert tour, with digital media next on the agenda. A business that big cannot rely on the relatively esoteric appeal of blues to pay the bills. "When we came into Chicago," said Hedrick, "we offended some people who misunderstood and thought we were saying we were *the* house of blues in Chicago. That's not what we're about, though. We're into the entertainment industry, and we're into music in all facets and capacities. We're not about blues. Blues is what we come from, as all music comes from, and we're a spin-off of the blues environment because that's, you know, the foundation of most music in America." As a distinctive hook that helps bring in customers for the resell, the blues content of the House of Blues has to feel like the real thing to a variety of customers, including—and here is the tricky part—a majority whose notion of the real thing derives from blues-derived rock, the Blues Brothers, and similarly second- or third-order sources. This state of affairs gave Hedrick a case of authenticity anxiety. "We try to maintain the integrity of the concept," he told me. "We're trying to balance the business with the philosophy of the company. I don't want it to be strictly business, strictly corporation, because it loses its edge and becomes corporate and you get all these suits, you know, you get all your ya-yas coming in here. We want to maintain our edge, being a little funky."

"Funky" was clearly a corporate buzzword at the House of Blues. So was "cool." The theme for the next House of Blues tour had not been chosen yet, but, Hedrick assured me, "They will have a cool name for it. It *will* be cool." In the company's in-house culture, "cool" means "cool," but it also means "effective and in keeping with the brand, therefore conducive to profit." There is a similarly multiple message in the company's motto, "Unity in Diversity," and in the iconographic motley of Christian, Jewish, Islamic, Buddhist, animist, and other religious icons that adorns the music hall. Profit can be had in presenting a mix of musics and cultures that captures dollars from what Hedrick called "all different demographics," but the phrase also expresses a universalist mysticism that identifies music and related spiritual impulses as a force for social good. Of course, to the extent that the House of Blues succeeds in communicating this latter ecstatic message about the godliness of good tunes, the company's earnest desire to look beyond profit and loss to the greater good operates as a hook that brings in more business and thus more profit. The House of Blues proceeds on the admirable principle that people are superficially different but ultimately alike in their tendency toward the transcendent; the same might be said of dollars or, in this globalizing age, of different currencies.

The Chicago House of Blues forms a link in a corporate chain, but everyone I spoke to there insisted that it was not like the Hard Rock Cafe, Planet Hollywood, and similar enterprises. Hedrick had to leave to meet with an alderman, but on his way out he said, "That's what I'll leave you with. We make sure we don't cross that boundary where we become cookie-cutter—what's the word? I say it all the time." Adell O'Bryant, the young black public relations officer who was shepherding me around the House of Blues (and whose voice mail message ended, "Have a blessed day"), helped him out. "We're not themed," she said, with sweet conviction. "Yeah," said Hedrick, sitting down again, "we're not themed, and we're not a theme-branded entity, because then we'd fall into . . ." He let the sentence trail off, leaving me to imagine an unspeakably uncool fate, then set out to explain at length, a disquisition I feel obliged to reproduce in full:

See, we've had focus groups, and that's been a thing that comes out of them. Many people perceive retail as a negative, and I can understand that, because that started with Hard Rock. You'd walk through the retail to get into the store, and people perceived that as corporate, cookie-cutter. All the focus groups said, "That's why we think you're Disney, that's why we think you're Hard Rock, because you do things that they do." But we're not Hard Rock, we're not Planet Hollywood. The demographic changes every single night in this building, and it doesn't there. You may be in our B. B.'s Blues Restaurant and see on the screen that this German band, Rammstein, is playing upstairs, and you might want to check them out. It's an entertainment complex, and maybe that's where the Disney thing comes from. But all the looks are different [in the House of Blues chain]. Disney has a consistent look. If you didn't have a sign on this building, there's no way in hell you'd think it was a House of Blues. You look at the House of Blues in L.A., it looks like a giant tin shack in the South. Each place is different.

It was a masterpiece of business-speak, the ideas moving like giant squids in the murk of spin control, almost appearing and then diving deep out of sight again. This much was clear, though: focus groups and the calculated variation of exteriors from one store to the next—Unity in Diversity—had kept the chain from becoming too corporate.

It was also clear that the history-invoking and symbolic functions of the blues—a bluesy feel as a guarantor of both the corporation's investment in art for art's sake and its awareness of the link between roots music and prosocial politics—had to take priority over live blues at the House of Blues. Guitars, other memorabilia, and images of blues artists lined the venue's walls and ceilings, but actual blues played by living people was too specialized a genre, too small a market, to sustain an operation that size. Buddy Guy's Legends, with a capacity of almost four hundred (four times that of the Checkerboard), was the most successful blues venue downtown, but the House of Blues dwarfed it. "Buddy Guy won't play here on a public date because he views us as competition, but I don't see it that way," said Michael Yerke, who took over when Hedrick finally left. Yerke, who booked music for the House of Blues, presented a variant of his boss's appearance: similarly lean and black-shirted, but blue-jeaned, longer-haired, and more edgy-looking, as befits someone who works more closely with the talent. "I don't see us in competition. We have different-sized rooms. He's got a pretty small place; we have a capacity of thirteen hundred here in the music hall. We may do occasional blues shows in there, but there's only maybe a dozen blues acts that can fill it." Filling a room that size—and doing it night after night—obliged him to regard the blues as a minor element of the programming mix, despite its prominent place in the name and self-presentation of the business. Classic and alternative rock, metal, rap, techno, soul, and funk drew more and bigger crowds—usually younger ones, too. Bruce Iglauer, of Alligator Records, does not take the House of Blues to task for the disparity between its name and its booking policies. "It's been a good House of a Lot of Different Kinds of Music," he has said, and he praises the corporation for getting blues on rock radio through its sponsorship of blues shows.[19]

When the House of Blues did book a blues show in the main hall, Yerke usually packaged two or more big-name blues artists, any of whom, appearing individually, would be a major draw at even a North Side club. Downstairs, though, in the restaurant, less well-known blues musicians entertained diners while they ate. "We do blues in the restaurant five days a week during lunch, seven nights a week at night," he said. "It's all blues down there. You're not into the Otis Rushes and Lonnie Brookses down there, though; it's not big-name people." On the one hand, it had to be at least partially good news for blues musicians that there was work every day of the week at the House of Blues, and that they could do a lunchtime gig there—even if, as bluesman Fruteland Jackson assured me, it did not pay well and nobody paid attention to the music—and maybe still play a club that night. More generally, it had to be good news for Chicago that there was a big room with first-class sound and an adventurously eclectic booking policy that embraced the Insane Clown Posse, Rammstein, and Otis Rush (but only if he played with John Mayall). On the other hand, I had come face-to-face with the fact of Chicago blues as music to do lunch by.

THE ONE MOST IMPORTANT THING

You can hear the tangled and occasionally epic history of institutions, money, work, and urbanism moving on and under the surface of Chicago blues. If you could not hear the story in the music, there would be little point in telling it. First and last, what matters about blues is the way it sounds and what that sound does to people.

Sitting in the darkened room upstairs at Legends, in a retrospective mood after his visit with the gifted blues-rock whippersnapper Jonny Lang in Minnesota (and with no guitar at hand to curb the flow of words), Buddy Guy got to talking about how the music itself had changed in the half century he had been playing it. He still had flying on his mind after his long day of traveling. "It's just like the old airplane compared to the one you got now," he said, meaning that the blues today was the same old blues in principle—it starts on the ground, it rises and soars, it returns to the ground—but much changed in form and speed. That got him started on a riff that traveled, like an airborne time machine, all the way back to Louisiana in the 1940s. "These young people out there—well, I got this young man Jonny Lang on one of my cuts. This young man, when I first heard him I thought he's got to be thirty-something years old, and he's just sixteen years old. That's how fast musicians are now. When I learned to play, I couldn't watch it on *tee*vee, there wasn't such thing as *on* teevee, so I tried to figure it out myself. Now they got instruction videos." He was warming to the subject, gesturing with his big, strong-fingered hands. "I think it's human beings itself now. You talk to a kid now in preschool, and they almost know as much as I did when I was in, like, third grade. They're just smarter now. I think people are just smarter than they was in my day. When I see 'em play, I look at 'em and I say, 'What the hell did you *play?*

And I done had a guitar in my hand long before you was born and I didn't find that note on there.' I just told Jonny that about four hours ago in Minnesota." Guy had arrived at his point, and he poked a finger at me to emphasize it. "It's just like when I came along I was, like, *under* Muddy Waters and B. B. King and just wailing, and they looked at me and said, 'Wow, that note you played . . . '"

In addition to making the always-popular observation that kids today grow up fast and have an intimate understanding of technological innovations that befuddle and amaze their elders, Guy was telling a hopeful story about blues culture renewing itself as it always had. Every generation of masters confronts apprentices on the make who learn the old ways but also push the masters and the music to new sounds, new feeling. When Guy came north to Chicago as a young man in the 1950s, burning up with raw talent, he found a city alive with accomplished musicians making vibrant music. There he found his style by mating the jazzy, gospel-inflected virtuosity identified with King to the electrified urban variant of hard Delta drive that formed the backbone of Muddy Waters's blues. Following his penchant for musical noise, he added to the blend his own experimental interest in distortion and feedback, his singular musical syntax, and a unique feel for the tension between the electric guitar's ringing metallic bite and its capacity for warmer, more humane tones.

Guy became a master in his own right, imitated by a generation of blues and rock guitarists. Now a second generation of apprentices has come up, led by guitar heroes, like Lang, who can hit the big time when they are younger than Guy was when he headed north to Chicago. Guy wanted to learn from his apprentices, though, rather than risk becoming a museum piece. "Still learning," he said, "*still* learning. I watch Jonny Lang and see something, and when I finish with you I'm goin' out back [to play guitar], if everybody leave me alone for a while." Musicians need to hear one another, and they need to practice. That reminded him of another case in point. "I brought Eric Clapton here, man, about three years ago when he played at the United Center. He said, 'If I go down there to your club with you, can I be left alone?' Because most fans don't think we need an hour of our own life. Everybody wants an autograph, everybody wants to ask you a question. But we learn to *play* by *listening*. And Eric come and saw this guy—which passed away, bless his soul, a couple of months ago—and he was playing slide. This slide player looked over, and you could see he was saying to himself, 'Oh, how I feel, Buddy Guy and Eric Clapton sitting there watching me,' but Eric said, 'Who *is* that man?' Because he was playing slide and singing, and he was amazing."

Guy was describing an ideal model of how a cultural form should extend itself, with practitioners supporting and revising one another in a running exchange, a kind of insider subset of the transactions between artists and audiences. Institutions like blues clubs and record labels give musicians ways to encounter one another and the traditions of the form. Shaped in these institutions with as much or as little care as the bottom line dictates, the music flows and changes as tradition and innovation, old hands and rising talents, react to one another.

There is, of course, another way to look at change: as decline. Guy was implicitly arguing against stories that present Chicago blues as losing its way, drained of genuine feeling and originality, consenting to the status of proto-rock or neo-Dixieland. Guy's relatively sanguine story, the decline narratives that oppose it, and the history I have been mapping all place explanatory frames around the continuing development of a genre and one of its leading exponents.

Guy's music fills that frame. Before considering what has changed in his music, let us begin with what has remained constant. The two structuring constants discernible throughout his body of work are a desire to see audiences blown away and a desire to explore his instrument's capacities, even at the expense of generic rigor. If Guy would have made a great edge-music experimentalist, he also would have made a great classical violinist—not a scrupulous technician or a maker of rich tonalities, but one of those pitiless virtuosos who brings down the house by abusing tempo, phrasing, and other evidence of composers' intent as he drags strangely altered masterpieces scratching and clawing from his instrument. Guy's taxing style veers away from fluidity to seek out defamiliarizing surprise. Always pushing up and out, trying to haul the listener up yet another ecstatic peak, Guy's performances do not make for comfortable experiences. Because he is at once a needy and a demanding artist, it can be hard work to listen to him—especially his guitar playing, which has always been troubled, hurried, gorgeously awkward, and bent on making something terrible and cathartic happen in the listener. Bruce Iglauer, who admires Guy's passion but also thinks he plays too many notes, has insightfully summed up Guy's musical persona and the technical flourishes that orchestrate it:

Buddy is able to summon up, apparently at will, an intensity of emotion that would be the envy of any great artist. If blues is, above all, emotion, and an expression of emotion, Buddy is by that standard a great artist, because his music, when it connects, is overwhelmingly emotional—both his playing and his singing. . . . Like his stuttering, the musical stuttering. The length of time he can pause, the way he'll lay a silence against a flurry of notes, the way a note that apparently is randomly chosen from a run suddenly becomes important as though the thought or feeling had just leaped into his hands, and he can't control it. So, he'll worry about or squeeze or shake a note that wouldn't appear to be a note a normal blues player would choose to land on and work with. There's a sense of discovery with Buddy—not always, but sometimes—that his hands are doing things his mind isn't controlling. The intellect is overwhelmed by emotions.[20]

That laying of intellect against emotion and the impulses toward ecstasy and abstraction that drive it are constants of Guy's musical intelligence, traits that I accept (and that he seems to accept) as givens largely beyond my explanatory reach. But given those constants, much has changed in his half century of music making, in his recordings and in live performances. Bracketing some obvious changes—technological advances and retreats, shifts in production practices, the move from singles to albums—the most important shift in his music, one more broadly emblematic of Chicago blues since 1960, has been a rebalancing of the relationship between instrument and voice.

Guy has led the way in effecting the genre's single most important formal mutation: the rising proportional importance of guitar and the corresponding decline in the importance of singing. This is what people mean, often imprecisely, when they say that Chicago blues is turning into guitar rock. When I talked about it with Bruce Iglauer, a schizophrenically decline-minded booster, he gestured at a pile of packages against one wall of his office in Alligator Records' cramped headquarters and said, "See that? Those are audition recordings. I guarantee you that for 70 percent of those my letter back will say, 'If you had taken as much time thinking about your singing as your guitar playing, you would have a tape that I might want to listen to.' Singing is the *one* most important thing in Chicago blues, and it's getting hard to find people—any people, black or white—who can sing in this style." This problem of devoting disproportionate attention to guitar chops is especially acute among men, who dominate the blues talent pool (although there have been more female guitar aces of late). Men also dominate the audience, "and boys do tend to place a high value on being good with your hands," notes Francis Davis.[21] Fittingly, some of Alligator's best, and best-selling, blues singers have been women who do not play guitar: especially Koko Taylor, one of the label's warhorses, and, more recently, Shemekia Copeland, its latest star.

Iglauer emphasized the importance of constant training and rein-
forcement at an early age in a singer's development. "Most real blues
singers, their singing has a great deal to do with gospel singing, and
most of the vocal training and ear training they're getting—to bend
notes and hold notes and so on—they're getting as children. And not
from records; from people singing live in church, around the house, and
so on." He insisted that early training mattered most; coming to blues
in college was too late. White people were for the most part unable to
sing the blues, Iglauer believed, not because they were white but because they started too late. He cited himself as an example. "I've im-
mersed myself in blues for almost thirty years of my life. If anybody
should be able to sing blues among white people, I should. I'm awful.
I started too late. I grew up—I'll tell you what I can sing because I
learned to sing it when I was really little. I can sing just like Gordon
Macrae. I can sing all the Rodgers and Hammerstein you'd ever want to
hear, and I can sing it really well." To prove the point, and at my urging, he sang a couple of choruses of "You've Got to Be Carefully
Taught" with exemplary verve and a pleasing vibrato.[22]

Buddy Guy *did* have the kind of sustained early exposure Iglauer describes, and he can sing blues masterfully, but mostly he plays a lot of
loud, fast, often very unvocal electric guitar, and that goes a long way
toward defining the generic standard in Chicago blues these days. It is
no longer possible to say that most of this guitar playing advertises itself as an extension of the human voice raised in song. That identity between voice and instrument was once a fundamental element of Delta
style and early Chicago style. It helped to define the Delta and Chicago
blues signal, an indicator that musician and audience were communicating on a blues frequency. The rebalancing of that relationship has
produced much of what purists hear as interference and dismiss as "too
many notes" or "noise."

We can, following an argument made by Iglauer, trace the decline of
singing in the genre to the decreasing southernness of African American culture, especially church singing culture, in postmigration Chicago. And we can factor in the defunding of music education in public
schools—a failure of arts education that "blues in the schools" programs
have tried to reverse. Perhaps we should also trace the fading authority of
the genre's original formula rules to the fading of the shock of urbanization and industrialization as compelling subject and aesthetic condition. That shock has been largely replaced by less urgent impulses—historical nostalgia for industrial urbanism, second-order concern for the

fate of the blues tradition, exploration of the blues roots of rock, and distant mythologizing regard for an agrarian order with which most people in today's Chicago blues world have had no direct contact.

We can trace the expansion of the guitar's role to the classic rock aesthetic that has made the guitar solo paramount in the musical calculus of ecstatic experience. Commercially and artistically, blues has become junior partner in the blues-rock synthesis that has recruited the lion's share of Guy's audience since the 1960s. The guitar, not the voice, comes first in this new regime, a primacy reinforced by two-going-on-three generations of steep technical escalation pursued by musicians that the embattled saxophonist A. C. Reed has dismissed in song as "guitar freaks."[23] It bears noting that "guitar freak" constitutes a kind of chosen ethnicity that often supersedes other social distinctions, encouraging the flow of influence and licks across genre lines and the color line. During the sustained development of what Iglauer calls "instrumental heroism" on the guitar since the mid-1960s, rockers have caught up to and in many ways eclipsed their blues mentors. "Whereas the quality of the average rock-and-roll guitar player now can be pretty amazing," he said, "the quality of the average rock-and-roll guitar player in 1968 was that B. B. King could cut him to shreds while taking a piss with the other hand. That's no longer the case."

Given the concatenation of circumstances driving the swing from voice to guitar, it should come as no surprise that Buddy Guy—a guitar freak who listens to a variety of other guitar players, who remains perpetually eager to lead a willing audience toward ecstasy, who is always happy to take thirty or forty exploratory choruses of guitar solo comes at least halfway to his rock-trained audience's aesthetic ground by playing extended solos that depart significantly from blues orthodoxy as defined in the 1950s.

But, in keeping with a policy of constructive skepticism toward any decline or booster narrative, I hesitate to accept the characterization of Guy's stylistic evolution as a simple case of focus-group musicianship. With plenty of research, interviewing, and twenty-four years of close attention to Buddy Guy's live and recorded music to back me up, I can say with confidence that his will to abstraction forms a potent artistic impulse that was going to find expression one way or another. I would not pretend to account for that impulse, but I can place its consequences in a historical and generic context that should give pause to those eager to dismiss Guy as a musical opportunist who sold his blues soul for a bigger audience.

Guy has always tried to push past the conventional boundaries of blues sound. In the 1950s, before he even came to Chicago, he was already experimenting with feedback, distortion, and other effects that injured the sensibilities of some of his elders. The blues, of course, has a distinguished tradition of noise-making and experimentation, but that tradition often produces tension where it encounters generic orthodoxies. In the early 1960s, as a respected Chicago sideman, he tried to introduce some of these effects at the Chess Records studios, only to be curbed by Muddy Waters, Willie Dixon, and especially Leonard Chess. "Actually," he told an interviewer in the early 1990s, "a lot of sustained notes that you hear us all doing now—and Hendrix said he was getting this from me—I was doing out in the public early on. Chess Records called it *noise,* they wouldn't let me cut it. They was telling me, 'Who's going to listen to that noise?'"[24] Until the rise of rock and soul and the postindustrial transformation of city life changed the map of popular culture, the Chicago blues establishment remained institutionally strong enough to police Buddy Guy's tendency toward "out" playing. Record producers, club owners, and artistic kingpins could point to the bottom line—sales of a proven product to a loyal audience—to curb what they heard as his excesses.

One way to write the cultural history of music is to trace the authority with which different people can say "You are hurting my ears" at any given historical moment. Before the mid-1960s, Guy's departures from generic norms tended to hurt the ears of some people who had the power to stop him from doing it at least some of the time. Even as late as the late 1960s, Junior Wells, Guy's regular performing partner for many years, was still in the peremptory habit of clamping his hand on the fretboard of Guy's guitar, deadening the strings, when he felt it was time for a solo to come to an end. Guy, the guitar hero, would in time become the more celebrated of the two, but Wells, a harmonica master and forceful singer, had been in Chicago longer than Guy and was a more established band leader. In the late 1960s, the fraternal struggle between them tended to come out about even or slightly in Wells's favor, putting a fruitful edge on the music they made together. With the triumph of the guitar in the 1970s and after, though, nobody has the authority any longer to police Guy. (Wells died in 1998, mourned as a grand old man of the blues but very much in Guy's shadow.) It would be blasphemous for anyone, even B. B. King, to suggest that Guy cut short a solo, let alone to touch the fetishized instrument while Guy was playing it.

Even when restrained by senior bluesmen or blues formula—perhaps especially *because* he so manifestly came up against those restraints—Guy's pressing at the boundaries of blues genre made him a mentor to the founding generation of rock guitar heroes. These men, most of them younger than Guy and many of them British, listened to and emulated the exciting music he made as a young man in the 1950s and 1960s. Guy was not playing rock (even though some of his peers in Chicago thought he was), but he was attempting explorations rooted in and extending beyond Chicago blues norms, a model for the rockers' project. From the 1970s through the 1990s, Guy led the way in redefining Chicago orthodoxy in partnership with fans who had built their musical intelligence around just those rock guitar heroes who imitated him in the 1960s. Also, and not incidentally, Guy took financial control over his career—by buying Legends, by controlling the rights to his compositions, by signing a good recording contract (aided by old and new acolytes, from Eric Clapton to Jonny Lang, who helped sell his CDs by playing on them). So Guy has put himself in a position to let himself go, unpoliced, where he always wanted to go and to please his core audience by doing it. He is not hurting their ears, and he is not making noise; rather, he is broadcasting a signal they are equipped to receive, satisfying their demand for blues that rocks.

"Journalists miss the point of Buddy playing a Clapton tune or a Hendrix tune," argues Scott Holt, the young white Tennesseean with astounding guitar chops and modest singing skills who has backed Guy for more than a decade, "He's not being lazy, he's not pandering. He's showing how that stuff *liberated* him to play the way he always felt. And he's showing you the connections backwards and forwards." This is a case of reflexive influence—the rock-star students first imitated the bluesman teacher, stealing his thunder when he was in his prime, and then influenced his career and music as they helped him secure long-delayed rewards—but it is also a case of the prevailing musical aesthetic coming into alignment with an individual artist's long-standing proclivities.

Sit down with a collection of Buddy Guy's recordings, and you can hear those proclivities producing music of changing form and valence as the historical frame around it shifts over time. In his singles of the 1950s and early 1960s, you can hear Guy and his handlers at Chess and other independent labels casting about for the right niche. He plays some straight, powerful Chicago blues on the Otis Rush and Magic Sam models but also some R & B and novelty songs—dance music related to early Chicago soul. Guy's peculiar musical genius does not fit comfortably within the limits defined by the three-minute single, the sub-genre formulas available at the time, or the marketing imaginations of the Chess brothers and their competitors.

Guy strikes a better bargain with the business on *A Man and the Blues,* the album he made for Vanguard soon after parting ways with Chess in 1967. Supported and constrained by a top-of-the-line Chicago ensemble, Guy paid more attention to orthodox strictures than he usually did in live performances at the time. The key collaborator was Otis Spann, a veteran of the Muddy Waters band, who was the Chicago scene's master pianist and a hoarsely eloquent singer in his own right. Spann played inspiring piano behind Guy, creating especially with his left hand a dark, furrowed backdrop that grounded Guy's singing and cleanly picked guitar work, both of which, in Guy's younger days, tended toward the keening upper registers then regarded as B. B. King territory. On the dirgelike "One Room Country Shack," Spann's brooding, surging work gets so good that Guy makes a vocal show of urging him on: "Otis, you make me feel so good this morning, play it. . . . Play it!" The collaboration produced a superb album of late classic Chicago blues, an engaging mix of slow tunes in the second-wave Chicago style and uptempo dance songs that offer Guy's oddly angled readings of contemporary R & B styles (the Motown tune "Money," for instance; "Jam on a Monday Morning," which owes something to "Land of a Thousand Dances"; and Guy's rocking version of "Mary Had a Little Lamb"). It works beautifully because the band of Chicago regulars builds a solid, nuanced structure through which Guy weaves his impassioned vocals and fleet, string-bending guitar work. He shows flashes of wildness—letting roller-coaster singing lines escalate into shrieks, striking a perfectly out-of-time and out-of-tune clank from his guitar during "Jam on a Monday Morning"—but in this context Guy sounds all the more vital as he rattles the bars of the genre's norms. And if there is a great deal of solo guitar on the album, it all takes shape around singing. He plays conversational, expressive guitar as an introduction to, extension of, or conclusion to what he expresses with his singing voice.

In Guy's subsequent recordings of the 1970s and after, first for minor independents like the British label JSP and eventually for Silvertone in the 1990s, his voice darkens and dips more often into the lower range, his increasingly rapid-fire guitar playing expands to fill the soundscape, he fools around with fuzzboxes and other rock-flavored ef-

fects, and his bands fall back to give him room. There are no more Otis
Spanns willing to stand up to Guy's guitar playing until one gets to the
Silvertone CDs of the 1990s, when rock stars like Jeff Beck and Mark
Knopfler bring a different but equally audible authority to collabora-
tions with him.

During the late 1970s—in the second act of this story, when the industrial blues synthesis had lost most of its cohesive force and the
postindustrial blues synthesis had not quite jelled yet—Buddy Guy produced a masterpiece. The album, entitled *Stone Crazy* and released in
the United States by Alligator in 1981, occupies an uneasy overlap between the syntheses, giving it more than even the usual Buddy Guy
edginess. Side 1 opens with a couple of minutes of snarling, roaring, distorted guitar, with Guy snarling and roaring semiwordlessly behind it—
powerful, unsettling music that sets the tone for the record. It is vintage
Guy: a series of fevered expeditions up and down the fingerboard, vocal register, dynamic range, and emotional ladder, with even the standard Chicago-style licks arriving in unfamiliar places and in odd rhythmic order. It is also good, if strange, Chicago blues: in structure (the
formulaic *what*), in feel (the ineffable *how*), and in the traditional (if tur-
bocharged) melodic and harmonic figures of Chicago blues one is often
surprised to discern in the heaving mass of notes. On *Stone Crazy,* the
music's tendency toward escape velocity always comes up against an insistence on blues phrasings, on making a blues guitar tell a story in
twelve- and sixteen-bar chapters.

Done on the thinnest of shoestrings and in exile, *Stone Crazy* indi-
cates the state of the old order. Guy, who had no record contract at the
time and was touring to keep the Checkerboard afloat, recorded the album (first released in France as *The Blues Giant*) in a few hours one afternoon in a French studio between gigs. It was done in single takes,
performance-style, with no fancy production and no rock stars sitting
in. He played with a Chicago bar band composed of his brother Phil on
second guitar, Ray Allison on drums, and the bassist J. W. Williams.
Four of the six tunes on the album are slow blues, most are originals,
and there is not a "Sweet Home Chicago" singalong in the bunch. Guy
makes no concession to blues-rock sensibilities in his musical choices.

But *Stone Crazy* also suggests the possibility of a new-order music
that has an ear for rock guitar but is still recognizably Chicago blues.
Guy lets himself go long on guitar in extended songs, working the
edges of the noise field and wrestling blues lines into novel shapes. With
room and time to explore, he finds a depth of fresh feeling inside and

behind blues formulas that still exert important influence. *Stone Crazy* draws a great deal of its energy from Guy's struggle to rein in his guitar playing just enough to sustain or at least gesture at the traditional balance of voice and guitar. You can feel the album's quality of middleness and transition; you can hear Guy's dueling impulses to both establish and push past an interesting generic limit. Since he became a guitar god, he has not always felt obliged to respect that limit, often just sailing right past without bothering to set it up, but on *Stone Crazy* he attends to compulsory figures before attempting quintuple axels. So a recognizable blues logic animates the web of sound connections he makes between voice and guitar, bringing out the verbal qualities of even his most forbidding instrumental work. He plays conversational fills rather than hot licks between sung lines, he reproduces a variety of groaning and shouting sounds on the guitar, and he indulges his habit of actually groaning and shouting semiwordlessly over his own playing. Laughing crazily and issuing officer-like calls to his doomed band to advance behind him into terra incognita as he takes yet another wildly original solo, Guy establishes the identity of voice and guitar in the face of its falling apart.

Stone Crazy has little to do with dance; it is concert music, and "difficult" concert music at that, as close in spirit to bebop as it might be to rock. Guy does most of his impassioned singing over an extremely muted band, which cranks up behind his solos, jerking from near silence to near noise. He comes down just this side of excess with miraculous consistency. Part of the credit goes to the band, Chicago troupers willing to stay with Guy every step of the way while insisting on blues structure. But most of the credit goes to Guy, who, often in a single take, makes a thousand finely nuanced choices at breakneck speed as he plunges into deep, unexplored waters. He does not sound at all like Muddy Waters, Otis Rush, or B. B. King, and he sounds even less like Eric Clapton or Jimi Hendrix. The listener might think to hear all of them evoked (rather than invoked), but in the end *Stone Crazy* sounds like Buddy Guy triumphant. Both guitar and voice are deeper, rougher, and more idiosyncratic than they were on *A Man and the Blues*. The middle-aged Guy, having extended his range since the 1960s, plumbs the affective depths of middle and lower registers that too many blues musicians abandon in the desire to wail up high. Listening to *A Man and the Blues* and *Stone Crazy* back-to-back, one can appreciate not only how Chicago blues changed but also how a young man's talent developed into the mastery of a mature artist.

If you had asked me in the late 1970s what the best way to hear Buddy Guy's music might be, I would have said that you should go to the Checkerboard. On good nights, his live shows navigated excitingly between blues musicianship and his idiosyncratic drives, but none of his recordings since 1968 had done justice to this stylistic balancing act. I would have said, further, that for the sake of understanding how Guy's style had developed, you should also listen to the records on which he and Junior Wells had collaborated in the 1960s and that you listen to *A Man and the Blues*. If you had asked me the same question again in 1981—how to hear Guy to best advantage—I would have urged you to get *Stone Crazy* and then go see him at the Checkerboard a few times to see if he could match it.

If you had asked me in 2001 how to hear Buddy Guy at his best, I would have said listen to the recordings: *A Man and the Blues* and *Stone Crazy* above all, but also some of his early singles and some cuts from his CDs of the 1990s. On the recent CDs, highly produced and featuring support from rock stars and big-time session musicians, he can be extraordinary, and he is always interesting, although at times he seems less inspired than he has been in the past. These recordings are, I hate to say, often more satisfying than his live performances have been of late. Removed in the studio from the immediate felt demands of the crowd, and with the leisure to reel in excesses and refine his sound, Guy can attend to the craft he often abandons during a live show in favor of raw emotion. As a craftsman in the studio, he seems paradoxically liberated by the constraint of having to produce professional-sounding music on a CD. In front of an ecstasy-seeking audience, he feels both enabled and obliged to go wild, with the usual result that he defeats both the sound mix and the blues song structures responsible for conveying his musical intelligence to the audience's ears.

Most of my ecstatic experiences of Buddy Guy in concert happened in the late 1970s and early 1980s, which gives me pause. Was he better then, or was I easier to please? That most of those episodes took place when I was a chronically bewildered teenager (with some aesthetic convictions, like a fondness for the collected works of Michael Moorcock, that embarrass me now) makes me suspect that perhaps I would feel differently about them if I could transport my adult self a couple of decades into the past to hang out with my moderately rotten teenage self at the Checkerboard. I might realize, seeing Guy again as he was, that he is a more professional musician now than he was then. His greater fame, the fancier venues at which he plays, and the momentum of heftier investment backing his performances oblige him to be that way. He can no longer end a set by saying "Fuck it" and yanking his guitar cord out of the speaker in midsong with a headache-inducing crash, which he used to do at the Checkerboard. He can no longer play a half-hour version of "Chicken Heads" and spend fifteen minutes of it arguing with a drunk seated within striking distance of him while the band vamps on the song's main groove. A more competent purveyor of product now, he arrives ready to give satisfaction every time out in pretty much the same way. But some of what makes him a more polished and popular entertainer makes him a less affecting musician. I often find a niche-marketed, prepackaged inevitability in his live performances that tends to preclude experiment and to encourage guitar heroism at the expense of blues craft. His principal audience craves its blues as rock has understood the blues since the 1960s: guitar pyrotechnics comes before songcraft, the ritual display of what parades itself as emotional truth comes before the art of giving an old song a new reading or a new song an inner life, and there can be little incentive to get inside the music when what both audience and performer want is for Guy to take us all higher, higher, higher.

So Guy can be a frustration to me. Making my way home, skull abuzz, from receiving yet another muddily mixed hammering from his guitar at a live show, I ask myself if I am selfish to look back with fondness to the days when Guy was struggling, angrily and sometimes dispiritedly, to win the recognition he knew he deserved. I liked his music better then. Voice and guitar were usually in better balance, and Guy was poised on an interesting frontier between constraint and exploration. But he liked his situation then rather less than he likes it now. If you ask him, he will tell you so, and he will tell you he is making better music now. Musicians, like boxers, feel obliged to consider themselves only smarter and more seasoned with the passage of time. "I've never been in better shape," a thirty-nine-year-old boxer will tell you, and in a sense he is right. But, selfish of me or not, I think the age of Buddy Guy's greatest musical accomplishment as a performing bluesman might have ended when he made it (relatively) big, when his touring became a way to support his Silvertone albums rather than a way to keep the Checkerboard alive. I think this is when he got better at producing the same predictable facsimile of thrills night after night. Not *because* he made it big (for a bluesman), but because the conditions of blues production asked less of him—or asked different things of him—than they had before. By this logic, the age of Buddy Guy's greatest musical accomplishment began when the conditions of blues production began to change in the early 1960s, when the industrial blues synthesis started to fall apart, when R & B and soul in various guises began to win away the old constituency of the blues and rock began to produce its new one. Guy's career, just taking off in that moment, plunged into the following quarter-century period of turmoil and often lean times, and he made some remarkable music out of the material provided to him by the blues in transition. As the older strictures of Chicago blues orthodoxy loosened in the 1960s, Guy emerged as an avant-gardist, albeit one with close ties to the founding fathers; and as the outlines of a new Chicago blues orthodoxy took shape and began to harden in the 1980s, a mature and road-tested Guy was already far out ahead of the field—a pioneer to whom a generation of new apprentices has looked for a model of how it ought to be done.

That history helps explain the form of a typical Buddy Guy set. He opens with a classic Chicago shuffle and then a slow blues (often Eddie Boyd's "Five Long Years"), traditional tunes that feature his most forceful singing and most orthodox, controlled guitar playing of the evening. As the set proceeds, he sings less, and his solos become vast washes of sound with recognizable Chicago blues figures buried deeper and deeper within them as his guitar playing begins to lose contact with the defining generic ground from which it departed. After a while, when his audience begins to feel disoriented, Guy presents his history of the Chicago blues tradition in a medley that links Muddy Waters to Stevie Ray Vaughan. His set is a palimpsest, a layered model of Chicago blues history: from industrial to postindustrial synthesis, from vocal to guitar music, from folk origins to assimilation by rock, from a form of popular culture grounded in the Black Metropolis to a museum-quality roots concert music housed in the precincts of the information-handling classes.

A BLUESY CONDITION

I first encountered Buddy Guy in the late 1970s, when I was entering high school and trying to find a way between the period's two popular musical monoliths, which dominated teen culture. On one side, looming up like Stonehenge, was classic rock, the unremitting bombast of which had already worn out my patience. On the other side, perhaps even more imposing (on the South Side of Chicago, anyway), was the soul-funk combine, which I liked as music but which made what I regarded as unreasonable social demands regarding dance, dress, and comportment. New wave and punk rock made even more unreasonable demands. Expressing a desire to listen to them felt like rushing a fraternity. Blues, like jazz, offered an alternative world that came with a history to explore, opportunities for both connoisseurship and instrumental dabbling, and a social climate dominated by adults uninterested in adolescent melodrama—which encouraged me to take a welcome break from such melodrama myself. And, unlike jazz, blues commanded a good view of both rock and soul; well-worn aesthetic paths led back and forth from blues to the other genres.

So I found my way to the Checkerboard Lounge on Forty-third Street, where a thirteen-year-old could get in and order drinks, no questions asked, and where Buddy Guy presided over a remarkable collection of musical talent spanning the postwar period. From time to time you could catch first-wave postwar codifiers, like Muddy Waters or Willie Dixon. There were representatives of Guy's generation, the second wave that refined Chicago blues: like Junior Wells, the subtle guitar master Sammy Lawhorn, and the impassioned Texas transplant Fenton Robinson (whose spare, elegant version of "I'm Going to Chicago" was being piped in to welcome travelers at O'Hare Airport in the late 1990s). Magic Slim exemplified the third wave. His band, the Teardrops, played weeknights at the Checkerboard for years. There were younger apprentices, ranging from new traditionalists like John Primer and Valerie Wellington to progressive revisionists like Dion Payton and the 43rd Street Blues Band. There were local characters like the half brothers Lefty Dizz and Johnny Dollar, respectively the gentlest and most ill-tempered musicians around. Lefty Dizz, who resembled the Cat in the Hat both in appearance and in his gift for turning a dull evening into a chaotic good time, ran the Monday night jam. (He also played my senior prom.) Touring blues stars and Guy's rock-star disciples would drop in late after playing shows on the North Side or at suburban arenas. And, often enough, there was Buddy Guy, who kept a guitar behind the bar and would get it out and plug in when somebody else played well enough to be considered a challenge. He was at the height of his powers and his career frustration back then, the moment when he recorded *Stone Crazy,* and it made for supercharged music. Unlike arena-sized musical scenes, the Checkerboard scene happened on the human scale. It cost two dollars to get in most nights; drinks were a buck and change; and, when the weather allowed, during set breaks musicians and audience alike went outside and stood around on the sidewalk talking shop, a living portrait of the overlap between industrial and postindustrial blues syntheses.

Late one winter night in 1979, after an evening at the Checkerboard, I got a ride back as far as Hyde Park and set out to walk the rest of the way home to South Shore through Jackson Park. It was one of my favorite walks; plus, I had spent all my money at the club. Too cold to bother with my usual cautious practice of keeping to the shadows of the tree line, I walked briskly down the median strip of the park drive, alone under the lights except for sparse late traffic. After a while, a cab driver pulled over and generously offered to take me home free of charge. He was an older black gentleman, gray-haired, driving a giant red-and-white American land cruiser of late 1960s vintage. I was chilled, despite having ingested antifreeze in various forms earlier in the evening, so I accepted his offer.

We rolled through the Olmstedian reaches of Jackson Park, the South Side's grandest park, which had been the site of the World's Columbian Exposition in 1893. It occurs to me now (and certainly did not then) that the exposition of 1893 was all about the profound cultural consequences of economic and social transformation—not the postindustrial but an earlier version, the industrial transformation of culture, complete with its own racial and musical dimensions mapped on a schematic urban landscape. To our left were lagoons on the site of the White City, the exposition's model in plaster of the beautiful life that factory machines would produce. To the right was the Midway, along which had been arranged an exotic display of the exploitable peoples of the world. The young Edgar Rice Burroughs had driven up and down the Midway, demonstrating a prototype automobile; Buffalo Bill made theater of the exposition's racial politics, and the aging Frederick Douglass made a speech in protest of them. There had been musical performers, too: Scott Joplin, for instance, and Little Egypt, who either did or did not dance the Hootchy Kootchy to beguiling tunes, but became famous for it in any case. (Generations later, Chicago bluesmen would be singing a new, re-gendered set of beguiling tunes about hoochie koochie.) It was all long gone. The Golden Lady, a reduced replica of the statue that presided over the exposition, oxidized peacefully with arms upraised in a landscape of groves and water, her back turned to a parking lot where rough customers in the sex and drug businesses circled all night in their cars.

The cabbie and I got to talking about where I had been that night, and he became enthusiastic about young people taking up and extending blues traditions. A sixtyish black working man of southern birth (as he told me) and a young, white information-handler-to-be, we were, after all, representatives of Chicago's two principal blues constituencies. He said, "There's a lot of good new blues out there," and I agreed, thinking of several up-and-coming musicians who frequented the Checkerboard and hoped to be discovered there as Buddy Guy once was at the Blue Flame, but the cabbie was headed in another direction. He said, "People don't realize it, but Aerosmith and Steve Miller and Foghat— that's *blues*. That's some good blues." From my position of authority— a fourteen-year-old genre purist stretched out on the backseat, looking up at the rose-colored urban night sky through the cab's rear window— I remonstrated with him. I told him that wasn't blues, not even close, and to think of it as blues was an insult to Magic Slim, Otis Rush, and the rest of the hardcore Chicago stylists. "You got to *listen*," he urged me. "Aerosmith and them are playing some serious blues. They change it around some, that's all, so the young people will like it." I thought at first that he was simply going out of his way to establish common ground by extolling music he assumed I liked, but he convinced me that he truly heard classic rock as blues—that he regarded the blues-rock synthesis as a viable aesthetic enlivened by the two-way traffic of influence, not as an artistic catastrophe arcing ever-downward in a one-way decline. I was having none of it, but he was doing me a favor, and I thought it would be churlish to argue further. Also, I felt awkward telling a black southerner of a certain age what was and was not blues. When we got through the park and into South Shore, I asked him to drop me up the block from my house to facilitate my skulking in undetected. When I got out, I thanked him, and he entreated me to abandon my hidebound doctrinaire position. His parting words were "Give those white boys a chance."

I was reminded of him when I talked to Buddy Guy about the changing situation of Chicago blues, specifically when I asked Guy about playing for the rock-trained audiences he commands these days. He took my question to be about playing for white people, and he asserted, as he usually does, a universalist truism: "Music has no color," he said. "I never think of music like that." But then he fixed me with an odd look, serious around the mouth but less so around the eyes, and said, "I was born and raised in the South. My mama and daddy told me before they died, they said, 'Son, you're grown. If you marry a *elephant* and bring her home—if you love her, we like her. *You* got to sleep with her, *I* ain't.'" There was, to say the least, a double edge to the anecdote. His parents urged him, as the cabbie urged me, to be tolerant and open-minded, and Guy has prospered in the end by being tolerant and open-minded about the parameters of blues genre and the aesthetic, racial, and class politics of the blues business. But Guy's rendering of his parents' advice also suggests a warning that any resulting alliances he might make, with amorous elephants or adoring blues-rock fans, would constitute making his own bed, in which he would then have to lie.

His music reposes in a bed of changes and contradictions—a complicated situation, both decline and renaissance and also neither. You can hear it in the music.

Chicago blues is the urgently immediate music it always was; Chicago blues has become something new, strange, and nostalgic.

Chicago blues is a local art form, Chicago blues is music for tourists.

Chicago blues does not pay the bills; Chicago blues is a vital hook for the big-time resell of culture.

Chicago blues is an atavistic industrial art form; Chicago blues is a revitalized postindustrial art form.

Chicago blues is black music; Chicago blues is not black music.

Chicago blues is in decline; Chicago blues is booming.

Chicago blues is all right; Chicago blues is not all right; it's in a distinctly bluesy condition.

3

GRITTINESS

*The New York—made movies have provided a permanent record of
the city in breakdown. I doubt if at any other time in American
movie history there has been such a close relationship between the
life on the screen and the life of a portion of the audience.... [I]t's*
there *in the theatre, particularly at late shows, and you feel that
the violence on the screen may at any moment touch off violence
in the theatre. The audience is explosively* live. *It's like being at a
prizefight or a miniature Altamont.*

Pauline Kael, from her review of *The French Connection*

*Even when we were cops on the street, Eddie was always the actor
and I was always the producer.*

Sonny Grosso on working with Eddie Egan, his partner

ENTERING THE OFFICES OF Grosso-Jacobson Productions, high up
in an office tower in midtown Manhattan, I passed a receptionist and a
wall-mounted row of promotional shots for the company's television
shows and made-for-television movies. In those pictures, square-jawed
hunks and simmering babes stand tall in the face of crime, weapons at
hand. Guided by Salvatore "Sonny" Grosso, who was a detective in the
New York Police Department for twenty years before he became a producer, Grosso-Jacobson makes formula television, unapologetically
cranking out crime-themed cultural sausage links with a minimum out-
lay of cost and artistic pretense. At its studio in Toronto, where many
of the shows have been shot, the premium has always been on keeping
the assembly line in motion. Roll in a palm tree on wheels to mark a

scene as set in Miami; roll away the palm tree and bring in a pushcart to shift the scene to New York. Wherever the action is supposed to happen, the cops are honest, the crooks are not, and justice gets done. Elsewhere in the offices of Grosso-Jacobson hang grainier, murkier images, posters for 1970s crime movies on which Grosso worked when he broke into the business. Compared with the promotional shots for the more recent television productions, the older posters seem downright arty in their ambiguity—especially the poster for *The French Connection,* in which Gene Hackman, playing an NYPD detective closely modeled on Grosso's notorious partner Eddie Egan, shoots an unarmed Frenchman in the back on the stairway of an elevated train platform.

A laboriously stenciled old sign hangs on Grosso's office door: 27TH DETECTIVE SQUAD. DETECTIVE ON DUTY. PLEASE TURN KNOB AND WALK IN FOR ASSISTANCE. USE NO HYPOS. OUR COPS ARE TOPS. The office, commanding a panoramic view of Queens and Brooklyn across the East River, is crowded with police paraphernalia, gifts from pals, and images of the sainted Joe DiMaggio and Marilyn Monroe. A purple sash hangs in one corner; Grosso wore it in 1996 when he was grand marshal of the parade for the festival of Our Lady of Mount Carmel, the Madonna of 115th Street in East Harlem, his old home parish. Grosso does business with gusto at a big desk crowded with mail, scripts, and a small VCR and monitor. He yells for assistants to bring him things, he looks at tapes, he takes phone calls. "Look," he was saying into the phone when I went to see him on a winter afternoon in 2000, "if he doesn't give a fuck about Malta and he doesn't give a fuck about a million dollars, then he should be shooting in Canada. Instead he's talking about Malta. What the fuck? You know?"

Gray-haired now, in his sixties, Grosso retains an air of physical competence. He has always been good with his hands—he boxed as a young man, studied karate, and gave and took his share of punishment in his twenty years as a cop—although in latter years he has slowed down, eaten many robust meals, and had health troubles. Something irreducibly vigilant, careful to the point of worry, remains in his unmistakably Italian face. Behind his rough, generous manner is a certain hardness that comes of experience in imposing his will on other people. He still carries his NYPD-issued sidearm. He will adjust it to a more comfortable position on his waist when he sits down to dinner, or pull up his shirt to show it to an interviewer. "I still got this," he once said to me, flashing the piece. "If I don't like what you write, I'll kill ya." We both laughed politely. He makes a policy of advertising the gun's presence to remind old adversaries, should there be any left in condition to consider getting even, that it is still a bad idea to tangle with him. But the effect is curiously touching. In an age of semiautomatic pseudo-cannons and seventeen-shot clips, the short-barreled .38 revolver has the old-timey look of a dueling pistol.

Grosso grew up in working-class, white-ethnic sections of Harlem—first in Italian East Harlem, then in Vinegar Hill, on the West Side—in the period that bridged the Great Depression, World War II, and the postwar boom. His father drove a truck and died young, obliging Sonny to begin supporting the family when he was still in his teens. He describes the working life that confronted young men from his neighborhood as one of "building things, mostly, but with the police department there was economic stability," meaning job security and a city pension—plus excitement, of course. He was his family's first cop, joining the department in 1956, and that occupational choice represented a significant imaginative departure from the norm. Being a cop was physical work, especially when it got rough, but it was also bureaucratic, analytical, and improvisatory, so it seemed wildly different from the shopfloor labor his peers expected to perform their whole lives. His unlikely second profession—making movies and television shows—was still so far over the horizon when he became a cop that it was impossible then for him to imagine undertaking it. Only when the city and the culture business changed in the 1960s did the possibility of this second working life, even further removed from "building things," suggest itself to him.

Grosso, who left East Harlem long ago, maintains an attachment to his old neighborhood as best he can. "I'm not a big switcher," he says. The ritual centerpiece of his week is Monday night dinner at Rao's, the spaghetti-bender's mecca on East 114th Street frequented by insiders in politics, organized crime, and other forms of show business. He grew up nearby and has been eating there for forty years, so he is received as family, with embraces and exclamations all around. When I was at Rao's with him and a big tableful of guests, dinner was interrupted a dozen times by childhood friends and latter-day acquaintances of Grosso's, a couple of reporters and a local news anchorman who stopped by to say hello, and a young tenor named Michael Amante who rose to belt out "O Sole Mio" and "I'll Never Fall in Love Again," with festive diners joining in on the chorus. A middle-aged lug in loose-fitting clothes at a neighboring table wryly half raised his glass of wine to Grosso, who nodded in return. Grosso muttered to me that he had had a hand in putting away the lug, as well as a couple of other men in the place, for a stretch in the joint. No hard feelings; everybody had just been doing his job. The bentnoses and their imitators at Rao's knew that Grosso is a regular guy, even if he is "on the other side of the street," as they say.

The nightly informal pageant of ethnicity at Rao's, one of the last remaining Italian outposts north of East Ninety-sixth Street in what is now mostly a Spanish-speaking neighborhood, is staged for the benefit of its Italian American performers as much as for the others who come for the show (and to prove that they can land the toughest reservation in town). The version of the Old Neighborhood to which the pageant gestures, a relic of the urban villages settled by European immigrants who came to American cities to work with their hands, has become more an object of nostalgia than a social reality. Grosso is one of the dwindling minority of regulars at Rao's who learned how to act like an inner-city Italian American in the streets and tenements of the urban village, and not primarily from movies and television. His dinner rituals gesture at an order of white-ethnic life that has been in ever-shorter supply in New York City proper, especially in Manhattan, for exactly the same three decades that crime stories have kept more or less romantic versions of it continuously before us on the screen and the printed page. Memories of the way it probably used to be are embodied in the hearty food served at Rao's, in the wiseguy atmosphere, and especially in the old-school affect of Grosso and the onetime adversaries with whom he grew up. Everything about Grosso seems to say, This is how they made them, back in the day, in the urban villages of New York. As a self-conscious period piece, he is both typical enough and rare enough to merit landmark status. He has weathered high drama and hard knocks, achieving in latter years a stateliness that calls to mind those well-constructed prewar walk-ups, fire escapes zigzagging down their brick facades, that once predominated in Manhattan's landscape and now anchor the steel-and-glass boxes of twenty-first-century New York in the city's history.

Having moved out of the old neighborhood long ago and retired from the force in 1976, Grosso devotes his working hours to telling crime stories. As actor, writer, technical adviser, producer, and broker between the NYPD and Hollywood, he has helped to craft thousands of stories about the heroism and expertise of cops on the street. In a television and movie career spanning three decades so far, he has worked on or influenced a significant proportion of the popular crime fiction produced by the American media machine: police stories, gangster stories, private eye stories, courtroom dramas, procedurals, action, whodunits, true crime. His résumé goes all the way back to *The French Con-*

nection, the 1971 movie that set a generic pattern still followed by crime fiction—an influence evidenced in, for instance, the shaky-cam psychologizing of *Hill Street Blues* and *NYPD Blue,* the winking docudrama aesthetic of "reality" cop shows, Quentin Tarantino's application of high-art conceit to bottom-feeding popular formula, almost everything about Steven Soderbergh's *Traffic,* and the latest action movie's bid to add a new wrinkle to the rite of automotive pursuit through city streets.[1]

Exploiting the breakthrough made by *The French Connection* and its contemporaries, Grosso has helped to map and people the cultural terrain that opened up during the urban crisis of the 1960s and has shaped Americans' thinking about cities ever since. Already in 1977, even before Grosso had established himself as a producer, James Monaco observed that "Sonny Grosso has had a hand in most of the major cop films and television series of the 1970s" and jokingly speculated that someday scholars would discuss "Grossovian subtexts" in the period's police dramas.[2] Before he became the boss, Grosso worked on movies (among them *The Seven-Ups, Report to the Commissioner, The Godfather, The Brinks Job, Cruising),* television movies *(Foster and Laurie, The Marcus-Nelson Murders, To Kill a Cop),* and television shows *(Kojak, Baretta, The Rockford Files).* Since he became the boss, in partnership with Lawrence Jacobson, he has produced a number of made-for-television crime movies and hundreds of episodes of shows like *Night Heat, Secret Service, Strike Force, Counterstrike, Diamonds, True Blue, The Big Easy, Bellevue Emergency,* and the true-crime shows *Cop Talk* and *Top Cops.* (Even *Pee Wee's Playhouse,* the most anomalous of Grosso-Jacobson's few non-crime-related projects, has retrospectively taken on an aura of criminality because the show was canceled after the Sarasota police caught its star doing what comes naturally in an adult movie theater in 1991.) Grosso has also coauthored two books, *Murder at the Harlem Mosque* and *Point Blank,* and told me he was working on a third, *Real to Reel,* a memoir.

I began visiting Grosso in 1999 because I was curious about his role in refitting American crime stories to the task of representing an order of city life that succeeded his own. On that winter afternoon in 2000 we were talking in his office, between phone calls about Malta and other Hollywood emergencies, about what he characterizes as the "positive" tone of the police stories he produces. "If I was responsible for doing *all* the cop shows," he said, "every single one, then I'd be forced to do negative ones too. Just to be fair, because there's that side of it. But I'm not responsible for all of them, so I do positive stories. I leave all the crap to Sidney Lumet." Lumet's dramatic accounts of whistle-blowers Frank Serpico *(Serpico)* and Bob Leuci *(Prince of the City)* are the best-known corruption dramas, another type of crime movie that also flourished in the 1970s in the wake of sensational investigations by the Knapp Commission into misconduct in the NYPD. Decades after they were made, these movies still deeply offend Grosso, who sees them as glorifying stool pigeons. He believes that such high-profile corruption stories made it even harder to be a cop by further fraying the reputation, morale, and cohesion of a department already assailed on all sides. He does not deny that there was corruption; he just does not see why anybody would want to make or see a movie about it, although he does have a theory: "I guess Lumet, [Budd] Schulberg, people like that, Elia Kazan, they're informers, and they make movies about heroic informers." Leuci's testimony exposed widespread wrongdoing in the elite narcotics unit that Grosso had been instrumental in elevating to glory when he helped break the French Connection heroin-ring case in 1962. One element of the Leuci investigation (pursued with special fervor by a young prosecutor named Rudy Giuliani) struck particularly close to home: on one or more occasions sometime after the French Connection bust, somebody, almost certainly a police officer, entered the department's evidence-holding facility and stole most of the heroin that had been seized in the case. The shadow of that ultimately inconclusive investigation into the heroin theft fell across many detectives—including Grosso, whose reputation for honesty stood him in good stead. Other narcotics detectives' careers ended prematurely, and there was at least one related suicide. As for *Serpico,* Grosso complains that his own mother, after seeing the movie, asked him for reassurance that not all cops were corrupt. Partly in response, Grosso undertook to create heroes who unproblematically impose law and order on a world with a manifest tendency to devolve into chaos.

All the threads in this story—Grosso's two-stage career, New York and the Old Neighborhood in transition, the ongoing influence of the NYPD on the mutating forms of American crime stories—extend back to *The French Connection,* a fiction spun from selected facts of Grosso's biggest case. Principal credit for the exhaustive intelligence-gathering, surveillance, and investigation that led up to that bust went to Grosso and Eddie Egan, a notorious character whose exploits as a detective became the subject of a cycle of movies and who later went on to become a technical adviser and an actor himself. Grosso's contacts with federal

Sonny Grosso (left) and Eddie Egan in supporting roles—playing cops but not the cop characters based on themselves—in *The French Connection*. Courtesy of the Museum of Modern Art/Film Stills Archive.

narcotics investigators made it possible for the two partners to zero in on the drug traffickers, but the lore of the case (and the movie version) has one of Egan's spur-of-the moment hunches initiating the investigation: while hanging around off duty at the Copacabana with Grosso, Egan spotted a suspicious crew of revelers who turned out to be local mafiosi connected to an international heroin ring based in France. (It was after the partners happened upon the wiseguys at the Copacabana, Grosso says, that his federal contacts told him about their ongoing investigation of the drug ring.) Many people worked on the case, but Egan and Grosso became known as the street cops who made the biggest heroin seizure that anybody had heard of in 1962: 112 pounds of very pure product worth $32 million.

Even though *The French Connection*'s policemen seem to be concocted primarily out of warts and gall, and even though its quintessentially self-deflating 1970s ending allows the criminal mastermind known as Frog One and other leading villains to get away with their crimes, Grosso refuses to regard the movie based on his exploits as anything other than a monument to street policing. Mostly by showing in brutal mundane detail how cops did their jobs in difficult conditions, he believes, it scored a signal victory in the struggle to rehabilitate the police hero after that figure's reputation had fallen low in the late 1960s. "*The French Connection* came along and said, You may not like what we do or how we act, but this is *why* we act the way we do." He elaborated further in an interview with the BBC: "I think it turned the tables and turned the corner for police pictures, because if you go back before that it was Jack Webb saying, 'Just the facts.'" Grosso loves a surveillance scene in which detectives suffer out in the cold, making do with rancid coffee and a slice, while French drug smugglers eat a sumptuous restaurant meal. "You really have to examine it and say, 'Why are these guys out here, and why are these millionaires in there? We're all born the same way, we all come from a mother. What makes these guys do that, and these cops do *that?*' That to me symbolized what *The French Connection* is all about." [3] Others have seen a variety of competing contents in the morally, politically, and mythologically double-edged movie, which answers to descriptions ranging from law-and-order fantasy to absurdist critique of the liberal welfare state in self-contradictory collapse. [4]

The French Connection was all of that, in addition to being a five-time Oscar winner, a resounding financial success, and an important prototype for the soon-to-be-dominant genre of the action movie. The movie changed Sonny Grosso's life, opening the way for him to cross over from police work to the culture trades, but it was also a signal event in the thoroughly intertwined histories of crime fiction and American urbanism. It marked a turning point in the style and substance of crime stories, it caught the feel of New York in the throes of a great transformation, and it exemplified the consequences of crises of the 1960s that shook both Hollywood and the inner city.

THE SANTA CHASE

Sooner or later, a conversation with Grosso will find its way back to *The French Connection.* He got to telling me about recruiting a small-time miscreant named Matt the Parky to play a junkie—not a challenging thespian stretch for Matt the Parky—in a bar scene that occurs early in the movie. The workday had ended for the staff at Grosso-Jacobson Productions, and the deep quiet of a Tuesday evening in February had fallen over the office. The voice mail system was picking up incoming calls, so Grosso's phone had stopped ringing. The East River went dark in his east-facing bank of windows, the lights of Queens and Brooklyn coming on across the black stretch of water. I had a video of *The French Connection* with me, so Grosso inserted it into the VCR on his desk, and we watched the opening scenes that we both knew by heart.

The movie opens with a prefatory vignette in which a gunman murders a French police officer or informant in the vestibule of a Marseilles apartment house. The killer—played by Marcel Bozzuffi, who had previously played a right-wing paramilitary thug in *Z*—steps over the fresh corpse into the sunny street, pausing only to tear a chunk from the loaf of bread his victim dropped and take a bite of it. The gesture is too petulantly Gallic to be chilling: Bah, les flics! I nibble their baguettes, like so!

Next, though, a title announces "Brooklyn," and the camera arrives on the streets of New York, which look chilled to the bone, wintry-hard and forbidding, as they so often do in movies of the period. The interiors of the scene that follows were actually shot in a bar in Harlem, but most of the exteriors were shot in Brooklyn. A couple of narcotics detectives, Jimmy "Popeye" Doyle (played by Gene Hackman and modeled on Eddie Egan) and Buddy "Cloudy" Russo (played by Roy Scheider and modeled on Sonny Grosso), are staking out a bar on a gray December afternoon. The movie has a grainy texture and muted palette, as if high-quality light were in short supply in the inner city. It looks like a documentary but also like an art-house movie: French? Italian? A stylish southpaw political thriller on the order of *Z* or *The Battle of Algiers?* Soon, though, there will be a chase, and the Hollywood-trained moviegoer will be traveling briskly—although with some fancy new swerves and jumps—down a familiar narrative and aesthetic groove excavated by D. W. Griffith and company a long time ago.

Cloudy, posing as a pushcart vendor and wearing an apron over a lumber jacket, hunches up against the cold. Popeye is in full Santa regalia, with bell and charity collection bucket to complete the disguise, and some small black boys have gathered around him. While asking them whether they have been good and what they want for Christmas, Popeye sneaks a look through the front window of the crowded bar, in which black men are drinking and carrying on. The extras in that scene (Matt the Parky among them) are petty crooks, junkies, idlers, and other Harlem street characters recruited by Grosso and Egan with the promise of a day's honest work and a fleeting moment of cinematic fame. "We rounded up a bunch of guys we knew," Grosso told me, "guys we had busted for using and selling, guys we had gotten into programs, guys who were selling to support their habits. Mostly they were still trying to wipe snot from their nose." They certainly look right at home in a bar in the middle of the day. Popeye, peering in, cannot hear the hubbub and the loping soul jam on the jukebox, but we can. Two men in the bar, one wearing an army fatigue jacket, stand shoulder to shoulder in front of the jukebox; something passes between their hands. Popeye, having spotted the exchange through the window, abruptly rings his bell and leads the children in a chorus of "Jingle Bells." Reacting to that signal, Cloudy sheds his apron and enters the bar, where he begins rousting patrons.

The scene draws on Grosso and Egan's experience of raiding bars, one of the principal ways in which they piled up record numbers of narcotics arrests. The raids could be dramatic—cops charging through the front door, everybody in the place dumping the goods or trying to get away—and Egan sometimes added to the drama by conducting busts in costume. Among the disguises he had tried over the years were a pushcart vendor getup and a Santa suit, both of which he employed to get close to drug deals incognito. "Eddie loved hitting the bars," said Grosso, reminiscing in his office, "but I hated it. I hated the confrontation. You couldn't tell what was happening, all the people moving around, people getting mad because here we were disturbing their good time. Eddie loved it. He acted like a maniac, and everybody was scared of him." Egan, usually costumed only as the great Eddie Egan and having worked himself into a sort of huffing Method fury, would enter the bar and go straight to the jukebox, which he called "the piccolo." The sudden silence he produced by yanking out its plug brought everyone's attention around to him, his preferred condition in life. "Eddie was onstage," Grosso continued. "I would stay back by the bar and look. If I see somebody drop something, I grab him."

I asked Randy Jurgensen, an ex-detective and a boyhood friend of Grosso's from Harlem, about raiding bars with Grosso and Egan. Smaller and trimmer than Grosso, dark-haired and mustached, Jurgensen also worked on the French Connection case and then on *The French Connection,* and he also went into movie acting and production. As he remembered their raids, "Eddie would be yelling, 'Get up against the wall! Get over here! Do this! Do that! Hey, what the fuck did I just say? You fuck, you want me to break that arm?'" Jurgensen, a good mimic, imitated Egan's voice as a choked bluster that communicated equal parts rage and theatrical fervor. "And Sonny was always the guy that enforced it. He'd be saying, 'All right, you heard what he said, get over here.'" He did Grosso's voice as lower, gravelly, commanding but calmer. "Eddie would say, 'Nobody talk,' and then of course somebody would talk, so Sonny would go up in their face and say, 'He told you not to talk.'" Once, raiding a bar on 110th Street, Eddie told a woman to shut up. Jurgensen shook his head, remembering. "She said, 'Sheee-iiit,' she's like in slow motion, and Sonny says, 'He told you. . . . ' I don't know where it came from, but she swung, broke Sonny's nose, clocked him, all the blood was coming down over the pool table."

Cloudy, Grosso's fictional alter ego, gets hurt in the movie's bar-rousting scene, too. His search of the bar's patrons continues until the man in the fatigue jacket makes a break for it, bursting from the front door with Cloudy in pursuit. Popeye, blowing his Santa cover, shouts "Hold it! Freeze!" and joins his partner in momentarily cornering the suspect, who produces a knife, cuts Cloudy on the forearm, and breaks loose.

Time for that chase. The detectives pursue their man on foot through the streets of Brooklyn past rowhouses and walk-ups in a run-down area of Bedford-Stuyvesant just below the junction of Broadway and Flushing Avenue, territory that Egan and Grosso once worked. The three men dart through traffic and pass some pedestrians, and at one point an elevated train rumbles in the background (an early promise of a more spectacular chase to come later on in the movie), but a desolate urban stillness surrounds them. The camera, mostly handheld and car-mounted, scrambles to keep up and occasionally gets ahead of the runners. The effect is as if an extraordinarily lucky and competent documentary crew had been trolling the streets and happened on the action. A telephoto lens and a nifty sound close-up catch Popeye, who appears to be getting a stitch in his side, huffing and cursing as he falls behind. His Santa hat falls off; his beard hangs askew around his neck like a bib. Tiring, the cops fade from sprinting to middle-distance speed. The fugitive appears to be sustaining an all-out effort, his face in a rictus and his natural pasted back as if by terrific g-force, but he cannot seem to get more than half a block ahead of his pursuers. Finally, in an extended handheld long shot, he cuts across a weedy vacant lot, where he turns his ankle on a piece of detritus and collapses, apparently felled by the same Hollywood logic that requires an athletic young woman to stumble so that the plodding slasher pursuing her can catch up. Or maybe the fugitive has just been winded by all that sprinting. The detectives stagger up and give the fallen man a beating. Popeye picks up a rock and appears ready to break bones, but Cloudy makes him stop.

After an edit, the three of them appear around the corner of a building, the detectives now dragging their prisoner with his hands cuffed behind his back. We assume that they are just around the corner from the vacant lot in Bed-Stuy, but actually they are back on location in Harlem, on 119th Street between First and Second Avenues, not far from Rao's and across the street from the building in which Grosso lived as a child. The detectives haul their prisoner past an open trash fire into a burned-out space between two buildings, where they abuse him further and shove him against a wall to interrogate him. Cloudy, despite his wound and despite having just kicked the cuffed prisoner in the back when he was down, plays the good cop, asking plausible questions about a heroin connection named Joe the Barber. Popeye plays the bad cop, insisting that the prisoner admit to picking his feet in Poughkeepsie—one of Eddie Egan's double-talk routines for confusing and intimidating a prisoner, priming him to admit to more comprehensible charges. The bewildered prisoner clearly believes him to be insane, an impression reinforced by the dissonant juxtaposition of Popeye's disarranged Santa suit with his apparent eagerness to punch the man's lights out. The camera closes in, tightening the frame on Popeye's face and his expressive hands—the left clutching the suspect's clothes under his chin, the right raised in a threatening fist, pointing in accusation, demanding admissions of guilt with a gimme gesture. Having established control of both the camera and the interrogation, Popeye bullies the bloodied prisoner into admitting that he has indeed been to Poughkeepsie, then proceeds to the next logical step: "You've been there, right? You sat on the edge of the bed, didn't you? You took off your shoes, you put your fingers between your toes, and picked your feet, didn't you? Now say it!" Once the prisoner has stammered "Yes," an admission of guilt in the abstract that seems to rob him of any remaining will to resist, Popeye brings the sequence to a close: "Now, I'm gonna bust your ass for those three bags, and I'm gonna nail you for picking your feet in Poughkeepsie."

The French Connection is best known for another chase, occurring later in the movie, widely regarded as The Greatest Car Chase of All Time. In that elegantly frantic sequence, Popeye commandeers a citizen's car and roars through crowded streets in pursuit of Frog Two, the French assassin played by Marcel Bozzuffi, who has hijacked an elevated train after accidentally shooting a woman pushing a stroller with a bullet intended for Popeye. That chase, a pure action sequence with the merest fanciful sliver of a basis in the facts of the original case, has always been the movie's most famous scene, a quintessentially early-1970s

Popeye (Gene Hackman, in Santa suit) and Cloudy (Roy Scheider) interrogate a suspect (Alan Weeks) after a chase on foot. Courtesy of the Museum of Modern Art/Film Stills Archive.

episode in which the city seems to be out of control on the grand scale: cars crashing and then crashing again, trains crashing, a drug-dealing assassin suddenly in charge of the subway, deranged cops and crooks hijacking vehicles and shooting at each other without regard for the lives of the innocent bystanders diving for cover all around them.[5] If Popeye purports to be an agent of law and order, his wheel-wrenching, screaming near miss of a second woman pushing a stroller suggests that the extreme remedy might be at least as threatening as the rampant disease of criminal disorder. When the movie was released in 1971, audiences and critics floored by its innovative escalation of suspense technique tended to identify with the train's motorman, who suffers a heart attack in mid-chase. Who wouldn't? But, memorable and even shocking though it may be, the car chase mostly elaborates what we already know by that point in the movie: the city is going to hell, and its inhabitants have been thrown into a primal scramble for what is left of it; Popeye's obsessive motivation has little to do with the rule of law; moral certitude and clean-edged justice have become quaint notions; and the movie looks and feels like a stylistic cross between a Hollywood genre film, a foreign art movie, and a documentary.

The Santa chase, which establishes all these principles as it blueprints *The French Connection*'s treatment of its subject, cuts much closer than the car chase to the center of the movie's world. A more modestly human-scaled précis of that world, the Santa chase also offers a more intimate and—curiously, considering the nastiness that transpires in it—a more humane account of the inner city in a peculiarly troubled moment. It serves as a sort of thesis statement, from which the rest of the movie proceeds as extended development: the protracted surveillance of gangsters, domestic and foreign, who seem to rule the world; the infighting among overworked cops and federal agents; the grim spareness of the investigators' lives contrasted to the gangsters' opulence; the endless standing around in the cold; the big car chase and the climactic shootout and bust; the anticlimactic escape to Europe of Frog One and the successful squirming of various other perpetrators through loopholes in the legal system; the cops' return to the futile business of busting hopeless junkies in the ghetto. All of this springs from and eventually returns to the routines of breaking the law and making the law in the inner city's burned-over districts, a world first introduced when Popeye and Cloudy chase down and nail their man for those three bags of heroin and for picking his feet in Poughkeepsie.

BLOCK 1728

That chase is one of thousands of movie and television episodes of the 1970s in which cops and robbers pursue each other through the inner city. Picture them in their mad period vines—flare-pantsed avatars of Achilles and Hector circling the walls of Troy—tearing through traffic and down debris-strewn alleys. White supercops chase drug dealers, mafiosi, and revolutionaries. Black private eyes and insurgent black Caesars chase corrupt white cops and Syndicate hoods. Good cops chase bad ones, and vice versa. The platform-shoed archpimp Priest sprints past the obligatory frenzied dogs and leaps a high fence in hot pursuit of a strung-out mugger in *Superfly*'s operatic "Junkie Chase" overture. The seriously messed-up Wambaugh cops on *Police Story* and the not-messed-up-enough heroes of *Starsky and Hutch, SWAT,* or *Police Woman* ("Freeze, turkey!") chase a variety of street corner entrepreneurs, radical brothers and sisters, psychotic acidheads, flashback-prone Vietnam vets, pseudocorporate racketeers, and other recurring villains on the inner-city frontier. The permutations extend to the horizon of the crime genres' imagination in the aftermath of the 1960s.

Seen in light of that moment, the pursuers seem intent on beating some answers out of the pursued. The violence of *The French Connection*'s Santa chase proceeds from the question, Who's selling drugs? But American crime stories tend to dig beneath the surface crimes that drive the plot; they unearth deep structural wrongs, an order of violence more diffuse than murder or robbery. So the deeper-reaching, potentially more disquieting question is, Who's responsible for this mess? Who did this to the world of the movie? *The French Connection* ends up hauling in the period's usual suspects, all of them guilty: unrestrained private capital, a resilient but weak citizenry, and a compromised state.

Chases in spaces make places. The camera, tracking the pursuit, pieces together an implicit account of the city and its history. The Santa chase, like many others of the period, reveals glimpses of a landscape once occupied by the industrial working class. Bedford-Stuyvesant and East Harlem, processed into one seamless inner-city terrain by the camera and editor, provide types of all those neighborhoods once inhabited by immigrants and migrants who came to American cities to find a place in the manufacturing economy. Densely packed walk-up apartment buildings in New York, like rowhouses in Philadelphia or bungalows in Chicago, have that epic compressed into their recognizable form.[6] By 1970, blacks and Hispanics had largely replaced white ethnics in places like Bed-Stuy: postindustrial ghettos, descended from industrial slums (increasingly remembered as idyllic urban villages) and marked with scars of urban renewal and across-the-board disinvestment that happened in the 1950s and 1960s. The flow of capital out of these neighborhoods produced vacant lots and urban ruins—signs of deeper, harder-to-identify social trauma on a grand scale—as well as rises in the violent, face-to-face street criminality that was easier to conceive of and identify as a social problem.

Sonny Grosso retold this story to me in his thumbnail history of Italian Harlem: "I watched my neighborhood disappear in the late fifties and early sixties." Grosso, whose old neighborhood was also part of his beat when he was a uniform cop and then a narcotics detective, makes heroin the principal villain, as do many others who mourn the fall of the urban village. Another Harlem guy of Grosso's generation nicknamed Sonny, Claude Brown from 146th Street, told the same story about black Harlem in *Manchild in the Promised Land:* "Heroin had just about taken over Harlem. It seemed to be a kind of plague. . . . If anybody had asked me around the latter part of 1957 what I thought had made the greatest impression on my generation in Harlem, I would have said, 'Drugs.'"[7] Because the heroin plague and associated criminal activity helped to break down the fabric of neighborhood life, heroin came to serve—as did, in different ways, the street gang, the high-rise housing project, and the automobile—as available scapegoat and symbolic shorthand for the effects of giant processes remaking the inner city: ethnic and racial succession, suburbanization, deindustrialization and job loss, shifts in policing and governance, urban renewal and other forms of redevelopment, all adding up to the disappearance from the inner city of a traditional structure of opportunity that once characterized industrial urbanism. Heroin became a way to think about, and not think about, the despair induced by sweeping structural changes in the inner city.

So did crime. During the generally recognized urban crisis that lasted from about 1965 to about 1970, criminal violence—especially in the form of the riot, the mugging, and police brutality—became institutionalized as the text in which pertinent urban contents might be read (or buried). Most often, those contents included the situation of American racial order, the evacuation of opportunity from inner cities in a suburbanizing age, and the failure of the New Deal coalition and the activist caretaker state to which it was committed. The exact nature of that failure depends on who told the story and when. Scanning from political left to right, it can be a failure to stick up for the people against big capital, a failure to provide decent housing and opportunity for all, a failure to get tough with punks—in any case, a failure.[8]

By the early 1970s, transformed neighborhoods like East Harlem and Bed-Stuy had inspired a thorough revision of imaginative geography, giving rise to a generic inner city in which the meanings of these changes could be staged and parsed. Consider one element of that generic landscape, the gap between buildings (on Grosso's old block in Harlem) in which the cops beat and then interrogate their prisoner. *The*

French Connection helped make that gap a visual cliché by showing that blight is good for chases. Like Monument Valley, it creates open foregrounds and expressive backdrops, and that landscape resonates with meanings, among them various accounts of the inner city's and the liberal welfare state's decline. Reading the gap between the buildings, starting again from the political left, one can say that this is the landscape of the war on the poor. A trash fire still burns from the figurative bomb that militant capital dropped on the industrial slum to clear ground for the postindustrial ghetto. The cops are there to keep the survivors under control, adding repressive insult to economic and political injury. From the center, one might read the gap as what remains for the welfare state to do, the gap left where the impulse of urban renewal met the counterimpulse to discredit it as wasteful or regressive. The cops, agents of both impulses, are there to impose order by protecting law-abiding citizens, as well as controlling the deviant. Read from the right, the fire becomes a campfire on a new frontier opened by the state's misguided efforts at social engineering and now devolving into barbarism, a terrain populated by savages so morally incontinent that they burn down their own neighborhoods. This terrain, mythologically continuous with the nineteenth-century western range, provided the logical new turf of migrants from the Western like Clint Eastwood and Charles Bronson—who were pushed to find new territory as the Western, with its resonance of race war and empire, suffered a generic crisis in the age of the Vietnam War.[9] If the cops cannot impose law and order, they can at least exact a measure of Western-style vengeance. *The French Connection,* being a movie of its moment as well as a money-making enterprise, wants to have it all three ways at once, plus whatever else works for you.

Picking and choosing stock elements from the complexity of different inner-city neighborhoods, popular formula invented a composite place called the Ghetto, a generic wasteland remaining after the traditional urban village was overrun in the 1950s and 1960s by a cast of barbarians that, depending on the teller, can embrace city planners and gentry as well as junkies. The Ghetto can be spectacularly engrossing in its own right, but the crime story, with its logic of unearthing deep crime, also trades upon cultural memories of that which the Ghetto supposedly supplanted: the urban village and the industrial cityscape in which it thrived. Hardworking people of modest means used to live decently here, the story goes—white people, in many versions, but in other versions they are black, Hispanic, Asian American. In any case, you know the details of the story. Yes, they did not have much, but they respected authority and understood themselves to form a community, and they had hope for the future; they left their doors unlocked, they slept in the park on hot summer nights, women could walk down the street unmolested at night, and so on. Then the neighborhood began to break up. Newcomers moved in, good jobs disappeared, drugs and guns proliferated, crime and racial conflict became what mattered most about cities, and everything changed. Variants of this master story disagree about causes and effects, but as a body of narratives they agree on more than their various tellers (say, black nationalists and enthusiastic participants in white flight) would care to admit. The before-and-after quality of the basic account was central to the way American popular culture imagined the emerging postindustrial inner city in the 1960s and 1970s—and still imagines it in its maturity today—even if the simplifications that produced the Ghetto tended to reduce the image of the older city to ruins so fragmentary that they could not evoke the close-grained, lived details of the industrial urbanism that the landscape once housed.

The French Connection, a crime movie speeding through the landscape in the grip of terrific narrative drive, can spare only a gesture at this hinted-at lost city. The Santa chase encourages you to say to yourself, "What happened to *that* neighborhood?" Looking at the ruins, you know how everybody in the movie got so tough, crazy, or weak: things used to be better; now they are worse. To fill out this schematic history suggested by the movie's setting, consider another, larger gap in the landscape explored during the chase. When the cops catch up to their man in a vacant lot, just before the action is silently transposed back to East Harlem for the interrogation scene staged between buildings, the camera frames the three of them in a square-block-sized hole in the urban fabric of Brooklyn—a gap that tells a story of the inner city's transformation.

After leading the cops north up Sumner Avenue, the fugitive makes a desperate left turn onto Ellery Street and cuts across a large vacant lot toward Hopkins, but he does not get very far before falling. You get a feel for the neighborhood's textures and architecture in glimpses of the low-rise buildings that the three men run past; and you can see in the background, framing the scene, some large structures that tell the story in shorthand: a building with a smokestack and postwar high-rises bracketing the All Saints Roman Catholic Church. You can fill in the blank spaces in the foreground with urban renewal, capital flight, lost jobs, absentee landlords, firebugs, and residents who tried to hang on to their place in the city. The movie, arriving in the gap between industrial and postindustrial cities, simultaneously erases and conjures the past. The gap serves as a clean slate, a ritual stage on which stock types play out recast editions of the usual frontier dramas, but it also suggests something that used to be there and is now gone: a dense, busy block crowded with walk-up buildings and the lives, enterprises, and stories that they contained.

This section of northern Bedford-Stuyvesant, wedged between Williamsburg and Bushwick, was once part of a typical landscape of industrial urbanism. Germans and eastern Europeans predominated in the early twentieth century; then it was a mostly Jewish and Italian neighborhood; then, starting in the 1950s, increasingly Hispanic and black. It is, in other words, an example of the urban place that has been serially inhabited by immigrants and migrants attempting the difficult transit between the Old Country—or an American hinterland—and the shopfloors that sometimes became avenues for entry into the American middle class. In the vicinity there were a few larger factories—producers of stoves and paper boxes, a leather works, a chemical plant, a brewery—and many small manufacturers of all kinds, especially in the clothing trades. Along with places of worship, rail lines, businesses, schools, and a web of voluntary associations typical of immigrant and migrant communities, these manufacturing enterprises anchored a way of life.

One can call up vestiges of that order by reconstructing the history of the square block—officially designated Block 1728, bounded by Ellery, Hopkins, Sumner, and Throop—that by 1971 had become the vacant lot in which Popeye and Cloudy catch the fugitive. In the 1920s, it was dominated by Jews, many of them in the business of making and selling clothes, with a few Italians scattered among them. On that block in 1929 there were two synagogues, Fiternick's Russian and Turkish Baths (on a site previously occupied by Industrial School Number 5), a steam printer, the Great Northern Tire Works, the Industrial Cloak Company, and a blacksmith named Alex Wexler. Just across Ellery Street were the Siegel Knitting Works and the Washwell Apron Manufacturing Company. Small enterprises—tailors and seamstresses, machinists, a variety of skilled tradespeople—filled almost every building. Important local institutions along Sumner Avenue helped provide the structure of civil society in the urban village, among them the offices of the Joint Board of the Dress and Waist Makers Union, the Brooklyn

Waiters Union Local Number 2, and the Fior Di Marsala Mutual Benefit Society and Credit Union. More Italians moved into the neighborhood in the 1930s, and by 1955 most of the people in the area had names that ended in vowels: there were still Jews in the neighborhood, and Italians still dominated, but Hispanics were arriving in force.[10] A look at the phone directory shows the layering of populations: Guadalupe Santiago had moved in next to the A-1 Metal Spinning Company; Carmen Pagan and Salvatore Asaro lived on either side of the Ford Metal Store Front Company; the Cuba Rico Pastry Shop had opened two doors down from the Fior Di Marsala, bracketing Max Machlovitz between them. Synagogues departed, and the Catholic church remained, as is usually the case, and in the 1960s Spanish-language evangelical churches moved into storefronts on the east side of Sumner Avenue.[11]

This kind of succession, similar to the turnover that occurred in Sonny Grosso's East Harlem, is typical for New York (and many other industrial cities, especially in the Northeast and Midwest), with new waves of in-migrants crowding in on the heels of the old, mixing with and replacing them in the neighborhood's streets, candy stores, shopfloors, and houses of worship. The sequenced, layered arrival of new populations has been one of the most important, most dynamic aspects of American urbanism—perhaps the best thing about our cities. But after World War II, when the very existence of cities arranged on the industrial model began to be seen as a major social problem in a suburbanizing age, the changing form and function of the inner city— edged with the calculus of race—caught up with Bedford-Stuyvesant. Arriving Hispanic and black workers found that the way of life that had been instrumental in drawing them to the industrial city was rapidly eroding, especially in the increasingly deindustrialized remnants of the urban villages that had once been organized around factories. Instead, government encouraged the evacuation of capital and opportunity from these parts of the inner city and then responded with policies designed to house and maintain those in the working class—and its conceptual evil twin, the "underclass"—who had not been pushed out already by the process of clearing ground for postindustrial infrastructure. In the 1950s, the city wiped out several square blocks just south of Block 1728 to make room for the Sumner Houses, 1,099 units of public housing in a series of squat buildings set slantwise to the street. Block 1728 was next.

By 1970, Block 1728 was a clean slate, a vacant lot, condemned and razed to make room for a medical center, a forbidding copper-and-gold-colored metal-and-glass building completed in 1972. The crew for *The French Connection* shot the Santa chase on that vacant lot in the winter of 1970–1971, after the block had been leveled but before work began on the new building. It was a handy stretch of desolation, framed by evocative buildings, in which to stage an extended handheld long shot in which Santa hits a black man with a rock. That bizarre, perhaps darkly hilarious gesture suggests urban devolution from welfare state (what do you want for Christmas?) to state of nature (the marginally more powerful hit the less powerful with rocks) to through-the-looking-glass state of insanity (you ever pick your feet in Poughkeepsie?). The rock in Popeye's hand is a shard of the history of Block 1728, which is in turn a fragment of the greater history of industrial urbanism's rise and fall. The three running men traverse the zone of overlap—rendered as a gap—between the latter part of that history and the emergence of a new landscape and a new urbanism housed in it. If that history cannot be recovered in detail in the movie, even the most action-fixated viewer can see that something momentous has happened to the city through which the characters move. And even the most obtuse consumer of American movies, television, newspapers, magazines, and other popular media circa 1971 would have had a vague sense that city life had recently entered a period of wrenching transformation.

The French Connection is a popular adventure fantasy and perhaps an art movie, not a planning document or a sociological study. The movie wants to present a good tale well told, and New York City provides a resonant setting for the action. But that setting and its resonances cannot help but infuse the action with meaning. Director William Friedkin, who knew exactly nothing about the neighborhood's history, sent out his location scouts to find him urban bleakness, they found Block 1728, and he used the location because it looked right for his purposes. But part of the rightness of the block's look resided precisely in the big picture of urban transformation that such landscapes evoke. And crime, having become a central metaphor and content in which to read that transformation, was an inherently big-picture subject in the sense that Americans had already fallen into the habit of using it as symbolic shorthand for a whole complex of interrelated urban subjects that included class and race and inequality, economic change, the proper role of government, the tension between public life and private rights, and what happened to the urban village. Friedkin used New York settings to tell a particular story, but the movie he made—and the many others that explored similar territory in the 1970s—drew upon and helped to tell a

Sonny Grosso, Roy Scheider, Gene Hackman, and Eddie Egan (from left to right) during a break in shooting on Block 1728. Photo: *New York Daily News.* © 1999 Daily News L.P.

larger story about the emergence of postindustrial urbanism. That larger story lends its substance to *The French Connection,* sometimes in ways that break the surface of the movie, sometimes in ways so muted and compressed that the viewer comes away only with a vague sense of something big moving beneath the surface of a new-order police procedural.

THE FORMULA FOR GRITTINESS

More than a generation after it was made, *The French Connection* is un- mistakably a period piece. Its early-1970s feel comes off the screen in near-palpable waves. Part of that feel proceeds from the movie's con- tent: the postindustrial inner city rising from the ruins of the industrial, the junk trade storming to cultural center stage, the blend of finger-in- the-dike absurdity and Western-style heroism in the characterization of street cops. Intimations of deeper crisis and chaos can be found in the hot pursuits through wintry streetscapes, the naturals and sideburns, the wide-bodied cars, and the words of a man in the know who says,

"Everything's everything, baby." You are reminded that things seemed particularly shaky and rough in America's big cities back then, and that, although the streetfighting of the 1960s had abated, fresh shocks to American confidence waited in the wings. Coming attractions include Watergate, the oil bust, final defeat in Vietnam, the near bankruptcy of New York and other cities, "stagflation," and an escalating domestic arms race associated with the street corner drug trade. But the movie's period feel proceeds just as much from its style of presentation. Friedkin did find terrific material to work with, but he also drew creatively upon a variety of sources, precedents, and talents in formulating an expressive style appropriate to that material. He and his colleagues played crucial parts in a significant revision of Hollywood's imaginative habits, doing much to develop and codify the movie industry's formal apparatus for exploring the postindustrial city.

The French Connection has a classic Hollywood structure, a chase plot involving highly motivated characters competing to achieve clearly defined goals, but it also draws upon a variety of other formal traditions that had blossomed since World War II and were finding their way into Hollywood—among them television news, documentary, underground film, and especially the French New Wave, Italian neorealism, and other foreign cinemas. Intensive use of handheld cameras, telephoto lenses, and natural light all mimic cinema vérité, as if the moviemakers had chased after unscripted action already under way in the inner city. Lingering close-ups of unglamorous faces and the pervasiveness of informal acting styles, mixing improvisation with verbatim transcriptions of street talk, work against the grain of Hollywood tradition and raise echoes of both European art movies and the television news. Inspired by Godard and Antonioni, Friedkin and his editor, Jerry Greenberg, consciously tried to interject a dose of New Wave discontinuity into standard Hollywood rhythms: jumpy transitions, creative mismatches of sound and image, and a refusal to fall into textbook editing patterns that repeat familiar angles.

Not only was the movie shot on eighty-six locations in New York, but its formal properties emphasize the fact of location shooting. Scenes like the Santa chase typify the ways that the new urban cinema of the 1970s, having freed itself from the soundstage on which most city movies of previous eras were filmed, is always nudging you to notice its location aesthetic. "Hey," the movie says, "we're in the street! Look! The camera's chasing the action! Buses and trucks are getting in the way!" The "traffic wipe," in which passing vehicles obscure the camera's view of the action for an anxious second or two, became a visual cliché after *The French Connection:* the omniscient Hollywood camera's (and viewer's) momentary lapse into urban confusion strikes exactly the period pitch. Even the severe winter of 1970–1971, which froze equipment and shortened tempers during the shoot, reinforced not only the starkness of the movie's social vision but also its location aesthetic. Popeye, Cloudy, and the rest are so obviously half frozen that one cannot forget how much of this movie was made in the street.

The look and feel of the movie have been labeled for posterity with a standard keyword, "gritty," which is understood to convey thematic "grittiness," just as the stylized darkness of film noir is understood to convey thematic darkness. Owen Roizman, the cinematographer, told me, "When we shot *The French Connection,* I always had in mind, Keep it not-pretty. Keep it gritty." Roizman got the job because he shared Friedkin's interest in crafting a new look by being creative with existing technology, and because he had not worked on a feature before and was relatively free of conventional Hollywood habits. The main camera operator, a Cuban expatriate named Enrique "Ricky" Bravo, had a knack for catching complex action with a handheld camera—in the pre-Steadicam age—without undue swinging and jerking of the frame (a skill Bravo developed, says Friedkin with typical hyperbole, when "he photographed the revolution at Castro's side"). Roizman recalled that the equipment "wasn't anything new, but how we used it was often new, and it was new to bring this to features. People had been doing some of this on documentaries for years." They used a BNC noiseless camera for sound scenes and an Arriflex 35 camera for scenes in which sound could be synched in later. They chose old lenses that had "a slight creaminess to them," rather than the Panavision lens so perfect for achieving the preternaturally clean Hollywood look. Roizman estimated that "maybe 70 percent of the camera work was handheld," a proportion unheard of in American feature films prior to that time (but increasingly common in movies and on television after *The French Connection*), and the telephoto lens had the effect of putting the audience on the street while also creating the feeling of surveillance from afar. "There was literally no makeup that I can recall," Roizman said, and, breaking with Hollywood's usual bath-of-radiance approach to lighting, they used available light outdoors during the day. At night they deployed larger setups, but always guided by the imperative to approximate New York's "natural" nighttime light sources. When shooting indoors, they tried as much as possible to mimic available light sources with mobile zip lights and creative work-arounds. For instance, in a scene in a bar's bathroom, Roizman replaced the existing bulb with a brighter bulb that he coated with hairspray to cut flare. "Nobody was doing this kind of thing on features then," concluded Roizman—and he, of all the surviving key figures in the making of *The French Connection,* is perhaps least given to self-congratulatory overstatement.

Most important when it comes to achieving grittiness, the film stock was exposed and processed to achieve a grainy look. "We degraded the film," Roizman explained. "When you expose a film, there's a middle-of-the-road exposure for greatest detail in highlights and shadows, and the middle tones fall into place, but what we shot was underexposed, partly because we used natural light so much and the film wasn't as fast as it is now, and that takes away detail in shadows." Force-developing the film, by leaving it in the developer longer, overcompensated for the underexposure. Finally, "If you print it light enough to get the right brightness, you get 'milk' in the shadows. You get grain." You get, in other words, visual grittiness, a palette of grays and grains that came to be associated with moral and political grayness, and with a weary sense of complexity inspired by hard social facts that do not reduce to easy fictional answers. That palette and the ambiguous attitude it evokes say "early 1970s" as definitively as do the wah-wah pedal, improvised-sounding dialogue, and a telephoto shot of our hero Popeye checking his glove for frozen snot after wiping his nose with it during a frigid stakeout.[12]

Roizman's formula for grittiness was part of the more comprehensive formula for the movie's success: an urgent subject, expressive settings, and an original style, both elegiac and forward-looking, that combined to capture the feel of an anxious historical moment in the capital city of American culture. The movie gives expression to a typically tense admixture of attitudes toward the inner city after the urban crisis. A sense of the thickness of urban layering mixes with a tendency to assume that there is nothing left of the Old Neighborhood but ruins. Intimate fascination mixes with distancing fear. Appreciation of criminal spectacle mixes with a yearning for law and order. Awareness of the hard facts of social failure mixes with a desire to recoup that failure in popular fantasy. These are not just thematic tendencies; they take root in the technical and stylistic decision making that gave the movie its distinctive feel.

Viewers and reviewers responded to that feel as conveying the essence of the moment. Pauline Kael, for example, who despised *The French Connection* as an aesthetic object but recognized the movie's craftsmanship and importance, made her review of it an occasion to announce the arrival of "a new movie age of nightmare-realism" that captured "a new spirit of nervousness, anxious hopelessness, which is the true spirit of New York." Horrified but respectful, Kael placed *The French Connection* in the first rank of "New York–made movies" that "have provided a permanent record of the city in breakdown." Among those she had in mind were crime movies like *Klute, The Anderson Tapes, Midnight Cowboy, Shaft, Cotton Comes to Harlem,* and *The Panic in Needle Park.* "There's a sense of carnival about this urban-crisis city," Kael observed, that brought the city on the screen and the city around her uncomfortably—if excitingly—close together: "The panhandler in the movie who jostles the hero is just like the one who jostles you as you leave the movie theatre; the police sirens in the movie are screaming outside; the hookers and junkies in the freak show on the screen are indistinguishable from the ones in the freak show on the streets." Tracing the genesis of the nightmare-realist cinema to both social upheaval in the streets and financial crisis in Hollywood, Kael treated *The French Connection* as the bearer and exemplar of bad news about American culture in a low moment. The crime genres, like the urban police, had turned nasty to cope with hard times: "This picture says Popeye is a brutal son of a bitch who gets the dirty job done. So is the picture."[13]

PARTNERS

The inner-city social crisis of the late 1960s was the most widely recognized part of a longer and larger process of transformation, the passing of the industrial city and the emergence of its postindustrial successor. That process sharpened into a widely recognized five-year event called "the urban crisis" in the latter half of the 1960s, when it had proceeded far enough to become conceptually accessible as a deep problem underlying the harrowing news of the day—especially crime news—and the fictions that eventually arose to exploit it.

The notion of urban crisis also extends to mean a parallel crisis in representing the American city. People who did that work—those in the film and television industries, reporters, photographers, social scientists, historians, policy makers, writers and artists and intellectuals of all kinds—revised their habits of imagining the transformed cities that confronted them. That process of revision especially affected genres, such as literary realism or sociology, that had developed in significant part during the previous hundred years around the cultural work of representing the city.[14] Among those genres were crime stories, many of which had fancifully depicted the industrial city and its dangerous classes (be they rich or poor or somewhere in the middle). Plot the points and draw a line of development through them: George Lippard's mid-nineteenth-century mysteries of the city; dime-novel tales of detectives, mechanics, and millionaires; pulp fantasies of exotic adventure in the dangerous terrain of Chinatown, Little Italy, or the Black Metropolis; Dashiell Hammett's masterpiece of sublimated urban class war, *Red Harvest;* Warner Brothers' ethnic-gangster epics of the 1930s; film noirs of the 1940s and 1950s; postwar police procedurals; the lurid juvenile delinquent literature of the 1950s; Chester Himes's Harlem policiers; Batman's and Dick Tracy's development as high-tech, back-alley battlers of urban freaks; the Rust Belt to Sun Belt dynamic shared by the *Godfather* cycle and Elmore Leonard's urban Westerns. In short, one central strand of American crime stories has consistently made art out of the flows of people, capital, power, and ideas that made and unmade the industrial city. It follows, then, that postindustrial transformation inspired generic change in crime stories: new authors, revised stories, new stylistic syntheses.

But the urban crisis caught Hollywood unready. Its urban and crime film formulas, which had last been comprehensively overhauled just after the war in film noir, suddenly seemed obsolescent in the mid-1960s. Venetian blinds and wiseguy patter became quaint when new-model urban hobgoblins like junkies and the fuzz moved to cultural center stage and shaky news camera shots tracked what looked like civil war in the streets. American popular film tended to avoid the inner city at the height of the crisis, ceding priority to television and documentary, but by 1970, with audiences updated by other media in their thinking about the inner city as the stage for expressive violence, Hollywood felt ready to exploit the moment. Its new treatments of the city coalesced in 1971 and 1972, with crime predictably on the leading edge. We can trace the engagement of a major culture industry with a major social crisis in pattern-setting movies like *The French Connection, Dirty Harry, Superfly,* and *Shaft*—all four released in those two years, all four explicitly and implicitly copied in a sustained surge of movies that followed throughout the decade and gave rise to subsequent surges reaching to the present day. The elaboration of a revised cinematic style and the exploration of an urban world proceeded as linked projects; each can be plotted on the other.

Makers of movies and television shows needed guides to help them map the territory and turn the period's hot, apparently inchoate inner-city news into finished Hollywood product. Cops, like reporters and

criminals, were natural candidates for the job. American police departments and American crime fiction grew up together and in association
with one another—since, after all, both took the forms they did in response to the consequences of urbanization, industrialization, and immigration— and the line between police work and telling stories about
that work has always been more of a permeable membrane. Cops are
notoriously accomplished collectors and tellers of stories, and they have
unique access to content for which the culture business is always hungry, particularly in times of urban social crisis. In New York and Los Angeles, especially, cops can find their way with relative ease to the reporters, publishers, producers, agents, and other gatekeepers who can
give them access to culture making. The West Coast's most prominent
example has to be Joseph Wambaugh, whose best-selling books about
his experience as a policeman in Los Angeles led to movies and television shows that redefined the LAPD's relationship to Hollywood and
its role in popular culture.

New York, the nation's other principal center for the production of
popular culture, has a long-established place in the history of crime stories. The NYPD has traditionally provided links between the real thing
and its representations on page, stage, and screen. In many ways that
function has been informal, in the sense that individual cops and their
exploits tend to find their own ways into the crime-story business, often with a push from well-circulated stories about them in the New York
press. In other ways, that function has been surprisingly formalized,
going all the way back to the case of George Matsell, who in the 1840s
served as chief of police *and* had part ownership of the *Police Gazette,*
the sensational and much-imitated magazine that trolled New York's
demimonde for material. Among Matsell's informal and formal successors can be counted all the NYPD-bred makers of crime stories, from
George W. Walling, whose *Recollections of a New York Chief of Police*
(1887) keeps the debased evildoers and intrepid upholders of the law
coming in two steady streams, to Commissioner Lewis J. Valentine, who
left his post in 1945 to pursue a career in radio and the movies, to the
long roster of cops and ex-cops who have more recently stampeded
down the old trail reblazed by Sonny Grosso and Eddie Egan in the
1970s.[15] That roster includes Bill Clark, of *NYPD Blue,* who flew groups
of his former colleagues to Los Angeles to meet with screenwriters; Ken
Sanzel, who wrote *The Replacement Killers* and turned to directing with
the express intent of emulating the style of Don Siegel (who directed
Dirty Harry); and Jack Maple, the deputy commissioner who created

the Compstat crime-tracking system and went on to help create *The District*. The roster also includes the working police officers who have written essays for the *New Yorker* and *Slate;* William J. Caunitz, a retired detective and best-selling mystery novelist; Dave Greenberg and Bob Hantz, immortalized in L. H. Whittemore's *The Supercops,* who played bit parts in the movie based on the book (as did one of Sonny Grosso's nemeses, Louis 17X Dupree, prime suspect in the infamous Harlem Mosque cop-killing case, who somehow ended up playing a police captain); the scores of cops and ex-cops who hold Screen Actors Guild cards and show up on small and large screens; and the officers of the NYPD's film and television squad, whose official task it is to ensure the smooth production of all kinds of filmed stories on the streets of New York.

Mayor John Lindsay belongs on the list, too, although he was never a police officer, and despite the strained relations between him and the department brought on by the Knapp Commission's inquiry into police corruption. Lindsay played an important part in bringing the NYPD into closer institutional contact with Hollywood. In the late 1960s, he initiated a concerted effort to attract commercial film and television production back to New York City, which since World War II had been a capital of avant-garde rather than mainstream cinema. Lindsay founded a city hall office to manage the process of obtaining permits and coordinating police assistance and other services to film crews, part of a larger effort to exploit the city's traditional role as a cultural center as it negotiated the arrival of the postindustrial age. As the city lost factory jobs and revenues, the culture business (like financial services and other nonmanufacturing sectors long established in New York) became ever more important.[16] Lindsay made a high-profile visit to the West Coast in 1967 to woo Hollywood executives, promising to "make life easy, simple, and beautiful, and throw open the city to producers from Hollywood with our special assets," and he followed up by securing institutional changes within city government that brought movie and television production back to New York in force.[17] Making *The French Connection,* for instance, William Friedkin received formal assistance from the city of New York in the way of permits, police services, and the loan of a precinct house, a subway station, and an elevated train line. But he also needed the kind of informal, off-the-record, sometimes frankly illegal assistance that Grosso and Egan could provide.

Professional storytellers made common cause with experts from the hands-on side of the policing-and-crime business to create *The French Connection,* helping to guide the crime story into a new phase in its long history. Phil D'Antoni, the producer, chose the young and relatively obscure Friedkin to direct and then shielded him from the studio's demands to hurry up and finish. Friedkin struck a fine balance between imposing his aesthetic will on volatile material and deferring to the artists, technicians, cops, and others assembled to work on the movie. Friedkin's collaborators included the movie professionals who formed his crew and his disparate stable of actors—Americans like Hackman and Scheider, as well as Europeans like Bozzuffi and Fernando Rey (who played Frog One and was hired by mistake: Friedkin wanted to hire the rough-looking Francisco Rabal, "the guy from *Belle de Jour*," but he or his minions in casting confused Rabal with the more refined Rey, who had also been in Luis Buñuel's movies). The collaborators also included a variety of experts in other fields. Functionaries of the accommodating Lindsay administration, the NYPD, and the Metropolitan Transit Authority cooperated with at least some of Friedkin's requests. Ernest Tidyman, the *New York Times* reporter who wrote the novel *Shaft*, drafted the screenplay. Jimmy Breslin, one of the nation's star newspaper columnists, contributed some lasting lines of dialogue during his extended audition for the role of Popeye Doyle. Fat Thomas Rand, a much-arrested bookie and wheelman, put his pachydermal knowledge of the city and its criminal element to use in choosing locations and extras. Add to that list all the cops, crooks, and other atmospheric types who gave the movie its street imprimatur; and, most of all, add Eddie Egan and Sonny Grosso, hardhanded policemen from the Old Neighborhood who must also count as principal authors of the movie. Without their many contributions, *The French Connection* would not have taken the pathbreaking form it did. They, more than anyone else, injected a potent dose of city life circa 1970 into what otherwise would have been just the grim little formula picture that the studio expected.

Beyond having helped break the case on which the script was based, Egan and Grosso put their mark on almost every aspect of the movie except cinematography and editing. They took the director and actors on ride-alongs and raids, educating them in the practices and culture of policing and the criminal underworld. They coached the stars and provided models for their characterizations. Along with Fat Thomas, they chose many of the locations, especially those on their beats in Harlem and Brooklyn. "Billy would say, 'Where did this happen?'" said Grosso, "and we'd show him and he'd shoot it there. He was a stickler for 'Where did it happen?'" In regular script meetings and informal conversations with Friedkin and Tidyman, and by letting Friedkin and his assistants follow them around and record what they said, they supplied much of the dialogue and local color in the screenplay. "That was strange," Grosso said. "Whatever we said, somebody would write it down, and then it would show up in the movie." They brought in criminals they knew as extras, as in the bar scene that precedes the Santa chase, and they also brought in two dozen moonlighting cops to provide advice, extra security, and traffic control, and to act as extras. In a second barroom raid by Popeye and Cloudy, for instance, the surly pharmaceutical- and weapon-dropping patrons are all played by black cops. Sometimes Egan and Grosso used their badges and the promise of a few bucks or fleeting fame to gather anonymous extras off the street, and they caused an infamous traffic jam on the Brooklyn Bridge when Friedkin needed one. They acted on camera in small roles, too (of which more in good time), which perhaps more than anything else caused them to be bitten by the moviemaking bug.

That is how Sonny Grosso came to cross over from the NYPD to Hollywood. The two great events of his professional life have been the French Connection case and the movie that fictionalized it. Working on the first made his career as a cop; working on the second initiated his career in Hollywood. If the fame he enjoyed because of the case and the movie made his superiors unhappy, even jealous, it also helped put him in a position to not give a damn what they thought. In 1976, after five years of dividing his time between policing the streets and helping to produce filmed crime stories, he crossed the line for good by retiring from the NYPD and committing himself to show business. That ended a strange period of his life in which he shuttled daily between worlds. "I used to go from crime scenes to crime-scenes-in-the-movies," he told me, "and I'd have all the cops that worked with me at both places. People on the street knew about it, too. You'd crash into a shooting gallery and they'd say, 'Is this a real bust or is this the movies?'"

The two great characters of Grosso's working life have been Eddie Egan and William Friedkin, two variations on the theme of the creative star driven and liberated by a near-delusory faith in the absolute rightness of his spur-of-the-moment whims as well as his deeply held convictions. Grosso played the good partner to both of them. Careful, worried, he minded the details that Egan and Friedkin glossed over in their rush to give expression to the different but equally selfish orders of inspiration that impelled them. When Grosso and Egan took Friedkin along to observe barroom drug raids in Harlem, Egan would charge in first and perform his usual bullying harangue with extra panache for the sake of Friedkin, who, entering third, eagerly took in the priceless raw material that would help turn him from sort-of-promising young director into white-hot auteur. Grosso came in second, right behind Egan and well before Friedkin, and managed the scene: making the customers in the bar do what Egan told them to do, patting down those whom Egan pointed out as "dirty," arresting them when Egan happened to be right, watching everybody's hands and his partners' backs.

PLAYING EDDIE EGAN

Before Friedkin entered the cops' lives, Eddie Egan was the only auteur Grosso knew. There is theater in being a cop, of course, and Egan chewed the scenery. He reveled in his long-running role as the Scourge of the Ghetto, declaimed in front of unplugged jukeboxes to barroom audiences in Harlem and Brooklyn. He performed in front of judges and juries, as all cops must, and did so with dramatic flair—trading barbs with defense attorneys, persuasively claiming superhuman powers of vision that allowed him to witness heroin deals from around corners or at long range in the dark, and, in one characteristically brazen episode, pretending expertise in sign language to plead guilty on behalf of some deaf-mute defendants. Egan also took to the stage proper with gusto. When performing in training exercises for rookies, he once threw himself so convincingly into the role of an uncooperative drug suspect in a search-and-seizure simulation that a young officer pistol-whipped him onstage, hurting him badly enough to send him to the hospital. When asked how he could do such a thing to a fellow officer in a make-believe drill, the rookie said, "I got carried away with the realism of the moment." As Grosso summed it up, "Even when we were cops on the street, Eddie was always the actor, and I was always the producer." Egan provided the inspiration; Grosso managed the setups, details, and aftermaths.

Egan, who died at the age of sixty-five in 1995, was a strange man, at once complicated and simple. He felt most comfortable when people thought he was crazy—because it made them fear him—and he seemed to make a point of rubbing people the wrong way, but by all reports he could also be charismatic and charming. I was talking about him with Randy Jurgensen in the Delightful Restaurant, a diner on First Avenue in East Harlem where three decades earlier the cops had met regularly with Friedkin and Ernest Tidyman to work on the screenplay. I remarked that both Jurgensen and Grosso—watchful, reserved men—tended to talk about the more extroverted Egan and Friedkin as men who took over, who assumed that the party could start only when they arrived and that it had to be a party in their honor. "Billy was that kind of person," Jurgensen said, "because Billy was knowledgeable, talented, and it's just okay. Eddie, on the other hand, you know, he took that position because he said it was so, and guys would say, 'Ah, fuck him, let him have his way,' you know?" So, I asked, *was* Eddie knowledgeable and talented? Was he a good cop? There was a pause. "You know what Eddie was?" said Jurgensen. "Eddie couldn't do the job easy. There's a way to do the job easy, you know how it is? You say to a guy, 'Okay, look, you tell me where you're getting your narcotics and I'm gonna do the best I can to help you out, I'm guaranteeing nothing's gonna happen to you.'" In other words, you let the guy believe what you need him to believe. "You can say to yourself, 'Did I try? Yeah. Did I knock myself out? No.'" That kind of deal making with criminals, whether or not the cop lives up to his promises, is business as usual. "Now, Eddie would say to the guy, 'I don't give a fuck, you're doin' two years and you're *still* gonna tell me what I need to know.' He went the hard way."

Egan was, paradoxically, both a grand mal egomaniac and a good partner. Jurgensen concluded, "With Eddie it was all I, I, I, me, me, me. But we were a lot safer. We were. We felt a lot better about ourselves because of cops like Eddie Egan. Absolutely." As Grosso told the BBC (overlooking the sucker punch he absorbed when trying to enforce Egan's will in that bar on 110th Street), "Nobody would fool around with us, nobody would fool with Eddie. If Eddie said 'Hold it,' they held it. If he said, 'Put your hands on your head,' they'd do it. I don't know what would happen today, but in those days they had a lot of respect for us."

Egan grew up in the neighborhoods of Queens—Woodside, then Hollis—in the 1930s and 1940s. Before becoming a cop he had played baseball well enough to have a minor-league run as an outfielder in the Yankees organization, and he had been a drill instructor in the marines. Big and imposing, with the rosy, slab-of-meat thickness of an athlete in decline, he radiated physical competence—except when it came to gunplay. He seemed to regard his sidearm as a dramatic noisemaker and prop, using it most often to fire over his head during raids, a practice that brought down ceiling plaster and made his partners nervous. Jurgensen said, "Eddie was good with his hands, and he was good with his mouth, and back then cops had to back up what they said. We had no radios, you were out there by yourself, and to be in control you had to make a guy pay physically when he stood up to you. But with a gun Eddie couldn't hit that fucking car if we stood in front of it." Egan's colleagues nicknamed him "Bullets" because he expended so many of them, especially in trying to hit a target at the practice range. He willfully misunderstood the nickname as a swashbuckler's badge of honor, but, said Jurgensen, "The truth of the matter—and he wore it well— is he couldn't shoot worth a shit." Reminiscing about his old partner in his high-rise office, looking out at Queens across the East River, Grosso said, "Eddie was great with his hands, a powerhouse, and he could take care of himself, but mostly he was fearless, just undaunted, the bravest cop you could imagine."

Egan's fearlessness, like most things that mattered about him, flowed from seemingly contradictory sources. One was an all-out commitment to the job as a higher calling. His sister, Maureen Massett, a nun in the Dominican order who works with elderly patients in the Bronx, described him to me as a passionately by-the-book moralist. "With Eddie," she said, "everything in life was right or wrong, black or white. In many ways he was very old-fashioned. He was a product of that time"—by which she meant the Depression-bred conventions, hard-boiled and conservative, of respectably lower-middle-class Irish Catholic Queens. When he saw his sister in latter years, for instance, he always asked, "Where's your habit?" as if he had caught her out of uniform (and something about "your habit" has the ring of interrogating a junkie). "It was cancer he had, that he died of," continued Sister Maureen, "and at the end it was clear it was hopeless, but of course he felt he was going to beat it. Like everything else in life, he was just going to have his way. His philosophy was you do the right thing, and that's it, it's taken care of. So he would say to me, 'Are you praying?' and I'd say, 'Yes, Eddie, I am,' and he'd say, 'That's all I need' "—as if, in the end, hanging on to life itself was a matter of playing by the book.

Those who knew Egan as a headstrong, often perversely inspired cop willing to ignore rules to satisfy his own curious sense of the right might be surprised to see "by the book" and "moralist" crop up in connection with him, but they would not gainsay his commitment to the NYPD. Egan, who had a complicated and often unhappy family history as a child and a series of self-destructing marriages as an adult, tended to slide out of regular familial arrangements and into institutions built around the effective male body: the Yankees farm system, the marines, and finally the NYPD, which, everyone agrees, became the true love of his life. Sister Maureen said, "He desperately wanted a family, he married three times, but the department was his family. When we would get together, which was not frequently, he was police department all the way." Egan seemed to draw courage from a deep well of loyalty and conviction created by the total investment of himself in the job and in the rule of the police over the streets.

"Eddie had a fixation," Grosso said. "He wanted junkies to know there's no sanctuary, no place beyond the law, no place beyond Eddie." He elaborated on the point in a BBC interview: "They're breaking the law and they're causing this horrible epidemic to spread all over the inner cities, and so he kept harassing them. That was his job, he felt." Also, Egan liked to mess with people, and he was confident that the near-universal filthiness of human souls made almost everyone guilty of something. He prided himself on being able to spot culpability in even the most innocent-seeming character. Owen Roizman, the cinematographer, tells a story about Egan leaving the shooting location when a snappily dressed passerby vaguely resembling Fernando Rey caught his eye. "He's dirty," said Egan, and that was the last the crew of *The French Connection* saw of their technical adviser for the day as he went off in pursuit. When Roizman asked him about it later, Egan said only, "Yeah, he was dirty." Jurgensen remembers Egan's gift for spotting the guilty as less than clairvoyant: "Eddie would always be saying, 'He's dirty, he's dirty,' and he was usually right, but in a neighborhood such as that"— meaning the high-crime areas in which they worked as detectives—"it's like the guy who says, 'Jeez, I think it's gonna rain today,' and he says it every day, then when it rains he says, 'I told you so.'" For Egan, being dirty seemed to be an existential condition, not just a matter of criminal possession of narcotics or weapons, and the condition was nearly universal. If he was a chronic self-aggrandizer, and if he was hard on his fellow human beings when they showed weakness, he did not burden himself with the conceit that he was necessarily cleaner than they were. Perhaps, in fact, it was the conviction of his own sinfulness that made him so sure he could spot it in others.

The other source of Egan's fearlessness seems to have been the opposite of selfless dedication to an institution: his contempt for everyone luckless enough not to be Eddie Egan. Even those few who loved him concede without argument that he was less than generous to others, full of himself, arrogant, pushy, perpetually hungry for the limelight and all of the credit. An equal-opportunity bigot, he filled the air around him with a comprehensive and wide-ranging field of epithets. Seeking to protect Egan from his reputation as an old-school racist, his former partners insist that the accusation does not do justice to the scope of his animus. "Eddie didn't hate black people especially," Grosso said. "There were all kinds of people he didn't like. It was more like the vocabulary of the attitude he had about who he was on the street. He had to prove he was tougher and crazier than everybody else, to make people afraid of him." For instance, Grosso noted, he used to bring Egan to Rao's back when the restaurant's owners prided themselves on serving the best steak in town, and Egan, who understood himself to be surrounded by grease-ball gangsters, would make a point of slathering ketchup on his perfect steak just to piss everybody off. Jurgensen told me, "The way Eddie hated an Italian was the way he hated a black, and I'm clearing that up, you understand?"

Egan was ambitious for promotions and celebrity, both of which he received at an impressive rate. He worked hard, driven by ego and by a selective moralism that made junkies the scapegoats for the transformation of the familiar world of midcentury New York into the crime-plagued inner city of the urban crisis. He became a very successful cop in the 1950s and early 1960s by enforcing his notion of the law in his bizarrely theatrical way.

That theatricality proved crucial to Egan's style of policing and to his and his partners' future crossover into the crime-story business—which for Egan was more a change of emphasis than a radical departure. Hard-case though he may have been, Egan was also a born entertainer. Sister Maureen said, "Our mother's mother was a very strict lady—scary, almost, you didn't want to cross her—but her husband, Grandpa Ryan, was the life of the party, always joking and carrying on. I always thought Eddie took after both of them in different ways. Those were the two parts of him." Egan loved to play dress-up, and he had a sharp sense of the comic grotesque. On the occasion that Egan costumed himself as a full-bearded Santa to finger junkies, Grosso explained, "He'd get next to the guy making the deal and ring his bell to signal me, and I'd grab the guy." They made several busts that way without blowing Egan's cover, but then a suspect eluded Grosso and ran into a crowded bar. "So Eddie runs into the bar, dressed as Santa, and grabs the guy. And everybody in there said, 'Hey, what's going on?' He pulls down his beard and they all went, 'It's Popeye!' But the best part of the Santa thing was when we arrested the main dealer. It turned out to be a man dressed like a woman in this leopard-skin getup. When the press came in to the precinct, there was Santa taking the statement, typing with two fingers, from a girl who's really a guy in a leopard-skin dress."

It was Egan, seeking a larger public and feeling himself destined to be a star, who cultivated the reporters, writers, Hollywood types, and other cop-watchers who turned the detectives into media figures—and eventually into makers of crime stories. Whether or not he was the most important player in breaking the French Connection case, Egan's character drew culture-makers to it. He worked on the writer Robin Moore to make sure that Moore's true-crime book about the case became a story about Egan and Grosso (who told me that his superiors detailed him to tag along with Egan "and make sure that hole-in-the-head doesn't say anything stupid to Moore that gets the department in trouble"). Egan overrode his partners' anxieties to make sure Friedkin and his actors got whatever firsthand experience they needed in order to make the movie. And he was the reason Friedkin thought the case would make an interesting movie; at bottom, it would be a character study of Egan. When the movie project was still a rumor, Egan had already posted on the bulletin board of his Brooklyn precinct a list of the actors he thought best suited to play him. Heading the list was Rod Taylor, the handsome stiff who starred in *The Time Machine* and *The Birds*. Even while breaking the case in 1962, Eddie already had the movie version in mind. "We had a problem with the warrants," Grosso recalled. "It was endangering the whole case, and we hadn't even found all the heroin yet. Me and Eddie had to go downtown to face the music. We're going into the precinct where there's all this brass and reporters waiting, and I say to him, you know, very worried, 'Uh, Eddie, what do you think?' And he says, 'Newman plays me; Gazzara plays you.'"

While Friedkin was planning the movie, Egan, Grosso, and Jurgensen took him along on raids. Friedkin lived at Eighty-sixth Street and Park Avenue then, ten blocks from the Realtors' Frontier that separated the Upper East Side from Spanish Harlem and East Harlem, Grosso's old neighborhood. The detectives would pick up Friedkin and, a few short minutes later, crash through the door of a bar or a junkies' pad. They tried to find a relatively safe place for the director within the routines they had worked out for these raids, keeping him out of the way as best they could, but the situation in any raid tended to be fluid and therefore hazardous. They could not anticipate every variable that cropped up in rooms full of illegal drugs and weapons and desperately scared, angry, stoned people. Danger aside, the ride-along observer got an eyeful not only of drama but also of human misery, some of which was too abject to put in even the most self-consciously gritty movie. On one of Friedkin's first raids, he wandered away down the hall from the main room of an apartment on 113th Street, where a dozen junkies were being rousted, and walked in on a woman who was shooting heroin into her vagina while sitting on the toilet. "She must have weighed two hundred pounds, she was swollen from the quinine," said Jurgensen, "and she said, 'Please, let me finish.' We just left her, took in the rest of them. It was right after that that Billy said, 'Do you know I live six minutes from here?' The whole city lived six minutes from a world they knew nothing about, they just didn't know it. Remember, this whole world of shooting galleries and heroin was still sort of secret back then. Even people who had been around, even people who lived in Harlem, they didn't know it."

Once Friedkin had hired Gene Hackman and Roy Scheider to play the roles of Popeye and Cloudy, the detectives took them along, too. Now they had to be even more careful, often leaving the actors outside until the raided bar or apartment had been secured. Roy Scheider told me, "We were never the first guys in the door, but we went into some pretty bad places where nobody knew we weren't cops. I remember we were in a bar with a bunch of badasses and the guy next to me was bumping me, feeling my arm, you know, squeezing the bicep, checking to see what I had in case he wanted to kick my ass." Scheider also remembers the swooping feeling of danger he felt when, in a bar after a bust, "Sonny said, 'Come here. I want to show you something.' He had me feel on top of the phone booth and there were guns, knives, just all kinds of things guys had thrown up there" when the cops charged in. The actors studied the cops' technique and style, and Egan and Grosso went so far as to let Hackman actually grab a petty heroin user or seller, pat him down, ask him if he picked his feet in Poughkeepsie, and take him for booking at the station. This went far outside the bounds of the law and department policy, but they had a movie to make.

During this process of education, which became mutual as the cops soaked up Hollywood knowledge, Scheider and Grosso took readily to one another. Both were fascinated and intimidated by the other's profession. As Grosso remembers it, "It was an attraction on both sides. It's a fair trade." Grosso took Scheider deep into the working life of a police detective, a kind of insider tour into street life and the exercise of power that noncops almost never get. "I had these guys in my neck of the woods," said Grosso, "in Harlem, in the shooting gallery, in the back stairwell of the Black Panther headquarters." In return, the Hollywood slummers gave Grosso entry into the movies, not only as a collaborator in the production but also as the idealized character played by

Scheider. Grosso was profoundly happy to work with Scheider and to be played by him. When the actors and cops met for the first time, in a cafeteria near the Twenty-eighth Precinct in Harlem, Grosso and Egan were so excited when the actors walked in that they jumped up from their table, and Grosso's gun flew out of its holster, clattering loudly on the floor. "He was humiliated when it happened," said Scheider, "but it's just that he was so nervous and thrilled to be working on a movie." Scheider and Grosso threw themselves enthusiastically into the business of turning actor into cop—and, as it turned out, cop into actor and eventually producer—for the purposes of the movie. Once shooting began, Grosso would give Scheider his watch, ring, badge, and gun at the beginning of every working day; Scheider would give them back when production was done for the day.

Hackman and Egan, on the other hand, were never so cozy. Playing Eddie Egan was difficult and in some ways awful work. Accomplishing that stretch not only demonstrated that Hackman was a great actor but also helped make him one, and Hackman had to overcome his own serious reservations about embarking on the project. Once Hackman had mastered the role, though, Egan used to stand around on location and shout, "He's more me than me!" between takes. It was a testament to Hackman's abilities, but also a needle inserted into the consciousness of a sensitive man who might have respected Egan's efficacy but never liked him much.

The differences between them, and Hackman's ultimate success in becoming Popeye by transcending and using those differences, have become an integral element of the mythos of the making of *The French Connection.* Interviews with the principals and accounts of working on the movie have detailed fundamental disagreements between Hackman and Egan about crime and punishment and just about everything else; Hackman's horror at Egan's casual abuse of citizens and the law; Egan's fear that Hackman was not a regular guy and therefore not man enough to play him; Hackman's persistence in trying to find some humanity in a monstrous character who Friedkin wanted him to play as an unredeemed, vicious slob.[18] The cops bridled at Hackman from the beginning, and they did not believe that he could ever become a creditable facsimile of Egan, whose ballbreaking habits put off even his fellow cops. When they met Hackman, he looked and acted like their idea of a bleeding-heart queer: he had a droopy handlebar mustache, he wore balloon-sleeve shirts and flare pants, he had recently appeared in *I Never Sang for My Father,* and they did not like his version of a New York accent. "We taught him to talk like us," remembered Grosso, "and one of the things Eddie used to say was 'Can you stand a toss?' Which means 'Are you carrying anything illegal?' Gene would say 'Cahn you stahnd a tahss?'" Grosso makes a face, as if somebody had put ketchup on his plate at Rao's. "What the fuck is that? 'Cahn you stahnd a tahss?'! Like he was from New England or something."

The cops understood Hackman's initial language problems to express his deeper unwillingness to adopt their worldview as unquestioningly as Friedkin and Scheider had. Friedkin, a city boy from Chicago and a lifelong police and lowlife buff, and Scheider, who had grown up in New Jersey and spent most of his life in and around New York, seemed to "get it," a phrase both Grosso and Jurgensen use to describe Friedkin's and Scheider's easy assimilation of the cops' speech and attitudes. The cops saw Hackman, though, as a liberal skeptic from the West Coast who regarded working with them (and their new pal Friedkin) as unpalatable but necessary aspects of his job. Grosso and Jurgensen, eager to credit the big-time Hollywood players who took an interest in their lives, like to proclaim that Friedkin would have made a good cop, or at least a good criminal, and they both say that Scheider learned his lessons swiftly and well, but they keep Hackman in a separate category. They agree that Hackman's becoming Eddie Egan was an actor's masterwork—and they tread lightly on the subject, not only because Hackman was a colleague, but also because they are movie and television people now and he remains a star—but they do not regard him as one of the fellows in the same way. Jurgensen, trying to find some way to say it, settled on a cop's faintest praise: "Gene would have been a very good social worker."

Scheider once asked Grosso what it was like to work with Egan, a man nobody else liked. Grosso's answer—"If I don't, who will?"—gave Scheider the key to unlock his role: "That's all I needed. The spine of my character was, 'I go with my partner.' That's all it took for me." Egan offered Hackman many such keys to himself, but Hackman hesitated to use them. Once, for instance, the actors were along for a ride with a prisoner who complained that his rights were being violated because Egan would not let him get a meal or make a phone call. Egan told the prisoner that people like him did not have rights. Hackman declared, "I can't do this, I can't play this guy," and got out of the car. Grosso, of course, was the one who went after him and tried to calm him down. "He's just acting," Grosso told him. "He's making these people think he's crazy." So, I said to Jurgensen after he told me the story, Eddie was giving this guy a hard time simply because he could. Jurgensen responded, "Eddie was being Eddie." But, I insisted, Hackman felt that Eddie was treating the guy like less than a man, less than a citizen. Jurgensen grimaced expressively and said, "Look, Eddie was being a cop. I don't want to go so far as to say thank God for people like Eddie Egan, but . . . " This last, unfinished sentence echoed remarks Hackman made to the effect that, while Eddie Egan might be an unsympathetic character, he did a dangerous, vital job with admirable skill.[19] Jurgensen told me, "Gene said more than once, 'Thank God for people like you. Thank God.'"

Everybody connected to the making of *The French Connection*, of course, thanked God for people like Eddie Egan because he, Grosso, and the local talent they recruited helped turn the movie into a cinematic landmark. In addition to all they did behind the scenes, they also acted on camera. For a brief period in preproduction, Friedkin even considered casting Egan and Grosso as themselves, but that brainstorm blew itself out to sea (like his plan to cast Jimmy Breslin as Popeye, which led to rehearsals that upset Egan, the Rod Taylor man). Instead, Egan and Grosso and their cronies contributed their atmospheric mugs and voices to the movie in supporting roles and walk-ons. Jurgensen had a talking cameo as a cop who stalls an angry Frenchman at the police garage while Popeye, Cloudy, and a guy named Irv (played by the actual guy named Irv who worked at the police garage) tear apart and then reassemble a Buick Invicta with heroin crammed under its rocker panels. Grosso appeared in several scenes, including the big shootout at the end, as a taciturn Fed named Klein. Egan, the born actor, played Lieutenant Simonson, Popeye and Cloudy's boss, a tasty role with plenty of lines. As Simonson, Egan got to chew out Popeye, reenacting from the other side the lectures he had received from put-upon superiors over the years. He also defended Popeye, and therefore himself, as "basically a good cop" in an awkward, unforced little gem of an exchange with another nonactor and fellow blowhard—the stunt man Bill Hickman, who not only drove Popeye's car during the dangerous parts of the big chase scene but also played a Fed who hates Popeye.

There is also a curiously sad bit of byplay in the movie—sad because it reminds one that Egan was a lonesome monster who achieved the second existence on the screen he wanted and was no less alone for it—when Egan-as-Simonson, sitting at his desk, calls to Hackman-as-Popeye as the latter leaves his office, "Popeye, you still picking your feet in Poughkeepsie?" "Picking your feet in Poughkeepsie," along with "Can you stand a toss?" and "What is this, a fucking hospital here?" and others, was one of Egan's signature phrases that made it into the movie. (His catchy narco-couplet, "Addicts in the cellar, sellers in the attic," did not.) Popeye stops, the two men look at each other for a moment, and then Popeye goes out the door, leaving the lieutenant to brood. A team of cultural theorists working double shifts for a month could not fully untangle the knot of Eganian subtext in that throwaway moment.

CONVERSIONS

Like the many cops, crooks, movie people, and moviegoers who tend to regard the movie version of any event as the definitive account of what happened, Egan and Grosso regarded *The French Connection,* fantasized car chase and all, as the official historical record of their exploits. Furthermore, they and the other cops who helped make the movie assumed that one good reason for lending that assistance was to buff up the NYPD's public image. So they objected when they thought Friedkin was doing something that made the police look bad. Grosso, for instance, did not like seeing Cloudy kick the handcuffed, kneeling dealer in the back after the Santa chase. Since Cloudy's injury in the movie had been inspired by a real-life incident in which a suspect slashed Grosso's arm with a knife, I asked Grosso if he hadn't kicked the guy who cut him. He smiled a thin little smile and answered, "The point was, I didn't think it should be in the movie." But, I said, it's just Roy Scheider, it's not really you. "No," he said, "it's me. I took it personally."

A much bigger blowup occurred over Popeye's use of the word "nigger." After the Santa sequence, after the arrestee has been booked and Popeye has changed out of his Santa suit, Cloudy appears in the precinct house with a bandaged arm, and Popeye tells him, "Never trust a nigger." Roy Scheider told me that Popeye's line brought down the house when he saw the movie just after it opened in a theater on East Eighty-sixth Street. "It was a half-black, half-white audience," he recalled, "and the *whole* audience broke into applause. I think for some of the people it was that at last whitey had made a movie that said what they knew cops had been saying. I mean, it was a big hit with African American audiences. And for other people, well, they thought Popeye was saying something true." The movie aims for exactly this kind of complexity, or two-facedness, which is then extended in the following lines. Cloudy responds, "He could have been white," and Popeye, never at a loss for a misanthropic aphorism, says, "Never trust anyone."

Sonny Grosso is, in effect, the author of those additional lines. He told me that, to his knowledge, the line "Never trust a nigger" was not in the script, that the first he knew of it was when the actors rehearsed the scene in the old First Precinct station house just prior to shooting it. When there was a pause in the rehearsal, Jurgensen and Grosso rushed to Friedkin to urge him to cut the line or use a different word. Jurgensen was so enraged that Grosso, always the reasonable one, shunted him aside and did the talking. Friedkin let him make his case at length, then stopped him cold by asking if in fact he and his colleagues never used the word. "You know," said Grosso when he told the story again to the BBC, "it's an uncomfortable thing when somebody puts you up against the wall like that. I said, 'I work with a lot of people, black people,' and I said, 'I don't think it has to be in the movie.' So he calls Eddie over and he says, 'Hackman's walking down the stairs and he says, Never trust a nigger. Do you say that?' And he [Egan] says 'Yeah,' and he walks away. I could have taken my gun out and killed him." In the version of the story Grosso told me more than once (with no BBC camera running), and in Jurgensen's and Friedkin's versions, Eddie answers Friedkin's question more emphatically: "A nigger's a nigger's a nigger." Grosso continued to argue, even though Egan had just completely undermined his case, and Friedkin finally asked what Grosso would say in response to the line. Grosso's answer made it into the movie as the next two lines.

Grosso and especially Jurgensen also objected to the climax of the famous car chase sequence, in which Popeye shoots the unarmed Frog Two in the back. That episode became a turning point in Jurgensen's life, the moment he crossed the always tenuous boundary between being a cop and the make-believe police business.

"I'm out in Brooklyn one day," remembered Jurgensen, who in addition to playing a bit part also took the director and actors on ride-alongs, provided technical advice, and helped with traffic control and security, "and here I see them rehearsing where Gene ends up and the Frenchman comes off the train." This is after Frog Two's hijacked elevated train has plowed into another train stopped at a station, forcing him to scuttle down a long flight of stairs leading to the street, where Popeye, having totaled the car he commandeered and nearly killed a score of citizens in transit, is waiting for him. Frog Two, who has lost his gun in the collision of trains, begins to descend the stairs, sees Popeye, and turns to run. Popeye shoots him in the back, precipitating a tumble to the base of the stairs at Popeye's feet. "You have to understand," Jurgensen told me, "I'm going into this business, I'm trying to grab as much as I can, but I'm still a cop. I'm going to be plenty of things, but I'm always going to be that. So I'm watching this scene and there's a break and I go over to Billy and say, just like this"—with naive conviction—" 'Billy, you can't shoot this guy, he doesn't have a gun.' " Jurgensen proposed an idealized revision in which "Gene says, you know, 'You're under arrest, I'm gonna read you your rights' and everything. I'm dead serious, I'm representing the police department. I want the guy standing at the top of stairs, and it's a life-threatening situation, and he's gonna have a gun." Friedkin, of course, shot the scene the way they had rehearsed it. After seeing the dailies, Jurgensen told Friedkin he had done a great disservice to the police department. "And I say, 'We don't shoot unarmed people, we don't shoot them in the back.' And he said, 'Eddie says it's okay.' "

Jurgensen, faced with a questionable shooting, wanted to plant a gun in Frog Two's hand and turn him around so that an ideal version of the incident would hold up in court as a justifiable use of deadly force. He had not yet accepted Hollywood's notion of justifiable use of deadly force—action that plays well on-screen, extends and perhaps twists the arc of the drama and character development, and inspires a reaction in an audience (the only jury worth discussing). But even as he objected to the scene, Jurgensen already had one foot across the line from one way of thinking to the other, and the other foot followed in good time. "We finish the picture," he continued. "Fast forward: I'm in the theater, this is the preview. There has to be a thousand people there. I'm in the back walking up and down. We go through the whole car chase and everything. There's that moment of silence, and Gene shoots him. And the people, they roar. Billy's in the audience, comes running up the aisle, he says"—hissing—" 'It fucking works for *them*. I told you it fucking works for *me*.' And I stood right there. He goes back down, then he comes back up and he says"—hissing—" 'I got something in the mail for you, the fucking poster.' Surer than shooting, it arrives in the mail, and there's Gene shooting the guy in the back. Couldn't believe it. From that day, I really never questioned, you know, any director."

It was a conversion experience, an episode Jurgensen can look back to when he wonders how he crossed over. It had to be a good shoot by Hollywood's standard: the audience loved the scene, the image of Popeye gunning down Frog Two made for a memorable poster, and the movie made a lot of money and won Oscars for Best Picture, Director, Actor, Screenplay, and Film Editing. Case closed.

Sonny Grosso, as always, paid attention to everyone and everything during the making of the movie. If he objected as strenuously as Jurgensen did to some aspects of the movie, he did less storming off the set and more deal making with the director, and he took copious mental notes. At his first production meeting, for which Friedkin and Phil D'Antoni had assigned him the familiar Herculean task of keeping Egan quiet, he looked up and down the table and wondered why the hell they needed twenty-five people to make a movie. Over the course of the production, he found out why they needed that many just to boss different aspects of the project, he figured out what they all did, and he began to learn the nuts and bolts of how they did their jobs. In the years that followed—first as a moonlighting cop, then full-time after he left the force, he worked his way into the business and made a success of it. "He made his own bed that way," said Friedkin, "but it all began because word got around: if you want to make a cop film in New York, see Sonny and Eddie."

At the beginning of this transition, though, Grosso was a stranger in a strange land in which a foreign language was spoken. If the cops educated the Hollywood visitors in cop talk, street slang, and the quirks of Egan's idiolect, the cops had to learn movie people's cant. One day during the shooting of the movie, Grosso was taken aside by Kenny Utt, an associate producer with whom he would work again in coming years. As Grosso tells it, Utt seemed angry. "He said, 'You wanna do this movie? You wanna do this fucking movie?' I said, 'Whaddaya mean?' He said, 'Stay away from Billy. We're running out of colors.' I have no fucking idea of what he's talking about. So I went and asked a few people why Kenny was all mad at me, and he was talking about the script." Script revisions were printed on colored paper, a different color for each round of revisions. "Every time Billy would go out with us, he'd see something and he'd change it." The production team was becoming anxious about the director's willingness to change the script from day to day to incorporate the cops' advice, storytelling, and pungent turns of phrase. Utt was flustered enough that he forgot Sonny had no idea what he was talking about, but Friedkin seemed to enjoy puzzling the cops with Hollywoodese on purpose. Grosso likes to tell the story about the time Friedkin turned to him, pointed out a man in the crowd, and said, "'On the day, he's Pasadena.' So he gets ready to shoot, he says, 'What's that guy doing there?' I said, 'Hell if I know.' He's saying, 'On the *day,* on the *day,* he's *Pasadena!*' I hadda learn a whole fucking language with him." It took a while for Grosso to catch on that "on the day" meant "right now," and "Pasadena" meant "nowhere," but he was a quick study. Years of doing the bars with Eddie Egan, the unpredictable gold-shield leading man, had taught Grosso the do-or-die importance of watching everybody's hands and listening to everybody—especially Friedkin, the insider who showed the detectives the way into the New Hollywood and the culture-making side of the police business.

INTO THE NEW HOLLYWOOD

In the late 1960s and early 1970s, William Friedkin exemplified the New Hollywood. He came up fast and seemingly out of nowhere—arriving as a director via on-the-job training in television and documentary, rather than film school or apprenticeship in feature film production—and he brought an eclectic range of influences to bear on the problem of making the industry's reliable formulas fresh for a new era. Friedkin's rise, and the coming of the new urban cinema heralded by *The French Connection,* demonstrates the artistic consequences not only of social crisis but also of developments in the movie industry that made it peculiarly ready to exploit the cultural moment with new styles—and to welcome Grosso and his partners to their new profession.

As Pauline Kael observed in her review of *The French Connection,* which she considered to be an example of how far Hollywood would go to regain the audience it had lost, the movie industry was suffering through an economic drought in 1971. "Almost all the major movie companies are now, like the smaller ones, marginal businesses," she wrote, with losses since 1968 calculated at $525 million. Noting that only Disney and AIP, "the producers of ghouls-on-wheels schlock pictures," were showing a profit, Kael suggested that movies like *The French Connection*—which she understood to be "an extraordinarily well-made" compilation of jolts calculated to zap audiences in the way that scientists stimulate lab rats—were both the economic answer and the artistic problem.[20] Among the reasons for the financial crisis were the continuing rise of television and the popular music industry, Hollywood's failure to recruit television-raised baby boomers as movie consumers on par with previous generations, and a widespread sense that American popular film had become stodgy and lagged behind other forms (especially television and music) and other national cinemas in engaging with current sensibilities. Also, Hollywood was deep into a period of restructuring traceable all the way back to the partial breakup in the 1950s of the studio system, a groundswell amplified by corporate buyouts of studios and a late-1960s call from within the industry to turn from escape to engagement.[21] The extended disruption of the business had allowed new faces and styles to push in from the margins. As is usually the case in Hollywood, aesthetics and economics constituted two sides of the same coin: 20th Century-Fox, the foundering studio that financed *The French Connection,* let Friedkin take stylistic risks because the innovations he pursued cost less than doing it the usual way. Had grittiness cost extra to achieve, he would have been out of luck.

In that moment, supercharged by the larger upheavals of the late 1960s that pushed Hollywood to go scrambling after "relevance" (after holding out against it for much of the previous decade), potent influences reached into its moviemaking practices from a number of sources. From television, which at that point was still considered a competitor rather than a branch office of the same business, a new generation of talent made its way into film. Also, the location aesthetic of new city movies like *The French Connection* drew upon the formal authority of the television news that had brought urban disorder into suburban living rooms. Foreign cinemas, both art movies and genre pictures, offered other standards for what was to be gained by revising, abusing, or reaching beyond the limits of the classical Hollywood style codified during the studio system's golden age. Younger Hollywood practitioners imbibed technique and attitudes, including a taste for implied social critique as an element of cutting-edge style, from Italian, Japanese, and especially French mentors (who also taught them new ways to love classical Hollywood, like auteur theory). Another set of influences proceeded from American underground film and documentary—the work of moviemakers like Frederick Wiseman, D. A. Pennebaker, or Shirley Clarke—which further weakened the monopoly of conventional lighting, acting, and continuity. And the establishment of film in the American university shaped new kinds of producers and consumers: film school graduates sought to impress their learning on Hollywood, which addressed itself to an influential new elite audience developed by the teaching of film and circulation of foreign movies. Also, Hollywood discovered its disproportionately important black urban audience and began casting about for ways to engage it.

This ferment helped shape careers as different as those of Clint Eastwood (who became the new John Wayne by way of television, Sergio Leone's baroque spaghetti Westerns, and a well-timed shift circa 1970 from the Western range to the inner city in crisis), Gordon Parks (best known as a documentary and art photographer, he directed *Shaft* and *The Supercops* and more recently made a Hitchcockian appearance in John Singleton's updated *Shaft,*) and William Friedkin. A thumbnail sketch of Friedkin's career shows how he arrived at a synthesis of elements that both stretched the limits of Hollywood convention and remained within them. Trained in television and documentary, Friedkin came under the influence of European directors in the 1960s as he made his way into Hollywood. In 1967, he explained to an interviewer, "The plotted film is on the way out and is no longer of interest to a serious director. . . . A new theater audience, I'm told, is under thirty and largely interested in abstract expression." He cited Antonioni, Resnais, Lelouche, and Fellini as "prophets of this new expression." He also said that Hollywood spent too much money on its movies.[22] Friedkin made these pronouncements with one feature to his credit: *Good Times,* a movie starring Sonny and Cher. After going on to make *The Night They Raided Minsky's, The Birthday Party,* and *The Boys in the Band,* he got the chance to direct *The French Connection,* which brought him Oscars, a reputation as one of the New Hollywood's most talented new directors, his pick of scripts, and, eventually, the opportunity to go into business with fellow young lions Francis Ford Coppola and Peter Bogdanovich in the short-lived Directors Company. He started talking about adapting and containing innovations of the 1960s within what he called Hollywood's traditional "clarity of presentation." He argued that "American films of the thirties and forties had clear story lines and strong characters. Then the New Wave of European filmmakers took over and we all went out and copied Godard and Fellini, forgetting where our roots were."[23] He later claimed that a dinner he had with Hollywood rootsman Howard Hawks had inspired him to go back to basics.

Friedkin's outside-in story narrates the process of fitting the look, feel, and question-raising of insurgent cinematic influences into the containing frame of postclassical Hollywood. That marriage of traditions produced new ways to do old things and gave *The French Connection* much of its artistic vitality. The linear plot, fast cutting, and action sequences juice up the very French drama of people standing around, talking, and eating that takes up much of the movie's screen time. The elaborately staged choreography and camera work discipline the improvisational quality of the acting. The plot's clear structure of conflict and pursuit offsets the informal documentary look. The heroes' head-busting imposition of law and order on the poor masks a half-proposed social critique in which purveyors of opiates exploit the urban working class while the state does more harm than good. These balances and contradictions impart an edge to the world of the movie, investing it with tensions that evoke the conventional portrait of the inner city after the urban crisis: bursting with contradiction, but contained.

And the figure of a French connection allows for a wholly imposed reading of the movie as a different sort of period piece, an allegory of artistic influence. In the movie, effete but sophisticated French drug dealers come to New York to sell heroin to the loutish but hardy American mafia, and American policemen try to stop them. This makes a neat portrait of the crime genres' exciting, ambiguously resolved encounter with New Wave influences. The junk comes from France to infect America and is disseminated throughout the world of the movie. The cops try to contain this foreign material but are only partially successful: the most important drug dealer escapes back to Europe, and the Americans go back to brutally entertaining generic business as usual. If the movie innovates in many ways, including French twists on Hollywood traditions, that novelty is domesticated by conventions of narrative and character with which Hawks or Griffith could have worked. A kind of stylistic violence and excitement inheres in the forcing together of cinematic impulses to build a new movie style for the postindustrial city.

Friedkin did not set out to make *The French Connection* in response to the urban crisis, nor did he consciously intend to revise popular crime genres with a new synthesis of theme and style. "But," he said to me, "I'll tell you this: we set out to make a great picture. That was in the back of all of our minds. We said whatever we gotta do here, we're gonna do. You'd be amazed that that's not a hard-and-fast rule in filmmaking. Usually you get through it, you know, or you're working with some people who can't cut it." At some point in the preproduction stage, he realized that the multiple talents of moviemakers and actors, the fraught historical moment, and the all-important contributions of Egan and Grosso could converge to make *The French Connection* something better and more lasting than a formulaic job of work. Most of the people who worked on the movie seem to share this sense of deep satisfaction in a job well done. They talk about it with the evident conviction that, at least once, they helped make a great movie. In 1970–1971, "a great movie" meant different things to the different participants. For Egan and Grosso and the colleagues they rounded up to help out, it meant helping to formulate a new-model movie cop for a new era, after the cowboy, the moralist, and the bureaucrat had been significantly delegitimated as models for police heroes in the late 1960s. For Friedkin, it meant finding a way to incorporate elements of insurgent styles into the traditional Hollywood feature—not only the documentary look that established the New Hollywood's street smarts in a street-obsessed moment but also the New Wave touches that made his claim as a serious artist.

I visited Friedkin in his suite in an understatedly fancy hotel on the Upper East Side in October 1999. He was in New York to loop Samuel Jackson's dialogue for his new movie, *The Rules of Engagement,* a conventional mix of military action and courtroom drama that would open the following spring, doing good business at the box office and making a step toward reestablishing him at long last as a working director. Offering food and drink, consenting to spend the whole evening in an extended interview, he was far more gracious than my reading of his biographies and interviews had led me to expect.[24] In the 1970s, Friedkin played the directorial star—inspired, mannerless, seized with a self-importance appropriate to *un grand génie* who could also rope them in at the box office. He took the movie industry by storm with *The French Connection* and then *The Exorcist,* inventive and profitable reinventions of the crime–cum–action movie and the horror movie that helped set the pattern for those genres—and, more generally, for the tone and style of film and television—in decades to come.[25]

But the moment of perfect fit between Friedkin's craft and Hollywood's need passed, and he did not follow up with what the industry considered a sustained first-rank career—although he did make interesting movies (like the underrated *Sorcerer,* a retelling of Clouzot's existential parable *Les Gages du Peur*), highly professional movies (like the heist fantasy *The Brinks Job,* a crisp little fable of the urban village set in Irish and Italian Boston), and even a notorious movie (the complex, hateful *Cruising,* based in part on Randy Jurgensen's pursuit of a murderer who preyed on male homosexuals). Two decades out of the limelight, a lasting marriage to studio kingpin Sherry Lansing, and the instant perspective brought on by a heart attack had apparently mellowed him. When I visited him in his hotel room in 1999, he looked like somebody's lawyer-dad on a dress-down day—pants cinched up too high, a polo shirt, a still-clever but no longer mean face that could easily belong to Steve Forbes's younger and cooler brother. Even though he still had a tendency to embellish his stories to make sure we never forget that he is a hardboiled street character whose burning talent and filmic sophistication carried him to the pinnacle of artistic achievement and commercial success, it still seemed to me that he had become a calmer, somewhat chastened fellow.[26] He might have had less to say with a movie camera than he did before, but he was probably a better man than when he was the New Hollywood's gifted young prince.

I wanted Friedkin to tell me about the synthesis of influences evident in *The French Connection,* which, most impressively of all his movies, plants his flag where the realm of high-culture aesthetics overlaps with the urban precincts of authenticity as Americans conventionally understand it: the subcultures of lowlife, the insular world of cops and robbers, the Ghetto and the Old Neighborhood. We ended up talking about his old neighborhood by the end of the evening, but he began with television.

At WGN, a local station in Chicago, Friedkin started in the mail room just after high school and graduated swiftly to floor manager and then director. He estimates he directed more than two thousand live shows, including drama, news, *Lunchtime Little Theater* with Bozo the Clown (who, along with a disturbing hand puppet named Garfield Goose, also directed by Friedkin, was one of the principal small-screen monsters of my Chicago childhood), telecasts of Chicago Cubs baseball and the Chicago Symphony Orchestra, even "the very first live courtroom show, called *They Stand Accused.*" [27] Friedkin left Chicago in 1965, moving to Los Angeles to make documentaries for David Wolper at ABC, including *The Thin Blue Line,* a survey of law enforcement. The house style aimed for grand overview with authoritative voice-over. "You never had a character study then," Friedkin said. But when he shot *The Thin Blue Line*—as when he had shot *The People vs. Paul Crump,* his first extended documentary, in Chicago—Friedkin was on the street and among cops and criminals with a camera. These were not just mundane ride-alongs, either: "There were riots in Rochester, racial riots, and I went up and covered that." So, in the sense that he was there with a camera, covering the law-and-order spectacles of the urban crisis, he was already in training for *The French Connection.* "The Wolper documentaries is where I learned how to induce that documentary style," he said, "'cause they are all fake in the sense that you go out there and set things up. You know, I'm doing a scene with El Cordobés, the bullfighter, and I want to get him putting on the suit of lights, so you have him put on the suit of lights and you shoot it three or four times from different angles, 'cause you only had one camera. Or guys riding in a patrol car: 'Okay, let's do it again, don't say so much this time,' or 'Point out that club over there,' you know. You're telling these guys what to do."

When the chance to direct *The French Connection* came along, he was actively seeking a feature in which he could try out the induced documentary style, much as Costa-Gavras had in *Z.* Friedkin called that movie "a revelation in terms of its style, like a perfect blend of documentary footage with theatricality. That's what I was going for." *Z* and *The Battle of Algiers,* celebrated documentary-style political thrillers of the late 1960s, were two of many movies Friedkin cited in the course of our interview: taut Hollywood genre pictures like *White Heat* and *Bullitt,* American masterpieces like *Citizen Kane,* New York location movies like *Naked City,* the French genre films of Melville and Verneuil, the stylish Italian horror pictures of Dario Argento, and the canon of "serious" European movies regularly invoked by American directors of his generation. Among his peers in the 1960s, he said, "the real argument in my day was whose style would triumph, Fellini or Godard. Most of the films I had seen were foreign films. I mean *Last Year at Marienbad* and *La Dolce Vita,* and the films of De Sica, and Rossellini's *Open City,* and *Paisan,* and *8½,* which was like nirvana. And of course *Breathless,* which killed us, which knocked us all out." These movies taught him, he said, to think beyond the limits of any single conventional style. "What they were telling you as a young filmmaker was anything worked, you could try anything on, almost anything cut. So you didn't have to do predictable editing. And most of the American films in that period and before had become very predictable in their editing techniques."

The trick, as he saw it, was to apply these lessons to the Hollywood movie without denaturing it. In a typical yoking of high-toned influence to visceral results, Friedkin cited Antonioni as the inspiration for *The French Connection*'s editing style, which was novel and propulsive enough to leave viewers gasping in 1971. On the one hand, the cutting of *The French Connection* was "mostly dictated by necessity" brought on by the movie's commitment to its location aesthetic. In any given shot, "the frame I end on, in the next frame something horrible happened"—an actor blew a line, a pedestrian blocked the camera, the light went bad—"and the frame I come in on, a lot of bad shit happened up to that point. So out of necessity comes a style, comes a rhythm." On the other hand, the movie does have a distinctive driving rhythm, produced in great part by its editing (for which Friedkin claims credit, although Jerry Greenberg won an Oscar for it, just as Friedkin claims credit for Ernest Tidyman's Oscar-winning screenplay).[28] "It was *meant* to be unpredictable," he says. "And I'll tell you, the guy who affected my editing techniques and shooting techniques more than anybody was Antonioni. Antonioni's movies are slow, but he almost never repeated a shot." Friedkin shifted back and forth in his seat, framing with his hands to illustrate a point he has made many times before. "He would never go over shoulder, over shoulder"—meaning that Antonioni did not switch back and forth between already established camera angles. "Here comes a scene and it goes and he shoots it, and when he's done with it, he goes to another angle, and that's it. Maybe a third angle, but he would never go back within the scene and do all this bullshit that is the stock-in-trade of American filmmaking. In that sense, Antonioni's films move laterally, like this"—here he made a left-to-right scanning gesture with one hand—"like the way you'd read a book. Most American films are not like you'd read a book; they're Ping-Pong games, and the rhythms are dictated by the way they're shot. You can have a master and two over-the-shoulders, and a couple of singles, whatever. You shot all that shit so you use it. And that's why they're all predictable. Antonioni's editing is not predictable."

He went on to point out that Antonioni was, like himself, also a documentary filmmaker, which led him to Alain Resnais's documentary *Night and Fog,* the editing style of which, he says, he and filmmakers of his generation "cribbed from unmercifully." From there he coasted into a summation, as if concluding a scholarly paper on the European roots of the American action film as manifest in the works of William David Friedkin: "The powerful editing influences on me were Godard, Resnais, and Antonioni, each for different reasons that I think I've expressed."

We had been exploring Friedkin's professional background—his pathway into the movie business and shaping artistic influences. But what about the historical moment in which the movie was made? Did he have a special sense of the politically, socially, and culturally fraught status of the inner city at the end of the 1960s? "No," he said, "I first became aware that this thing had political overtones when I was in Italy" to do press conferences in support of the movie. "Of course the Italian press is virulently political. I would get guys on the left saying, 'This is a fascist movie!' And I would get guys on the right saying, 'How else can these police operate? I mean look what they're up against!'" The American press, although often less forthright about its politics and usually constrained from getting too far outside the middle way defined by conservative liberalism and liberal conservatism, pursued a similar range of readings across the political spectrum.[29]

As for his own politics, Friedkin described himself, now as well as back in the 1960s and 1970s, as "a pragmatic liberal." This is not the same thing, he wanted to make clear, as "a knee-jerk liberal": he was against "licentiousness and license" and "the Clintons." But he was passionately allied to the New Deal social agenda associated with his political idols. "To me," he said, "the great heroes of American politics are

Franklin Roosevelt and Harry Truman." His love of Truman was ill defined, having something to do with the atomic bomb, but he diverged off the topic there—into a discussion of the Gulf War and how much he enjoyed his brief stay in Iraq in the 1970s when he was shooting *The Exorcist* (the connecting link being, I believe, that sometimes even decent men might find it necessary to blow up many individually blameless and personable foreigners). But his love of Roosevelt was a Chicago-bred Democrat's plainspoken love of the American welfare state in its finest hour: "Social Security. FDR left a legacy that has to this day benefited people. No matter what his patrician origins, or his real feelings, or the fact that he was getting a little head in the White House himself. I'm a dyed-in-the-wool New Dealer, and FDR is up with God. I benefited from that, and from the machine politics of the Democratic Party. I don't believe that the welfare state is the answer to all that ails us, but nevertheless I remain a liberal on social issues. There's a humanness, . . ." he started to say, and then let the sentence trail off.

The urban crisis of the 1960s seemed to many people to mark the collapse of the New Deal order and its vision of the welfare state, and cops like Popeye and Cloudy were on the front lines of that collapse in the inner city, where it hit hardest. The movie imagines a world in which nobody will be taken care of, especially not by a strangely directionless government that can only send out legbreakers to try to keep the streets under control. Popeye and Cloudy are, he said, "trying to put their fingers in the dike. And there's also that song in there, 'Everybody's Going to the Moon.' Everybody *was* going to the moon back then, one way or another. They were either getting high, or all they cared about was putting a man on the fuckin' moon." The Three Degrees, purveyors of the Philadelphia Sound that dominated urban soul after Motown and before hip-hop, perform the song early in the movie. They are the floor show at the Copacabana, where Popeye and Cloudy first spot Sal Boca, the American mafia's link to Frog One.

All politics, even those underlying *The French Connection*, are local. Friedkin's account of Roosevelt's New Deal order in crisis trails roots in his account of the Old Neighborhood in decline—a story much like Grosso's thumbnail history of East Harlem. Friedkin grew up "on the North Side of Chicago, around Sheridan Road and Lawrence Avenue," an area he has repeatedly and misleadingly described as "a fucking slum" (although even his largely uncritical biographer, Nat Segaloff, observes that "contrary to his memory, the area where the Friedkins lived was a comfortable, though hardly impressive, middle-class Jewish neighborhood").[30] Friedkin grew up in a slum to the extent that he feels the need to establish street credentials, but he grew up in an idyllic urban village to the extent that he wants to explain what happened to the inner city and what it means.

Yes, the story of the Old Neighborhood goes, we did not have much: "We lived in one room," and his parents' bed "came down out of the wall." But, the story continues, things were better then than they are now because we lived in a genuine community: "We lived in an apartment building where you could smell the neighbors' cooking and all the doors were open, we never locked our doors, there was very little crime within—I mean, all those places are now barred up. We had no air-conditioning, and neither did our neighbors, so along with them and thousands of people in the Chicago summers we would go sleep in the park." The new order arrived as a series of shocks in the 1960s, with drugs in the vanguard, breaking up the old order and changing the world forever: "And the difference, though, was there was not this drug-related wave of crime which had swept the big cities of America. For many years you haven't been able to walk in the park. Then, though it was poor and there was some crime, there were no drugs. People weren't crazy in the street. It was before Vietnam, before the national nervous breakdown, you know, Kennedy and Vietnam and Martin Luther King." As Friedkin and others tell it, the decline of New Deal America went hand in hand with the triumph of racial division over class-based community: "I lived with and went to school with a lot of blacks, and I was just as poor as they, and I was—I am—Jewish, and there were Italians, and Polish people, and Germans, with blacks, and there was no overt prejudice because we were all poor together. It was about class, not about ethnicity or background. My father never made more than fifty dollars a week."

This narrative of the New Deal coalition's collapse into impotence and malignity—a story elegant in its rise-and-fall motion from utopia to dystopia, obviously fanciful yet also not without power and truth—lies near the heart of urban political life in America. It also lies, not coincidentally, near the heart of *The French Connection,* which puts Old Neighborhood–bred cops in motion through the new order with exhilaratingly awful results.

A call from the hotel's lobby interrupted Friedkin: Sonny Grosso was downstairs, having dropped by for a visit. When Grosso got to the room, Friedkin shouted, "Sa'vaturre!" with impeccable mock-Sicilian diction, and they embraced. Grosso took a chair, adjusting his gun, while Friedkin called room service for pasta and wine. The storytelling began: the one about how Friedkin had to grease an important palm at the Transit Authority to get extraspecial treatment, the one about how Grosso and Egan used their badges to shanghai extras off the street, the one about how Friedkin tricked Grosso's mother into revealing her paranoid son's phone number and address, all the ones about how Egan managed to be such a swine and such a charmer at the same time. The director and the producer talked about their current projects— Friedkin's comeback feature and Grosso's latest television movie, an unabashedly tawdry little number about Mary Kay Letourneau, the teacher whose scandalous affair with a sixth grader produced two children and many headlines. Friedkin and Grosso felt good. A long time ago they had given each other the gift of their expertise, and each had profited in the exchange. If there was something bittersweet in realizing that their first collaboration turned out to be the best thing either one ever worked on, there was satisfaction in knowing that it had set them up for life in show business. *The French Connection* speaks so eloquently of its moment that it has held up over the years. It will probably hold up better and better as the urban crisis recedes into the same middle distance as the Great Depression that gave rise to the New Deal in the first place. Among the double features that might instructively bracket this period in popular culture—like, say, *The Public Enemy* and *Superfly*—*The Grapes of Wrath* and *The French Connection* make a better pair than at first one might expect.

The two old friends talked and laughed, egging each other on to tell stories for my tape recorder. When the last tape ran out, I took notes, then after a while I just listened. It had been a long evening. Passing (by way of the moon and Philadelphia) from Bozo the Clown, *The Thin Blue Line,* and Antonioni's editing technique to the Old Neighborhood, the heroin plague, and the crisis of the liberal welfare state, Friedkin had taken me back to the cold, windswept cultural and political terrain of urban America in the early 1970s—and there were Popeye and Cloudy out in the middle of it, stymied but hellbent, limned for posterity in available light by a handheld camera.

THE WORST TIME

"It was the worst time, I promise you, it was the worst time to be a cop," Randy Jurgensen told me. We were driving around Harlem the next day, a sunny Saturday in October 1999, checking out the neighborhood in which he grew up and the precinct in which he had worked. He was talking about 1970–1971, when he moonlighted on *The French Connection*. Jurgensen left the force in 1978, when, after a distinguished career that had lasted just short of twenty years, he fell out with his superiors over the department's handling of the Harlem Mosque case.[31] Since then he has worked in movies and television as an atmospheric bit player of tough guys on both sides of the law, and also in production.

Like Grosso, Jurgensen came from a working-class family. His parents were building supers in Vinegar Hill, and they worked at St. Luke's Hospital; they urged him to get a job "at United Parcels, or Saks, something established." Like Grosso, Jurgensen boxed in his youth (as had their fathers). Like Grosso, he saw police work as a good government job that offered a chance at upward mobility for a smart, ambitious young man who was good with his hands. And, like Grosso and Friedkin, he tells his own shorthand version of the Old Neighborhood's decline in the 1960s. Steering with one hand and pointing with the other, he said, "This is where I made my first Holy Communion, St. Joseph's, 125th and Morningside; and these projects, they weren't here. They built those later. That's what destroyed the neighborhood, finished off the neighborhood, which I was born and raised in." As part of that same transformation of his neighborhood, which was also his beat (he used to walk to work at the Twenty-eighth Precinct), his status in the community as a policeman also changed. When Jurgensen first joined up in the late 1950s, he felt respected. "My mother used to tell people, 'My son's a cop,' the way other people would say 'My son's a doctor.' And then, through the sixties, that went away, that truly disappeared."

In the latter part of the 1960s, he had to put up with "suspicions of the police department, being called pigs," and what he perceived as escalating violence against the police. He wanted to understand it, to put the change in perspective. "The police department was an arm, an extension of the establishment," he recognized, "and the establishment was being challenged, and not at the ballot box. They were so anti-Vietnam, so anti-Nixon, so anti-government, and they took it to the streets. Corruption is what the police department represented, not law and order. The police, you could reach out and touch them. That's what was happening. They began, honest to God, to set up police officers and kill them." By 1971, he continued, "we had in this city experienced firsthand the civil rights movement, which was a long time coming; we had experienced several riots, the last one being the Martin Luther King riot the day he was killed. We were going through a terrible, terrible, on-television-every-day corruption hearing called the Knapp Commission, where they were what I call cup-of-coffee corruption crazy. That was the atmosphere, the thoughts, the image of the New York City Police Department during that time. Morale was terrible. It was the worst time to be a cop in New York."

For Jurgensen, *The French Connection* ended this era of police anti-heroism and restored the New York cop to his rightful status. "So," he asked rhetorically, "did *The French Connection* single-handedly change the image of the cop, change how we were accepted on the street, in the area where I worked, in the police department that was the largest police department in the world? Yes, it did. And I lived it, I saw the change. After the movie came out, we became heroes again. That single picture. We became heroes to the people that it was important to us to become heroes to"—that is, police officers they worked with (although the brass downtown were not pleased with the attention paid to Grosso, Egan, and Jurgensen) and at least some of the people they policed. He told me a story about wiseguys on Arthur Avenue in the Bronx who could not be convinced that Grosso and Jurgensen were actually working on *The Seven-Ups,* a 1973 knockoff of *The French Connection* cowritten by Grosso. "One of the guys called Sonny over, and he said, 'We know you're the French Connection cops, we know that you're not making a movie, this is all a charade, you've just come up here to bust us.' That's the reputation we had," by which he means that they became known as supercops capable of pulling off any sort of ingenious trick to make a case. Once, walking through the Tombs with Grosso after making an arrest, he heard a voice shouting from a cell, "'Didn't you lock me up? Didn't you lock me up?' And Sonny said, 'Yeah.' The guy turned back to the cage and said, 'I *told* you we got busted by the French Connection cops!' It meant something in that cage."

Jurgensen's account has a wishfully simplified, almost magical quality—they respected us, then the world changed and made them despise us, then the movie made them respect us again—but it expresses his personal sense of *The French Connection* as a just reward for having endured one of the most difficult moments in the history of urban policing. The rise in street crime in the 1960s had coincided with a growing general impulse, registering in different forms across the political spectrum, to discredit the state's wisdom and ability to act constructively—to rebuild and govern inner cities, ameliorate injustice and inequality, and exercise its monopoly on legitimate violence via military intervention in Southeast Asia or police activity on the streets. By the end of the decade, police officers felt even more cornered than usual. In the North-

east, their salaries had fallen behind those of skilled laborers; they identified lack of public respect as their main on-the-job complaint (even
ranking it above Supreme Court decisions); generational conflicts divided departments between World War II–era old-timers and Vietnam-
era newcomers (like Jurgensen) who felt more at home in the culture
that emerged from the 1960s; violent encounters with antiwar protest-
ers and reporters had helped turn police brutality into front-page news;
and, at least in New York City, a series of murders of cops exacerbated
their impression that police work had gotten more dangerous at the
same time that it had fallen in prestige. In 1969, a report of the National
Commission on the Causes and Prevention of Violence described
American police as "overworked, undertrained, underpaid, and under-
educated," and, adds Christopher Wilson in his book *Cop Knowledge*
(on which I have drawn in composing this general portrait of embattled
urban police at the turn of the decade), "fully alienated from their own
citizenry."[32]

But it was also a very good time to be a cop, in the sense that Hollywood in general and William Friedkin in particular needed help to satisfy the popular craving for stories set in the postindustrial inner city. As
the expert guides crossed over into show business, they gained a second
existence on-screen. Once you know what they look like, you can find
Jurgensen and Grosso all over American crime cinema of the 1970s. Jurgensen plays a Fed grilling a bank robber in Friedkin's *The Brink's Job;*
in *Sorcerer,* he plays a hood who first helps Roy Scheider to escape to a
godforsaken Latin American country but then tracks him down, arriving to whack him as Scheider slowdances with a woman in a cantina in
the movie's closing scene. As cops in *Cruising,* Grosso and Jurgensen
conduct a tag-team interrogation and serve as Al Pacino's backup when
he goes undercover in search of a serial killer. ("You came in too soon,
Sonny," says Pacino to Grosso after one abortive bust, sounding less like
a fellow cop than like a fellow actor lamenting a blown cue.) They turn
up again as cops in *Report to the Commissioner* and as members of the
hit squad of machine gunners who put a couple of hundred bullets into
the writhing Sonny Corleone in a tollbooth ambush in *The Godfather.*
(Grosso tried to explain to Francis Ford Coppola that a bullet or three
of that caliber would put anybody down, but Coppola felt that it should
take several clips to fell Sonny Corleone.) Grosso told me that his gun
has its own cameo in *The Godfather,* as the pistol that Michael Corleone
(Pacino, again) retrieves from a restaurant bathroom and uses to assas-
sinate a corrupt police captain. Grosso also plays a counterfeiter who

gets busted at the beginning of *The Seven-Ups*. He and Jurgensen often turn up at the beginnings of movies, as if to place the seal of authenticity on what is to come.

Egan shows up all over the place, too. He left the force in 1971, soon after *The French Connection* came out, after getting into what Grosso calls "a scrape." The department accused Egan of improperly withholding small amounts of drugs and related materials seized in busts— a common practice, as Egan argued then and Grosso still argues now, among narcotics cops who had to deal with informants. The department and reporters also asked Egan about the millions of dollars' worth of French Connection heroin missing from the property clerk's office, but he denied any knowledge of that crime. Egan went straight into show business as a technical adviser, story consultant, and actor. He had parts in television shows—*Mannix, Police Story, Joe Forrester, Mike Hammer*—and in movies. He appears, for instance, near the beginning of *Prime Cut*, a curious 1972 movie about a war between the declining Chicago Irish mob and a wildcat gangster named Mary Ann—a man, played by Gene Hackman—who runs a meat-and-white-slavery business in Kansas. A tough guy played by Lee Marvin goes into a bar to get his orders, and there he meets Egan, playing a Chicago mob chief, who has had it with Mary Ann. "He's skimming his own cream and sticking Kansas right up my yass," complains Egan. "I need you to straighten him out." Egan looks persuasively put-upon, as if the sinister machinations of history causing the fall of the Irish mob do indeed give him a personal pain in his ass, but you can see how much he enjoys being in the movies.

Watching the movies based on Egan's character and career, you can also see that they afforded him a chance to give his own account of himself. As in *The French Connection*, Egan plays his own boss in *Badge 373* (1973), the credits of which identify the movie as "inspired by the exploits of Eddie Egan." Robert Duvall plays Eddie Ryan, a fantasy version of Egan. When Duvall's character gets into a scrape and has to turn in his gun while awaiting departmental trial, Egan takes the gun but says, "Eddie, you'll always be a cop to me." In another scene, Egan shows up at a detective's wake at Farenga's funeral home (where he would be waked himself, with Sonny Grosso paying all expenses, in 1995); he is coming up the stairs just as Duvall says, "Stick the mayor up yer ass" to a bigwig.

The passage on the stairs at Farenga's is emblematic. Egan does not have much to do or say on-screen in the movie, but he has rather more to say if we recognize the extent to which his spirit possesses Robert

Duvall. Especially in the movie's opening scene, a bust at a nightclub, Duvall speaks fluent Eganese: "Anything found on the floor belongs to you," and "Send him to the Circumcision Division and charge him with violation of the penis code," and "Look at yer arms, you got more tracks than the Long Island Railroad," and "Everybody goes when the whistle blows," and "Hey you! Hey, you little spic! Hey you! Where you goin'?" Pete Hamill, who wrote the screenplay (and shows up in the scene at Farenga's playing a reporter), told me, "I just basically hung around with him, to get the rhythm of his speech. He had left the police force and was living in Fort Lauderdale, trying to get into the movies. I couldn't tell how much was Egan and how much was a performance for me. Eddie was his own fictional creation." Through Hamill's screenplay and through Duvall, Egan got to say his piece, he got to be in a big chase (commandeering a bus when pursued by Puerto Rican gangsters), and he got to participate in the fantasy of identifying and dispatching a master criminal personally responsible for making a mess of New York City.

The same logic of ventriloquism applies to *French Connection II* (1975), in which Egan did not appear on-screen at all. Gene Hackman plays Popeye again, and this time he kills Frog One. First, though, Popeye must go to France, where he is kidnapped and forcibly addicted to heroin, then he must go through withdrawal in an extended cold turkey sequence. In the depths of self-pitying, drunken despair to which all this indignity sinks him, Popeye semicoherently explains the tragedy of his life to a French detective: he was a great baseball player, he had a tryout with the Yankees, but when he laid eyes on the young Mickey Mantle in spring training, he went right out and took the police exam. Mantle's name means nothing to the French detective. Pete Hamill, an uncredited script doctor, wrote the scene, borrowing large chunks of it verbatim from Egan's barroom storytelling. A certain pathetic humor inflects Popeye's failed baring of soul, ironizing the movie's presentation of Egan's preferred version of his life, but bear in mind that his version—including even exaggerated trivia like his account of his near-miss baseball career—*did* find its way into the movies. In the movies, Egan could not only shoot straight, drive like Bill Hickman, nail Frog One, and speak in the voices of superior officers to pardon his own excesses in the line of duty, he even got to explain why he was such a jerk in ways that demanded sympathy.

Compared with *The French Connection, Badge 373* and *French Connection II* are not very good movies. Trying to exploit the original's success, they end up processing it into derivative blandness relieved only by livid little touches of color—a directorial flourish, a memorable gesture, Hackman's maundering Mickey Mantle speech. But, mediocre or not, these movies of the 1970s (and *Popeye Doyle,* a movie made for television in 1986) did amount to a heroic cycle of Eddie Egan stories that were disseminated far and wide. Respected journalists (Hamill and Ernest Tidyman, and Jimmy Breslin, in a sense) wrote his dialogue, and two of Hollywood's most accomplished players of regular-guy characters played him. Furthermore, the cannibalizing of *The French Connection*—not only by other Eddie Egan movies but also by a much larger body of movies and television shows influenced by its authoritative synthesis of form and subject—meant that Egan's persona diffused widely into the crime genres' collective bloodstream. "There were fifty movies that ate off that plate," said Hamill, and he meant only the direct imitations, rip-offs, and homages. Not only did many more movies and television shows indirectly sample *The French Connection,* but even real cops, Hamill believed, felt its influence: "After it came out, cops turned into cowboys for a few years, everybody trying to be a hero." After all, they went to the movies too.

Egan and Grosso (and Jurgensen, and others among their associates) have become layered into the substance and style of crime stories, in the same way that a history of city life is layered into the settings and action of even the most ahistorical crime fantasies. The French Connection cops' presence can be decoded from the speech and actions of characters, from story lines and choices of locations, from bits of physical business and attitude that moviemakers now learn from other movies without even knowing their sources. Gene Hackman, asked by Pete Hamill about his improbable appeal as a movie star, once said,

I guess the audiences respond to the proletarian man they see in me: the working guy who's doing vicariously what they would like to do. I think that's why essentially *The French Connection* worked. I don't have any illusions about my being the only actor who could have played that. A lot of guys could have. And it really *is* a director's medium, as we all know. But I *was* the guy who played it, and I kind of reaped the harvest along with Billy and some other people. But if there's an attraction, that's what it is. "I know Gene Hackman." They're able to say that, in some funny kind of way, you know, "Yeah, I know who that guy is."[33]

The working men recognizable in the layers of Hackman's and Roy Scheider's performances—men who embodied an old-school urban competence and style so often labeled "gritty," men aggrieved but also inspired and led to new forms of work by the transformation of places like Block 1728 and East Harlem—were Eddie Egan and Sonny Grosso.

4

ROCKY MARCIANO'S GHOST

*Real landscapes are rugged; sensual; muddy; ordinary; inacces-
sible. They are filled with things that are dead, overgrown, and
imperfect—things that are too young and too old. But they have
life and are interesting because they are not perfect, and because
unexpected things happen.*

Patricia Johanson on art beyond the museum,
long before she came to Brockton

*Honest to God, I love the history of Brockton as much as anybody,
particularly the blue-collar stuff, but it's history. They buried the
horses and wagons a long time ago.*

Jack Yunits, mayor of Brockton

PATRICIA JOHANSON, AN internationally prominent landscape artist,
was locked out of her house. Not the house she lived in, which was in
upstate New York near Albany, but a vacant house she owned on Dover
Street in what was once an Italian section of Brockton, Massachusetts.
She and I walked around outside, peering in and trying doors and windows, but it was closed up tight. Her keys did not work because somebody had changed the locks—on *her* property, which requires nerve. It
was hard not to take this situation as indicative of how badly things had
turned out for her in Brockton after a promising start.

Compact, wood-shingled, with small square rooms, the two-family
house is the kind of building into which Brockton's immigrants have
been crowding for more than a century. It is unremarkable except for
the fact that Rocky Marciano grew up in it. Marciano, known as the

Brockton Blockbuster, held the heavyweight championship of the world from 1952 to 1956 and—unique among heavyweight champions—retired undefeated. (He died in a plane crash in 1969.) In 1997, shortly after the city of Brockton hired Johanson to help improve its long-depressed image and economy by formulating a master plan to integrate its disparate cultural and natural resources, she bought the semiderelict house to save it from collapsing into an unsalvageable state. She intended to restore the building to its condition circa 1950 and turn it into a Marciano museum anchoring a Rocky Marciano Trail, which would guide visitors and residents through a new Brockton. From the atmospheric ruins of the mill city that once upon a time produced shoes and Rocky Marciano would rise a green cultural center that both celebrated and laid to rest its industrial past.

That had been the idea, anyway. The plan called for the creation of new green spaces, historical attractions, and other civic assets, all to be under construction as early as 1998. But it was now high summer in 2000, and the plan was still just a sheaf of memoranda and a set of elegant drawings on oversized rolls of paper. The parks and historical sites were not under construction. The river was still overgrown, fenced off, and choked with refuse. The planned green streets were still just streets. The old Marciano house at 168 Dover Street remained vacant and largely unrenovated, and the mayor and other powerful players in town were not returning Johanson's phone calls. She had come to Brockton as a potential savior, courted by local officials and welcomed by boosters and functionaries, but the initial climate of cooperative goodwill on both sides had soon cooled and then chilled. An outsider with no prior interest in boxing, she had discovered Rocky Marciano during her research on Brockton and had become excited about the idea of him as a heroic exemplar of working-class virtue. She expected that making him the centerpiece of her master plan would attract a broad-based constituency in his hometown, but she had come to think that she had made a mistake. Some people in town felt that Rocky represented the outdated Brockton they sought to supplant, some people who were passionate about Rocky objected to an outsider's handling of their local hero, and many people did not much care about Rocky one way or the other.

Johanson, who has moved in exclusive artistic company since she was an undergraduate at Bennington College in the early 1960s, looks like an artist from central casting. A pale, animated woman with a flutey voice and a taste for simple black clothes, excruciatingly lean and intense to the point of seeming to vibrate in place, she is prone to conversational non sequitur and to outbursts of delighted laughter at unlikely moments. She seemed out of place on Dover Street, a block of modest prewar houses occupied by a variety of working people. It was hot and still; a tethered dog barked steadily in the next yard, where a shirtless guy was drinking a beer on his back steps; a few kids messed around on the basketball courts in the James Edgar Playground across the street. Johanson had been in nearby Boston, delivering copies of her Brockton plan to an art gallery for an upcoming exhibition, and had decided to have a look at the house she still owned. She had not been to Brockton since she had turned in her last piece of paperwork a year before, in July 1999, after withholding some of her work to pressure the recalcitrant city to pay her fee in full.

The clear evidence that somebody had been renovating the house made being locked out even more perplexing. Basement windows had been replaced, the building's exterior had been partially painted, a sink had been removed and discarded in the backyard. Through the windows we could see that the floors had been stripped, and blown-up reproductions of Marciano family photographs had been taped to the walls of first-floor rooms. Johanson was worried, since alterations to the exterior would make it harder to landmark the building, but more than that she was strangely touched—hurt, but also impressed. Her property rights had been egregiously violated, true, but whoever was working on the house was also apparently motivated by respect for Marciano's memory. The careful quality of the work and the long dog lead attached to a pipe in the overgrown backyard pointed to a likely suspect. "It has to be Mark," she said, wonderingly. "He's like me."

She had never met Mark Casieri in person, but he had sent her pictures of himself and his pit bulls a year before when he wrote to her about his enthusiasm for Marciano and for her plan. Casieri, a custodian at the post office, was a Brockton guy through and through, Italian and built for hard labor. He seemed to be sincere in his admiration for both Marciano and Johanson, and he seemed to be the only person in town who shared her desire to turn the house into a museum. He had called Johanson to ask if she would sell him the house, and she had liked the idea. "I thought I would sell it to somebody who loves it, who loves Rocky," she told me. "At least Mark would honor the house. Mark is the kind of guy—I spent hours on the phone talking to him about how they boxed in the backyard, hung up a bag in the tree, and Mark said, 'Yeah, we can do that!' He was very excited." He had offered a fair market price of $90,000 for the house but could not get a mortgage. So she had given him "a very lowball price, $75,000," and they thought they had a deal, but then that mortgage fell through, too. He had tried for months to raise the money, and more than once he had believed that the mortgage was about to be approved, but each time something had come up—as if someone powerful were scuttling his efforts behind the scenes. She had concluded that he had given up, but apparently he had not.

"Mark has a big heart," Johanson said as we inspected his handiwork on the house's front porch, "but it's not clear he can withstand the forces around him." She felt he was not cunning enough to operate in Brockton. He might not even be able to protect himself from those he considered his allies. "He seems like a nice guy," she said, "but my feeling is that he's going to be used by other people." The mayor—whom she regarded as having turned on her—had mentioned Casieri as a possible buyer or caretaker for the house way back in May 1998, according to her project notebook, and she found that sinister. She had heard, too, that Casieri was a friend of Peter Marciano Jr., a city council member and son of Rocky's youngest brother. "I don't know," she said, "everything in Brockton is very ingrown." But Casieri's troubles lining up a mortgage suggested that he was not an agent of nefarious forces; perhaps he was just a true believer like herself, similarly assailed by those forces. In any case, he was her last hope of seeing a crucial piece of her Brockton plan turned from unbuilt idea to concrete fact, even if he had broken into her house and changed the locks.

When Jack Yunits, mayor of Brockton, tried to describe Mark Casieri to me, he made an odd gesture, opposing his splayed hands in front of his chest as if he were holding an invisible, heavy, pulsating object about the size of a cinder block. "He's got a heart like this," said the mayor, "bigger than his head. He can do the work with his hands, a real throwback, like the old-time Italians. He was mad at me when I passed the pit bull ordinance, though." Mary Waldron, the mayor's chief of staff, made a similar gesture when she described Casieri in similar terms: "A bull, a Rocky type, a throwback. He's got a heart as big as city hall and the hands of a working man. He can do the work, but he needs money and a lawyer." Casieri had also gotten testy with her, complaining that the city was not cooperating with him. "He got mad," she said, "much as Pat Johanson got mad. They're so focused on what they're doing." Casieri wanted the mayor's help in securing a loan to buy the Marciano house from Johanson so he could restore the building. He intended to live on the second floor while operating the first floor as a Marciano museum like the one she had planned. Johanson's idea had become his dream, but he had encountered serial frustrations in trying to realize it.

The building needed extensive work that would cost at least as much as the purchase price, and Casieri could not secure a loan for the full amount, so he had taken a typically direct approach to solving the problem. He broke in and started renovating the house single-handedly in the hope of lowering the price tag on the needed repairs far enough so he could get a mortgage. He changed the locks, logically enough, to make sure he could get in and out while keeping the house secure. He presumed, to the extent that he thought about it, that if Johanson found out, she would understand he was acting to make possible a mutually desired result. Most mornings about nine o'clock in the spring and summer of 2000, after completing his night shift at the post office, he would go home, collect his three pit bulls, and then head to the Marciano house to put in five or six hours of work. Around three o'clock in the afternoon, it would be time to eat and then sleep; he would get up in time to be at the post office by midnight. He was knocking himself out on his own time to fix up a house he did not even own, but, as far as he was concerned, he had a problem that hard work could solve.

"When I was nine years old," Casieri told me, "I was carrying boulders for my father to build a stone wall down on Pennsylvania Avenue. There was a lady there, she thought I was too little, but when I was finished she said I'd done good work." Casieri is built along the lines of Rocky Marciano: broad through the chest, heavy-featured, dark, with a big crew cut head and strong, compact arms and legs. He stands close and speaks loudly, putting a thick hand on your arm to emphasize a point when he gets excited, and he likes to take his dogs everywhere, so I can see how he might have come on a little strong for the taste of the mayor and his staff. ("When he grabbed my arm," Mary Waldron told me, demonstrating by grabbing my arm and squeezing hard, "that was it: end of conversation.") Casieri told me the story of the stone wall no more than three minutes after we shook hands the first time we met. We were standing outside the house on Dover Street in August 2000, a couple of weeks after I had been there with Patricia Johanson and several months into his campaign of breaking and entering with intent to renovate. Wearing paint-stained baggy pants, a maroon polo shirt, and a Red Sox cap, he was dressed to do the kind of work he had been doing on the house for the past few months: stripping and painting the exterior, repairing and rebuilding porches and rails, replacing windows and doors, stripping and refinishing floors and walls, installing doorsills and sinks, tearing out fixtures large and small and replacing them with period-appropriate ones. He would need to hire professionals to install new plumbing, heating, and electrical systems, but he was doing most of the rest of it himself, as well as rubbish picking in search of what he called "old-school" materials. "I'm a good worker," he said. "I don't mind working, I've always done the work. My father worked all day cutting leather, and he built his own house, too, worked for a homebuilder." Casieri told me he cut leather himself, in a shoe factory, back in the 1970s when he was a teenage kid, but (like Marciano) he could not abide sitting at the machine and so quit after a couple of months. "But I did go on weekends to where my father worked," he added, almost apologetic for having skipped out on a job twenty years before, "to load bags in the truck."

Casieri, born in 1961, never met Rocky Marciano, but the long-dead champion dominates his life. The particular nature of Casieri's devotion seems to have three interlocking components. First, Marciano, perhaps more than any other fighter, is identified with boxing as a ritual display of and meditation on the virtues of body work. Describing Rocky's fighting style, Casieri said, "It was like working on the street, like a construction job. You could hit him with a pipe, he didn't care, he kept coming. Rocky was all business. That's what he said the key was. Total control of body and mind, at all times." Second, Casieri feels that the people of Brockton are in danger of forgetting Marciano, which would be an outrageous denial of their own history and an indicator of cancerous self-loathing. "I'm a Brockton person for life," he said, with the doughtiness of a local booster committed to reminding his neighbors— and himself—of their hometown's greatness. "Just the athletes that come out of this town," he said, shaking his head, "it's amazing." Third, the Marcianos' family life seems to exert a strong pull on Casieri. He wanted the Dover Street house to be a memorial not just to Rocky the fighter and native son but also to Rocky the good son. "All the pictures in the house," he said, "are going to be family-oriented," as opposed to the publicity pictures and KO shots you can find on the walls of the historical society or George's Cafe, an Italian restaurant and Rocky shrine a couple of blocks from the Dover Street house. Casieri had posted blown-up copies of Marciano family photos on the bare walls of the house to guide him in his labors, each picture showing members of the family in the room under renovation. The most important one was a shot of Rocky's mother overseeing her son as he ate spaghetti. Casieri had mounted it between the windows in the kitchen, just where he figured the table had been at which Rocky ate his meals a half century earlier. The point of the house as a memorial to Marciano was to show how the totality of a way of life built around shoemaking and the foundational virtues of the urban village, a way of life with echoes in Casieri's own family history, had produced its own unbeatable champion. "My father cut leather his whole life," said Casieri. "Rocky's father did that. That's what made Rocky: hard work, good food, and respect. And he stayed in training."

It is not enough to be good with your hands; you also have to be in condition to go the distance. Rocky Marciano, who famously trained for the long haul, embodied that home truth in life and retains at least some of his potency as a historical figure over the still-longer haul of posterity. Many people in Brockton do not care about him one way or the other, but some still do—as attested to by the patterns of local resistance and support, not just apathy, inspired by Patricia Johanson's Marciano-centered master plan for Brockton. Marciano's memory can still shape the working and imaginative lives of people as different from one another as Johanson and Casieri and Mayor Yunits, and it can still play a significant role in ongoing efforts to articulate the consequences of the city's past and the possibilities of its future. Like the epic hero Roland, who can be roused from his tomb by a call to defend France once more against the Moors or other invaders, Marciano can be invoked in difficult times. He stands for a way of life associated with places like Brockton and with spectacles like those afforded by the fight world, in which industrial urbanism took archetypal American forms. More often than one might think, talking about Rocky Marciano overlaps with talking about the industrial working class, especially (but not exclusively) that large element of it once constituted by immigrants from Europe who flocked to American cities in the nineteenth and early twentieth centuries. Culture, like the built landscape, is not always as liquid as capital. The manufacturing economy may no longer provide the primary material basis of working-class life in places like Brockton, as it did from the latter part of the nineteenth century until the latter part of the twentieth, but that era's legacy still gives meaning to the landscape, daily life, and struggles to determine what happens after the mills close. Talking about Marciano can be a way to talk about what has been gained and lost in the long, slow aging-out of industrial urbanism—which may explain why he seems to haunt present-day Brockton as it navigates the postindustrial crossroads. Part tutelary deity and part restless ghost, Rocky floats ectoplasmically through a changing social and cultural landscape that is both continuous with his world and increasingly alienated from it.

A Rocky proposal

CHAMP'S HOUSE: Patricia Johanson plans to turn Rocky Marciano's boarded-up boyhood home in Brockton into a living museum on the legendary fighter, below. *Staff photo by Mark Garfinkel*

She's making a museum of Marciano's old house

By JACK SULLIVAN

A world-renowned urban design artist, who couldn't tell a jab from an uppercut, has bought Rocky Marciano's condemned boyhood home in Brockton and plans to turn it into a free "living museum" dedicated to the undefeated heavyweight champion.

"Rocky is really the quintessential American hero," said Patricia Johanson, who was so moved after reading Marciano's biography she purchased the boarded-up house to save it from being gutted.

"We should honor Rocky, his family and all the people who grew up in Brockton. Rocky is the theme that connected everything in Brockton."

Johanson, brought in by a state grant to develop a beautification and cleanup program for the decaying city, has also proposed the "Rocky Marciano Trail." It would be Brockton's equivalent to the Freedom Trail and would connect schools, buildings and parks that Marciano frequented during his years in Brockton.

Peter Marciano Jr., said yesterday his family is glad the house where "Uncle Rock

Turn to Page 18

Patricia Johanson, the Marciano house, and Rocky on the front page of the *Boston Herald*, May 28, 1998. Reprinted with permission of the *Boston Herald*.

A HARD WORKER

In Brockton, one of several small cities scattered in an irregular arc around Boston that were once famous for their industrial production, some older residents still remember Rocky Marciano running through the streets. Few fighters have been as closely identified with their hometowns. It is generally understood in some less-than-precise way that Brockton made Marciano, hardening him for the work of prizefighting and inculcating the fundamentals of toughness so deeply that not even the celebrity and fortune he enjoyed as champion could tempt him to lapse from the faith. Only after he retired from boxing did he slacken, spending his last years in almost constant gratis travel to Las Vegas, Cuba, and anywhere else he could find free lunch and action; and it is fitting that he died far from home during one of his many leisure junkets. If gaining a livelihood through hard work goes together with Brockton in the Marciano story, it makes sense that idle hands and aimless play (and, finally, an early grave) should go together with Marciano's seeming compulsion to be away from Brockton once he retired and fell out of training.

As a fighter, Marciano enacted local virtues on the international stage. He was not big, quick, or slick, but he was canny in his apparent crudeness, and he outworked, outpunched, and outlasted everybody he fought. His style of constant attack was founded on a confidence that the other man could not match Marciano's conditioning, the details of which have acquired a kind of golden myth-historical burnish in collective memory: shoveling off the backyard of his parents' house at 168 Dover Street in midwinter to work the homemade heavy bag hanging from a tree; punching underwater in the pool at the YMCA to build power without becoming muscle-bound; sparring with anyone who had nerve enough to mix it up with a man who did not know how to pull his punches; taking daily ten- and fifteen-mile walks that he believed made him hardier than other men; taking twenty- and thirty-plus-mile walks to Quincy and Providence just for the joy of feeling his own inexhaustibility; and running, obsessively running miles and miles every day, sometimes tossing a football with his pal Allie Colombo as they ran, through the streets of Brockton. They went past the modest houses and three-deckers that housed the city's workers, past the brick and wood-frame factory buildings that once housed a significant portion of the American shoe industry, past larger houses built for managers and industrialists, past the edge of town into the green landscape of the Olmsted-style park named for shoe magnate and philanthropist D. W. Field.

Those who believe Rocky Marciano to be the greatest of all time, a significant proportion of whom feel the same way about Frank Sinatra, will not listen to the usual counterarguments: Marciano was too small and too slow, the undeniably great fighters he beat were also all over the hill, wiseguys took a suspiciously enthusiastic interest in his success, and so on. As a rule, Americans overrate both victory and perfection—especially in boxers, who can be made smarter and more resourceful in the ring by a measured dose of defeat—but Marciano's professional record of forty-nine victories without a loss has become something more than a statistic. It encases the fact of him in a field of still-potent magic. He was indeed short for heavyweight (5′11″), stubby-armed (compare his sixty-eight-inch reach with, say, Ali's eighty-two-inch reach), slope-shouldered, not particularly quick for a fighter, and, because he invested his balance and leverage so completely in the punches he threw, given to swinging and missing with exaggerated wildness. One can imagine a bigger, quicker, more conventionally sophisticated boxer making him pay for those liabilities and beating him. But that never quite happened, and he did beat everybody worth fighting in his era—including all-time greats Joe Louis and Archie Moore, talented champions Ezzard Charles (twice) and Jersey Joe Walcott (twice), and fellow rising star Roland La Starza (twice)—so it is hard to imagine Marciano as anything other than victorious.

None of his peers in the first rank of heavyweight champions, even those who might plausibly get the best of him in a hypothetical match of the two fighters in their primes, has a similar aura of perfection. Jack Johnson lost most famously to Jess Willard, a giant stiff, and the blemish taints Johnson's record whether or not he faked the defeat. Jack Dempsey moidalized Willard, but he got two boxing lessons from Gene Tunney, long count or no long count. Joe Louis, who held the title longer than anyone and often gets experts' vote for the greatest heavyweight of all time, was knocked out early in his career by Max Schmeling, and, during his comeback, by Marciano, who belted him through the ropes and into retirement. Sonny Liston's invincibility collapsed when he encountered Muhammad Ali, whose heart-stopping quickness and confidence tapped the lode of toxic bad feeling deep within Liston. In 1971, Ali himself stopped being perfect forever—and, by weathering the first of several life-changing beatings, thereby commenced to win the hearts and minds of those who despised him in the 1960s—when one of Joe Frazier's left hooks broke his jaw and put him on the seat of his pants. Larry Holmes beat a faded Ali, just as Marciano beat a faded Louis, but Holmes was still only 48–0, one short of Marciano's record, when he lost the first of two close and inconclusive fights by suspect decision to Michael Spinks, after which Holmes was beaten by Mike Tyson, Evander Holyfield, and others during a series of comebacks that extended into his fifties and the new century.[1]

Marciano won a couple of close decisions that might have gone the other way, he got cut up sometimes, and he could look loutish when sharper boxers made him miss and then hit him with counters, but he wore down every opponent he faced. Mostly because of one celebrated victory—in which he flattened Jersey Joe Walcott with a short right cross in the thirteenth round after Walcott, the reigning champion, had thoroughly outboxed him and was far ahead on points—Marciano is remembered as a one-punch knockout artist. The standard portrait has him toiling on through a barrage of his opponent's blows, relying on magnificent conditioning and sheer fighting character to bear him up under terrific punishment, in the hope of delivering the dramatic equalizer. This describes to a tee the style of Rocky Balboa, hero of the *Rocky* movie cycle, but when applied to Marciano it is wrong, or at least the emphasis is wrong.[2] Marciano was superbly conditioned, and he did have a remarkable chin—an amalgam of physiology, preparation, and an intangible quality of will and fighting sensibility one might as well call character—but he won bouts by the steady, long-term, almost drudging application of force. He fought on the perpetual advance, bent forward at the waist and tilted to one side in a crablike crouch that made him deceptively hard to hit for a slow, offense-minded fighter. That advance was usually careful rather than hell-for-leather, at least until he got in range to throw his celebrated overhand right (the "Susie Q" punch), left hooks, and less easily classified punches. Marciano was not a one-punch-and-out belter like Earnie Shavers or George Foreman, both of whom tended to tire in later rounds; rather, he threw an enormous number of heavy blows, round after round, keeping his work rate high and steady as the bout wore on. Most of those punches hit nonlethal targets like his opponent's gloves or arms or shoulders, or missed entirely, but they cumulatively drained energy from a man and prevented him from conducting his own sustained offensive fight. Pushing and mauling his opponent in the clinches, Marciano used his compact body—big legs, thick torso, low center of gravity—to the same draining effect.

Most of the men Marciano knocked out were spent from coping with that extended application of force—and, in coping with it, had been prevented from devoting themselves to beating up Marciano—by the time he actually nailed them flush with the punch or three that put them down. That is true of Joe Louis and Archie Moore, two wise old masters who started out well against him but did not last the distance. It is even true of Walcott, who was clearly beating Marciano before getting caught with that famous right cross in the thirteenth round, but who was also at least thirty-eight years old and had expended much of himself in lambasting the younger man and fending off his constant attack.

"Marciano was a hard worker," Wilbert "Skeeter" McClure told me over lunch one day in August 2000, and he meant it as the highest praise one can give to a fighter. "He could take a lot of pain and, no matter what, he kept punching. One of the things that made him unique in the history of boxing is that he would punch the arms on purpose, whatever he could hit, and hurt you so bad you couldn't use them." McClure, a fine middleweight of the 1950s and 1960s, said that his trainer had been in Archie Moore's corner when Moore fought Marciano in 1955. During that fight, Moore set a clever trap for Marciano and dropped him with a counterpunch in the second round, but Marciano bounced up and resumed his systematic pounding of the older man. "My trainer told me that Archie came back to the corner between rounds and said, 'I can't go on, my arms are too bruised up, they don't work.' And they just told him, 'Then go out like a champ.'" Moore got by mostly on wit and sand until the ninth, when Marciano clubbed him down for the count.

McClure and I were sitting over the remains of our meal in the Ground Round at Cleveland Circle in Boston. Even though the place was semideserted at an off-hour, the waitress kept coming back to ask if we wanted anything else, silently urging us to move on, but McClure likes to talk, and he does not like to be pushed around. A trim fellow of advanced middle years who sports the soup-strainer mustache favored by many of New England's older he-men, he has seen and done plenty of boxing over the last half century. He had a glorious amateur career, culminating in a gold medal at the 1960 Olympics, where he was a teammate of the young Cassius Clay. As a professional, McClure held his own in good company—although the record books state that he lost a split decision to Hurricane Carter and then earned a draw in the rematch, he says, "I beat Hurricane Carter both times, and he knows it"—but he blames bad business decisions and crooked management for limiting his chances at a title. He enjoyed general acclaim for his efforts to clean up and professionalize the seedy Massachusetts Boxing Commission when Governor William Weld put him in charge of it in the 1990s, although in the end political cronies of Weld's successor, Paul Cellucci, squeezed him out.

A self-identified "serious educational conservative" (he holds a doctorate in psychology and has a consulting business), McClure preaches discipline and order to reverse the pandemic decline, moral and pugilistic, he sees all around him. For him, Marciano totemically embodies a dying ethic of virtuous toughness, based in work, that McClure imbibed from birth. McClure, who is black, grew up in Toledo, far from Marciano's Italian neighborhood in Brockton, but a mill city is a mill city. Once we got to discussing the current crop of heavyweights, McClure stated his firm belief that Marciano would have slaughtered them all. "Athletes of today can't compare to ones in the past," he said, with feeling. "The old gyms produced tougher men. Not necessarily better boxers, but tougher. Fighters of my generation and before led hardscrabble lives, they were tough men who led tough lives, and they knew that struggle is good for you. They weren't in it for fame and big money. Boxing is so full of shit these days." McClure cited his father as a modest representative of the old school. "He worked in a foundry pouring steel, and then on the line at Ford Motor Company. That's what everybody did in Toledo. If they needed a fighter, he could get up out of a crowd, borrow gear, fight some guy on the card whose opponent didn't show up. I've met several men of his era like that. You could make twenty-five dollars a night. That was a lot of money back in the Depression." Even Skeeter's entry into the fight world as a boy had something to do with work. "When I was twelve years old, my friends took me to a gym above a union hall, Larry and Al's Gym. When the door opened, it opened a whole new world for me."

McClure had worked up to a summation. "That's my theory of vocational development: geography is destiny. I was afraid to grow up because I didn't want to do this hard work that my father did, and then I found the gym." Geography is destiny in the sense that Toledo, like Brockton, was the kind of industrial city in which a kid like McClure would be both inspired to look for alternatives to the shopfloor and likely to happen upon a gym.

A few days later, I met a couple of old-timers in Brockton who assured me that Rocky Marciano, too, wanted nothing to do with the grinding labor that undergirded the local working-class ethic of toughness. "He detested any kind of work, he really did," said Joe Fedele, who hung out with Marciano when they both were young. "It's true," added Anthony "Snap" Tartaglia, who dug ditches with Marciano for the gas company. "Deep down," said Snap, "I don't think he even liked to fight." Snap should know. He carried the bucket for Marciano in the early days, before professional trainers in New York took over his corner, and even sparred with the future champ. "I'm the only one who ever broke his nose," he said. "I did it with my head." The steady stream of boxers who came (and, in greatly reduced numbers, still come) out of blue-collar cities, heroes who still exemplify those cities in the popular imagination, often fought not because they loved to fight but because they would do anything rather than lock themselves into the factory life to which their parents, siblings, and friends had committed. "Anything" meant anything they were good at, especially anything that exploited the physical competence, the fetish for uncomplaining resilience, and the willingness to endure repetitive drudgery inculcated by life in such places. So, once upon a time, when boxing had greater prominence and institutional purchase in American life, "anything" often meant boxing. In particular, Snap and Fedele stressed, Marciano made it plain that he would rather fight than work in Brockton's shoe factories, where his father and other men of the neighborhood were employed. Seeing the factories' effect on them, plus a brief taste of the work for himself, was plenty. Marciano's biographer, Everett Skehan, reports that Izzy Gold, another old friend, said, "The Rock lasted less than two months in the shoe factory." Marciano told Gold he could not get the smell of leather or the noise of the machines out of his head, and that his food even tasted like leather. "I don't know how our fathers can stand it," Rocky said. "Imagine if you had to do this the rest of your life." [3]

I was sitting with Joe Fedele, Snap Tartaglia, and Charlie Tartaglia, Snap's nephew, in a booth in George's Cafe, near the old Marciano house. Charlie, current proprietor of George's Cafe (and a member of the state boxing commission, appointed by Skeeter McClure), had convened Fedele and Snap to talk about the old days with me. The two older men, senior-division Italian neighborhood guys of a type you can still find throughout urban America, were members of the small flying squad of Marciano survivors, ready to meet with writers, television crews, and anybody else interested in Brockton's most celebrated native son. "There might be ten people left here who knew Rocky," estimated Fedele, meaning people in town who knew Marciano when he was a kid, when he was poor, when he first won some fights in Providence and then in New York against regional bruisers like Bobby Quinn and Carmine Vingo, before Marciano became a national and then an international figure. When Marciano fought regularly in Providence in the late 1940s, he would meet his cornermen at George's Cafe before the bout for the drive to the venue. The following day, the victorious crew would gather there again to discuss it; Allie Colombo would smoke a cigar and read the sports section of the *Providence Journal*. Fedele and Snap, who were part of that crew, were still talking the talk fifty-plus years later. They lamented the passing of the Ward 2 clubhouse and reminisced about long-forgotten fighters. "Remember the *built* on him?" said Fedele. "Hey," said Snap, reminded of nice builts of yesteryear, "remember Vingo's girlfriend? *What* a *doll* she *was*."

"There was no real money in the business in those days," Charlie Tartaglia said. "It was TV that brought that all on." That got them talking about Rocky's shortsighted but passionate business sense. "He was a Depression baby," said Snap (or a Depression child, anyway—Marciano was born in 1923), "and they were poor, poorer than people knew. He would do *anything* for $500 in cash." The fellows told stories about Marciano's cash-centered fiscal imagination: his unwillingness to accept checks, even going so far as to take less money for a fight if he could get it in cash; the time, in latter years, that he forgot $20,000 worth of government bonds under the mattress of a hotel room; the time that he fought and won hours after walking away from a wreck that totaled the car in which he was riding and ejected Snap and Snap's brother George, the driver, onto the pavement. The purse on that icy evening in 1948 was $500.

Marciano may have detested the idea of a steady job, they agreed, but he had a poor boy's eye for money and a Brocktonian work ethic. "I always thought he was overtrained," said Snap, "but then he never could have beat Walcott if he wasn't so strong." Fedele added, "For fitness, he was a fanatic," to which Snap appended, delicately, "When Rocky trained, women . . . well, he was completely . . . Rocky didn't believe in that at all. Other fighters have sex right before a fight." Something about that awkward little discussion of diligence paired with masculine self-denial opened a floodgate of nostalgia. Those were the good old days, the fellows told me. There was no theft, people left their doors unlocked, everybody came out in the street to play, to do business, to talk to the neighbors. There was no television or air-conditioning to keep people indoors, no Little League and no big business in sports to take the elemental fun out of hard play. When Rocky was fighting, thousands

of people would gather downtown to follow the radio reports and celebrate together. You knew your neighbors then, but now? "Drugs," said
Charlie Tartaglia, "are the ruination of this country." Fedele nodded
and said, "Oh, what they've done to this country." But drugs were just
a symptom, Charlie explained. "It's a different city. There's only one
factory left—FootJoy, best golf shoes in the world. There's twenty
thousand Cape Verdeans. It's a different city." Snap, who had been
quiet for a while, added, "Back then, everybody we knew was poor. We
didn't think anything of it because nobody was different. I remember
Rocky delivered papers in the winter in his gym shoes with holes in
them. He was poorer than people thought." That seemed to settle it;
they all nodded, satisfied.

But, it turned out, Brockton had not changed completely since Marciano's time. The discussion of training, poverty, and the fights led them
naturally to the city's other champion for the ages, Marvelous Marvin
Hagler, the premier middleweight of the 1980s. Hagler ran on the
streets of Brockton, too, and covered the city's name with glory in the
ring. Combining a Marciano-like taste for concussion with a more classically elegant boxing style, Hagler held the title for almost seven years,
winning celebrated victories over Roberto Duran, Thomas Hearns, and
John "The Beast" Mugabi, among other formidable opponents, before
losing a highly debatable split decision to media darling Sugar Ray
Leonard. Hagler is neither Italian nor homegrown—he is black, and
he moved to Brockton from Newark in his teens, mostly because his
mother wanted to get him away from inner-city dangers—but the old-
timers at George's Cafe regarded him as exemplifying the qualities that
Brockton traditionally held most dear in Marciano and its men in general, be they white, black, or otherwise. Hagler retired from the ring in
1987 and left Brockton in the early 1990s. He lives in Italy, pursuing a
career in action movies. "He says he still runs up in the Alps, though,"
said Charlie Tartaglia, "and he's married to an Italian girl now. He still
comes back to visit sometimes. Marvin's a regular guy. I knew him back
when he was carrying hod for the Petronelli brothers." Goody and Pat
Petronelli, who operated a local gym, trained and managed Hagler
throughout his career; they also had a construction business, for which
Hagler worked before he made it big. "Marvin was in here to visit a few
months ago," said Charlie. "I told him, 'Remember when I saw you
down in West Bridgewater carrying hod?' and he said to me, 'These kids
today sign for $2 million up front. They don't carry no hod.'"

Especially among men of a certain age, discussions of Marciano and
his kind keep finding their way back to carrying hod, digging ditches,

or working on the line in a factory—to the forms and meanings of working-class life in industrial Brockton, or Toledo, or places like them. They keep finding their way back to the way things used to be, and to the changing world's tendency to pull the rug out from under regular guys like Snap, Joe, Charlie, Skeeter, Marvin, and even Rocky, low center of gravity and all, had he only lived long enough. He would have been seventy-seven in 2000.

BOOSTERS

Mark Casieri wanted me to appreciate and understand Brockton, to see its quiet greatness. Before we went for a tour of the city, though, I had to see the interior of the old Marciano house. First he had to gather his three dogs—a pair of classically proportioned, handsomely parti-colored brothers named Biggi and Charger, and their mother, Angel, who was fat enough to be almost tubular. "These are gentle pit bulls," he said as they swarmed around. Having seen the brothers splinter a thick branch in their mouths and growl menacingly at a girl who tossed a rolled-up circular onto the porch of the house next door ("They don't like it when people throw things," Casieri explained), I was not rushing into the dogs' embrace. Still, they had checked me out thoroughly from shoes to crotch when I arrived, and after an initial hazing they had decided to stop bristling at me, so I was no longer seized with a nearly uncontrollable urge to flinch every time they came near. "I got the mother from Mo Vaughn," Casieri told me with pride. Vaughn used to play first base and drive in runs for the Boston Red Sox. Casieri nudged Angel with his foot and she rolled over obligingly to show a tattoo, "Vaughn 42," on the bald pink skin of her underside. "Mo Vaughn lived around here. He used to hang out at George's. He gave Angel and the father to me when he went to Anaheim." Casieri told me later in the day that the dogs bedded down with him every afternoon: a heap of sleeping bruisers, resting up in the late afternoon and evening hours until midnight brought the start of another workday.

We went through the house, to which the Marchegianos moved in 1939, when Rocky was sixteen. (He changed the spelling of the family name to simplify matters of publicity when he began to rise in the fight world.) Walking through with Casieri, looking past the current dilapidation and mess to the way it was, I could imagine the density of family life—the parents, Pierino and Pasqualena, and their children, Rocco, Alice, Connie, Elizabeth, Louis, and later Peter. Casieri showed me the work he had been doing, preliminary but meaningful measures to re-turn a period feel to a building that had been renovated, acquired by a public housing agency, renovated again, occupied by various tenants, and then abandoned and allowed to fall into partial ruin before Patricia Johanson bought it. She had hired a contractor to do basic structural re-pairs to keep the house from falling down, but Casieri had begun at-tending to details. "See how this doorsill fits perfectly? I found it at the dump, didn't have to change a thing, it just drops right into the spot. Must have been made for a house like this." He had been rubbish pick-ing for months to collect items for the house. "I look in the Italian neighborhoods and the old Lithuanian village. I love the furniture, it's beautiful, and it still smells like when you visited your aunt's. Now, see this door? That's an old-school door, with the boards going across like this. The new ones, I just strip them for porcelain and glass doorknobs, but otherwise they're no good. But this door, this is old-school. Feel how heavy. Go ahead, open it. See how beautiful it swings? That means it's hung just right." He had secured a promise from Izzy Gold, Rocky's childhood friend, to touch up the mural of a fishing scene Gold painted long ago in the front entrance. And the kitchen was taking shape: Casieri had retrieved a glass door from the basement, he had wheedled a vintage Philco refrigerator from his family, and his scavenging had turned up a suitably populuxe wall clock and a ring-shaped fluorescent overhead light fixture. They were exactly the kinds of things I would have expected to see in my Sicilian grandmother's house in Queens. So, too, was the chipped, paint-spattered statuette of a saint posted on a windowsill in the bedroom. "I found that down cellar, too," he said.

"I'm placing things in the house now," he explained, "that show how it's gonna be when it's a museum, where the plaques will go. And I use the pictures to figure out how it was." He had talked with the Mar-ciano siblings who still lived in the area, and with family friends of the Marcianos, but he also studied the pictures to figure out *exactly* how things had been arranged. From them he had determined, for instance, that every December the family had moved its RCA Victor cabinet out of the front room to make space for the Christmas tree. He had figured out what the original windows had been like, before the latter-day in-stallation of a picture window. He wanted to restore the old windows and to have "the nice doily things hanging, like they used to have." The pictures themselves, suitably framed, would become exhibits in the mu-seum. Some were taken by professionals, especially Stanley Bauman, the local photographer who began documenting Rocky Marciano's life

"I want to restore it to the way things were when Rocky lived here. I want people to see where he came from and what it was like."
MARK CASIERI

Mark Casieri of Brockton checks an old photograph showing a detail of Rocky Marciano's Dover Street home in the 1950s.

Marciano's boyhood home lovingly restored

■ A city resident who purchased the late heavyweight champ's 168 Dover St. home estimates repairs will cost him $60,000.

By Nikki Vamosi
ENTERPRISE SPECIAL CORRESPONDENT

BROCKTON — Mark Casieri says he was mesmerized as a child by the boxing career of hometown hero Rocky Marciano.

Today, the 39-year-old city resident is channeling his respect for the late heavyweight champ into a restoration project at Marciano's boyhood home at 168 Dover St.

"I want to restore it to the way things were when Rocky lived here," Casieri said. "I want people to see where he came from and what it was like."

Casieri, who works for the post office, is purchasing the run-down homestead from environmental artist Patricia Johanson of New York for $75,000. Johanson changed her mind about restoring the house herself, he said.

He will officially become the new

Mark Casieri paints the new porch rails as he works to restore the two-story original home of Rocky Marciano to its former status.

ingly collecting 1950s household paraphernalia in addition to using authentic Marciano furniture found in the base-

and other locations frequented by Marciano.

"The (Rocky) trail is still in the talk-

Mark Casieri's (illegal) renovation of the Marciano house on the front page of the Brockton *Enterprise*'s local section. Reprinted with permission of the Enterprise Publishing Company.

long before anybody outside Brockton knew who Marciano was. Some of the pictures were family snaps, like the photo of Rocky's mother and sister that he had found in a locket in the basement. He had the picture blown up and mounted it on the wall in the kitchen, which was turning into a memorial to strong women. In addition to the locket picture, and the picture of Rocky eating spaghetti under his mother's supervision, he had also put up a picture of Patricia Johanson posing next to a cheetah, a shot taken in 1996 when she was working on a park in Nairobi. We looked at Johanson, slim and fair among the blocky, dark-haired Marcianos. "Patricia, she's my hero," he said. "That's where her plaque is going to go, right here in the kitchen," a place of honor. "She's the best, the best thing that happened to Rocky around here in a long time. She's so intelligent and she has a nice even voice, very refined. Doesn't she remind you of Janet Reno?"

Casieri had committed himself to the house; there was no turning back. "You can't have your own feelings in this," he said in a reflective moment. "It's about history; this is forever. I'm a bag of nerves about the whole thing." Johanson had warned him that people would turn on him, as they had turned on her. "She did everything she was supposed to do," he said, shaking his head, "and the city turned on her. They brought *her* in; they went and got *her*. She told me, 'They're going to turn on you at city hall.'" Casieri still hopefully counted Johanson as a friend and supporter, but he felt increasingly alone in a difficult world. City hall would not give him what he needed; his local friends wished him well but tended to disappear when there was heavy lifting to do at the house; mortgage brokers kept assuring him he was in good shape and then denying him a loan; and even Johanson, despite being his hero, might not like the fact that he was working on her property on the sly. "She's turned it over to me," he told me, as if wishing had made it so, but that was true only in spirit, if at all.

Casieri had done what he could, even attending evening classes at Brockton High for landlords and homeowners—"I missed my bowling night for *eight weeks*"—but he was caught up in the play of larger forces, and he could place complete confidence only in his own two hands. "I don't have control over the loan or politics or anything like that," he told me. "What I do have control over is making this house right. I can't complete a whole city project like Patricia, but I can lock in and complete this—the way it used to be, clapboards and everything." He could lock in on the house, but the house itself was in limbo.

When we were done looking at the house, we got into Casieri's big old Grand Marquis and went for a ride. He had the air-conditioning cranked all the way up and the windows wide open; the dogs in the backseat took turns breathing their hot pit bull breath on the back of my neck. We visited the stations of the cross in Marciano's Brockton: the house on Brook Street in which Rocky lived as a small child; George's Cafe; Petti's Market; the brick house on Harlan Circle that Rocky and his wife, Barbara, bought when they got married; Saint Patrick's Church; and the Hickey-Grenier Funeral Home, where Rocky was waked. Casieri noted as we drove by that Hickey's was not the appropriate funeral home for one of Brockton's Italians, who were waked at Pica's. "Barbara had him waked at the wrong place and buried in Florida"—clearly, also, the wrong place to inter one of the Rust Belt's most exquisite corpses. "She didn't get along with the family," he said, which explained these lapses from tradition.

Our tour of Marciano landmarks turned into a tour of the city. It was hot; people were out. We went through neighborhoods where kids were playing on the sidewalks, enjoying the last days before the start of school. There were plenty of young men and women on the streets, too, hanging out on stoops or leaning on parked cars and watching Casieri's slow-cruising Grand Marquis from the moment it came into view until it disappeared. A too-big guy on a too-small bike—a common sight in Brockton—wheeled by at close range, appraising the big fellow at the wheel, his pit bulls, and the gent in specs in the shotgun seat. We did not appear to be cops, not with the dogs aboard, and we could have been potential customers for the street corner drug trade that did business on a couple of the blocks we passed through. "It's not as bad as it was a few years ago," Casieri said to me, exchanging stony but cordial looks with local characters as we rolled past them, "but I still call the police to report crack dealers whenever I see them, which is pretty much every day."

Brockton is your basic mill city, situated in southeastern Massachusetts within a triangle formed by Boston, Providence, and Plymouth. Its population of just under one hundred thousand is a mix of white ethnics (descendants of the Irish, Italians, French, Swedes, Greeks, Lithuanians, Poles, European Jews, and others who came to Brockton in large numbers before 1920), blacks, Puerto Ricans and other Hispanics, and fast-growing numbers of "new" immigrants: Haitians and others from the Caribbean, Hmong and other Southeast Asians, and especially Portuguese speakers from Cape Verde. The mayor's Comprehensive Policy Plan describes contemporary Brockton as "evolving from a self-contained but declining industrial city to a retail/services/medical/educational resource for its own region."[4] The city's signature enterprise was shoemaking, which began as a cottage industry, boomed as a factory-based industry during the Civil War and after, and began to contract in the 1920s under pressure from competitive Mississippi Valley producers, the proliferation of shoe styles, and management's unwillingness to do business with strong unions—challenges that defeated the collective imagination of the city's increasingly hidebound captains of industry. In 1899, 91 of Brockton's 431 factories made shoes, and many of the others produced related goods such as nails, blacking, models, patterns, and shoemaking machinery. William L. Douglas and his competitor George Keith (whose company made the higher-priced "Walk-Over" shoes) were Brockton's biggest names in shoe production, heading a list that included Churchill and Alden, Snow, Field, Stacy-Adams, Packard, Taylor, and Eaton. The shoe factories alone employed more than fifteen thousand workers in 1909, perhaps the local shoe industry's peak year; in 1964, there were ten shoe factories employing about two thousand workers; at century's end, there was just FootJoy.[5] Many factory buildings and warehouses have been torn down, but survivors still cluster along the old industrial corridor that runs north-south through the center of the city, paralleling Main Street and the raised embankment of the main rail line. The older residential neighborhoods spread out east and west of the core, sited within walking distance of the mills and composed largely of wood-frame, multifamily houses. The neighborhoods developed after World War II, by contrast, tend to feature single-family slab houses and strip-style commercial zones. More affluent suburbs and towns surround Brockton, which, in addition to having produced a disproportionately high number of notoriously fierce athletes, is home to a disproportionately high percentage of Plymouth County's hospitals, government services, manufacturing, nonwhite residents, poverty, crime, and potentially exploitable urban texture.

In Brockton at the turn of the twenty-first century, there is some question about whether the city needs to invoke its traditional champions now, when it has consciously reached the postindustrial crossroads at last. On the one hand, an emphasis on Brockton's heroic history of body work—exemplified by shoemaking, Hagler, and especially Marciano—could provide not only a hook to attract interest from the region and beyond but also a guiding impulse of cultural continuity in a time of disorienting change. Brockton will find its way to renewed prosperity by valuing hard work and productivity, as always, and by selling itself as the home of such traditional virtues, even if the nature of the work and the workers must change in an era of high-tech production, a

service economy, and new immigrants. And if cultural tourism and a calculated celebration of local history have to become part of the business
equation in Brockton, as they have in other former mill cities like Lowell or New Bedford, then Brockton can call once more upon the hard-
working shoemakers and fighters who put it on the map in the first
place.

On the other hand, Marciano might be part of the problem to the
extent that an aggressively orthodox insistence on the industrial past
and its legacies contributes to Brockton's failure to come to terms with
a new urban era. The city's new-order boosters feel that Brockton needs
a new identity that relegates its incarnations as a shoemaking center and
City of Champions (the official municipal epithet) to historical quaintness. In their view, Brockton must shed or denature its traditionally forbidding aura of working-class toughness, especially because over the last
couple of generations that aura has modulated into a dead-end reputation typical of depressed Rust Belt cities. A tendency among the state's
television and print media to confine their reporting on Brockton to
drug-related murders and contact sports has helped the city to become
identified with insular backwardness, violence, and a dynastic high
school football program that manages paradoxically to make the city
look like a loser by winning. Armond Colombo, cousin of the late Allie
Colombo and husband of Rocky Marciano's sister Betty, has for three-
plus decades coached the black-clad Brockton Boxers (the team used to
be called the Shoe Makers), who reinforce the city's image as Tough
Town, USA, every time they take to the field in Rocky Marciano Stadium to crush the scions of less atavistically gritty communities. "I always thought that Brockton was something special," Colombo told an
interviewer in 1989. "There was a mystique about the Brockton athlete,
a Rocky-type athlete—tough, strong, hard-working, great determination." Colombo added that, in his opinion, "the three things Brockton
is known for are one, Rocky Marciano; two, Marvin Hagler; and three,
Brockton High football."[6]

In 2001, the principal of Brockton's Champion Charter School enjoyed a brief run as number four on that list when word got out that he
had taken two feuding teenage boys into the school's basement, told
them to remove their shoes and jewelry, and let them duke it out until
they were spent, at which point he declared a draw and had them shake
hands. The story went national, touching off a debate about the relative merits of old-school discipline ("He's a barbarian" versus "Hey, nobody got shot and the kids learned a lesson"). The story also tore off

any scabs that might have been forming on Brockton's bloody-knuckled civic persona.[7]

New-order boosters want to play down Brockton's reputation for competence in body work and associated violence, cultivating instead a forward-looking image to attract businesses and homeowners to an affordable city conveniently close to Boston. The costs of living and doing business in Boston—New England's capital of high-tech business, research, and education—had gotten so high by century's end that looking for bargains in the region made good sense. Brockton's reasonably priced single-family housing and loft buildings awaited exploitation, as did its underpaid workers and surprisingly good schools (surprising, that is, to those who believe what they see on the television news), and its convenient commuter rail connection to Boston's South Station, only half an hour away. A reputation less dominated by leather and a fetish for hard knocks might help attract interest in Brockton's assets.

Jack Yunits, mayor of Brockton and leader of the new-order boosters, felt torn between old and new. "Honest to God," he told me when I went to see him in September 2000, "I love the history of Brockton as much as anybody, particularly the blue-collar stuff, but it's *history*. They buried the horses and wagons a long time ago." We were sitting in his office in Brockton's city hall, a stately Richardsonian pile built in the 1890s. On the way to the mayor's office, I had passed through a grand hallway lined with the city's collection of Civil War paintings: huge, murky canvases depicting battles on land and sea, officers and drummer boys, the 54th Massachusetts swarming over the rampart of Fort Wagner, allegories of War and Peace featuring ivory-limbed women striking midair poses with flowing garments askew. History and martial vigor matter here; so does the fact that the soldiers in the paintings could plausibly be assumed to be wearing locally produced shoes. In the suite of rooms that constitutes the mayor's office, a sign welcomed visitors to the City of Champions. I felt Rocky's ghost brush past me when, walking through the office, I literally stumbled over a poster-sized shot of a downtown victory parade for Marciano that was propped against a desk.

Mayor Yunits, a personable fellow with the energy of a good salesman and an anchorman's abundance of sculpted hair, knew that Brockton had to adjust to a changing world. "America doesn't make things anymore," he said, "not like they used to. We're more of a facilitator now." He envisioned a very different Brockton, suited to that change in function, taking shape around us: a center for services; a green, pleasant bedroom community and "feeder city" for Boston; a regional cen-

A crowd on Main Street in downtown Brockton welcomes Rocky Marciano home in 1956. Photo: © Stanley A. Bauman.

ter for sports, museums, theater, and other attractions that would draw people from the neighborhoods and the surrounding area to downtown Brockton once more.

Downtown was the key. "Five years ago, it was a dump," the mayor admitted, and it was still relatively stark during the day and desolate at night, but downtown had begun to change, and he had big plans for it. "We're doing a lot of the right things," he said, including putting up better signs and otherwise improving the approaches to downtown by car; returning two-way traffic flow to Main Street (the Avenue of Champions); clarifying zoning laws to allow a mix of residents to liven up a depressed business district; opening new schools and a new courthouse; wooing high-tech companies; starting up a trolley service (buses, really, but cloaked in quaintness); solving the city's perennial water shortage to allow further development; and "greening" the long-abused Salisbury Brook. He dreamed of filling some of downtown's redbrick industrial building stock with Internet or other high-tech businesses and urban-hipster residents—artists, especially. These sexy pioneers would then help to attract other businesses and residents, who in turn would help to attract grocery stores, banks, restaurants, movie theaters, coffeehouses, and brew pubs ("We *need* one of those," he insisted), all of which in turn would attract and be supported by visitors from the neighborhoods, the region, and beyond.

Tourism in the traditional sense was not a significant part of this plan, but the city would have to be marketed to its own residents and to the region as a place to live, work, and visit. "If I were mayor of New Bedford," Yunits said, "tourism would be really important and central, but not in Brockton. We're not a destination." But, he added, "People will need to have a great impression of Brockton," and as part of constructing such an impression a tourist-friendly makeover would be necessary, "so tourism will be an enhancement." What, besides a revived downtown, did Brockton have to offer in this regard? Its history, mostly, and here we encountered familiar figures: Rocky Marciano, Shoe City, the City of Champions. The city planned a historical walking trail based on Marciano's running route, and there were plans to put up three statues. One would be a long-discussed statue of Marciano. One would commemorate the thirteen firemen who died when the roof of Brockton's Strand Theater collapsed during a fire in 1941. As I had noted when dining out in Erie, Pennsylvania, old-time firemen are like human trolleys. They seem to incarnate horse-and-wagon manhood, beer in buckets, History itself. The third statue would honor Thomas Edison, who did some of his most significant work in Brockton in the late nineteenth century. It was in Brockton that Edison created his three-wire system, the first safe, commercially practical arrangement for generating and distributing electrical power. Some people in town, including Gerald Beals, the historical society's authority on local history, favored adjusting the city's usable past by decreasing emphasis on Marciano and increasing emphasis on Edison. The handiness and ingenuity associated with Edison, the Bill Gates of the late nineteenth century, gestured not only at Brockton's industrial history but also at a future of technological sophistication. Maybe Edison would make a better poster boy than Marciano for postindustrial Brockton.

Mayor Yunits agreed, at least in part. "The days of the Marcianos and Haglers are gone," he said. "Kids aren't hungry like that. They fought to get the hell out of poverty. Marciano didn't want to work in shoe factories, Hagler never had a dime." Then he disagreed with himself, pointing out there were plenty of Cape Verdeans in town who fit the traditional Brockton profile: "poor, hardworking immigrants, strong-willed, with tight families and communities, here for the right reason, with a real work ethic and basic skills. In that sense, the quality of the Brocktonian hasn't changed. The skin color has, but not the way the quiet majority live." He then switched back to arguing his original point: all those continuities, including the fact that Cape Verdeans' employers "tell us that they're very skilled with their hands," did not necessarily add up to boxers. "They're more into soccer," the mayor said, "and, anyway, things are different than they were back then; they know they need to get an education, stay in school." There were still manufacturing jobs in Brockton, but when I asked him to picture the average high school graduate looking for a future in town, he talked about service work and college. The days were gone when hard-pressed sons of Brockton's working class felt compelled to choose between body work and fighting.

But people knew Brockton primarily for its shoe factories and its fighters, which made for a tricky negotiation of past and present. As Mary Waldron, Yunits's chief of staff, put it, "Rocky Marciano is one of our hooks"; but, the mayor added, "We're going to try to soften the edge a little bit." The trick was to gesture at the fighters, the shoes, the local prowess in rough sports—all understood to express the city's work ethic—while emphasizing less aggressive aspects of its tradition, like good housing, good schools, and culture that does not put on the elitist airs prevalent up north in Boston. Waldron said, "We haven't won a state football championship in years, but still we're Big Bad Brockton. The arts people at Brockton High keep saying, 'Hey, we're champions, too.' The jazz band, the theater, they win competitions and prizes, too. We need to make that part of the City of Champions."

Brockton's new-order boosters, aligned behind Yunits, were convinced that selling Brockton would always mean selling its long association with hard work. "Our people are known for hard work and a work ethic," said Arthur Markos, the big, cordial man who ran the Brockton Twenty-First Century Corporation. Chris Cooney, the young president of the chamber of commerce, agreed. "Available labor is why we're on the map," he said. "That, and transit, allows a company to come here inexpensively because it translates into better wages," by which Cooney meant lower wages, which is of course better from the employer's point of view. Both men wished to ensure Brockton's future economic health by marketing that historically pedigreed, adequately educated, underpriced labor to a diverse group of service providers and manufacturers. (No more one-industry town: "I think we learned from our mistake," said Cooney.) Markos and Cooney also accepted the absolute necessity of the downtown revival envisioned by Yunits as the other principal component in the city's comeback. And they recognized that this revival, although it may return Brockton's center to its golden-age function as a lively core of civic life, could only take place if they succeed in changing the city's image and its local culture.

Both Markos and Cooney were relatively new in town when I talked to them in the summer of 2000. Markos had come to Brockton three and a half years earlier from Providence; Cooney, who is from Connecticut, had recently been hired away from a chamber of commerce on Cape Cod. A non–New Englander like me might regard them as essentially locals, but in Brockton they were outsiders (the same goes for Mary Waldron, who is from Chicopee, in western Massachusetts) with enough ironic distance from the city's ways to be selectively critical in guiding it toward recovery. Markos admitted that the city's government had been a mess in the recent past. "The late eighties and early nineties were terrible. Brockton was bankrupt, basically. A state board oversaw the city's finances. Forty percent of city workers were laid off. The city couldn't pay bills. The chief of police says there were Friday nights when only one car was on duty for a city of twenty-two square miles." The city's chronic water shortage, exacerbated by a long history of refusing to consider long-term solutions, had also been a drag on the economy. "In the 1980s," Cooney said, "the city was denying construction permits because of the water supply. We missed the whole Mass Miracle. It got so bad, people stopped asking. I mean, to take a small example, a restaurant couldn't expand and build a new bathroom." But, they both said, things had improved of late. "The city had to be tighter, more careful" under the state board's scrutiny, Markos told me. "And about eight years ago business leaders decided to boost the economic development effort. Yunits led that—he was a lawyer, then—and now he's mayor." Cooney also expressed confidence that Mayor Yunits, who had initiated many schemes and followed through on at least some of them, had finally brokered a viable solution to the water problem. Plans for a desalinization plant would have to pass environmental muster, but the outlook was, for once, promising.

Brockton's bad relationship with water extends to its long-suffering rivers, too. On a warm afternoon in late September 2000, I went for a walk with Chris Cooney to trace the route of a planned pedestrian way along the Salisbury Brook, a smallish river that has been so thoroughly cut up, fenced off, obscured, dumped in, and neglected that it flowed almost incognito through downtown Brockton. The Yunits administration had already begun to cobble together stretches of public land along the river and easements carved from private land to enable the creation of a landscaped riverfront corridor that would turn an eyesore into an accessible amenity. The riverway was still a drawing on paper at that point, though. During our walk we had difficulty getting to the water at all, or moving along next to it for any distance, because the banks were choked with plant growth and refuse, and because fences, buildings, and street bridges broke up our progress. The river and its banks gave copious evidence of having been pressed into service as informal barroom, bathroom, and garbage dump. Wherever the current passed under a street bridge, we found a partial dam of branches, leaves, and junk· bottles, clothes, hubcaps, plastic containers, a computer monitor, unidentifiable metal objects, cinder blocks, a couple of shopping carts. The shopping carts must have made a big splash going in.

It was cool and green under the overhanging trees at the river's edge, and the shallow water, eddying around the detritus, made a restful sound. It was beautiful if you squinted a little. "We're a canvas waiting to be painted on," Cooney told me, meaning that Brockton had resources in abundance, even a potentially pretty river, and that the boosters' task would be to attract those willing to take a relatively low-cost risk to exploit the opportunity. He said, "Renewing downtown is all about a critical mass—the river, market rate housing, quality shops and services, safety, people with money." I asked if the city's history was part of that critical mass. "That's always the question here," he answered. "It's, like, do we embrace the shoes, or give them the boot?" When we got back to the brick building that houses the offices of the chamber of commerce, right across the street from city hall, he showed me a room in the building where a high-tech company was installing a new fiber-optic switching station. In the late nineteenth century, the building had housed Edison's cutting-edge power plant; now it housed the chamber of commerce and a vital piece of postindustrial infrastructure. The building was the mayor's ideal of a recharged, economically vital, historically resonant but forward-looking downtown in a nutshell—so far, only in a nutshell.

THE RECIPE

Jack Yunits, Mary Waldron, Arthur Markos, Chris Cooney, and the rest of Brockton's new-order boosters shared a vision of economic development via selective exploitation of a city's traditional strengths and its existing built environment, as opposed to wholesale clearance and suburbanization. Frank Keefe, the state's master of downtown revivals, is one of the principal formulators and exponents of that vision. Keefe made his name in the early 1970s as city planning director in Lowell, then as director of the Office of State Planning and chairman of Governor Dukakis's development cabinet in the late 1970s. A fast-talking, natty fellow in his midfifties, with an air of worldly optimism and slightly rakish old-ivory-colored hair, Keefe has been instrumental in remaking cities as both a public servant and a businessman. He went on to serve as the state's chief fiscal and administrative officer under Governor Weld in the 1980s, and these days he is back in the private planning and development business as a one-man enterprise called the Keefe Company. When I visited him to talk about Brockton and the transformation of industrial cities, his small office on School Street in downtown Boston was piled high with plans, reports, and artists' renderings related to his latest project, a hotel and upscale housing in Boston's Kenmore Square.

"Lowell's the first successful city"—in Massachusetts, he meant—"at transmogrifying into something different, but based on its past." Senator Paul Tsongas made it possible by funneling life-giving federal funds into Lowell, but the city's public and private players also pursued creative answers to the question of what a textile-making city does when it stops spinning. Among the answers were the conversion of mill buildings into apartments, lofts, office space, and a National Park Service heritage park based on the city's industrial history; also a sports museum, a minor league baseball team (the Spinners, natch), real trolleys on rails, restored canals, and a peaceful little park named for native son Jack Kerouac in which skateboarders clatter back and forth while visitors read excerpts from his works inscribed on rectangular slabs. Lowell is not perfect—it is still depressed in many ways, and at this writing it is not yet clear that tourism pays its own way—but its center is alive after it had been written off for dead, and for that reason other cities in similar situations have studied its example. "As director of state planning under Dukakis," Keefe said, "I transported the model to other cities. We had successes, one of which Brockton isn't." In order to explain why that was so, he had to take me back to the genesis of the Lowell model, its wider application, and its failure so far to find footing in Brockton.

Keefe framed his account within the nationwide, federally driven impulse to clear industrial cities' "obsolete" elements in the decades after World War II. "The economy of Massachusetts hadn't been in great shape from the twenties on, and folks forgot in the sixties and seventies, when in cities the stories were all bad, that downtowns were for more than just shopping. Urban renewal nearly destroyed cities by treating downtown as a shopping center." That meant clearing not only downtown apartment buildings but also factory buildings, warehouses, workers' housing, railways, working waterfronts—all the infrastructure fitted to the circulation of raw materials and their conversion into finished goods. It meant suburbanizing cities with highways, parking lots, and strip malls, all acting to break up the traditional downtown. "The best thing that happened was that Nixon froze HUD in 1973," Keefe said. "The original plan in Lowell was to knock down the mills, fill in the canals, build parking lots and malls. But Nixon froze the money, and that allowed voices of reason to be heard. That sixties generation of political leaders was trained to be negative, just blast everything. The response to them was a generation that said, 'This is a great thing, our past.' Even the hack pols realized that people felt this was important. We opened a mill converted to elderly housing, and people who had worked there lived there. They said, 'This is great; this is important.'"

Keefe's experience in Lowell produced what he calls "a recipe" for revitalizing downtowns by working with the grain of a city's deep structure and against the grain of urban renewal. Operating through a series of interlocking public-private partnerships capable of bringing to bear the resources of both sectors, the recipe calls for a mixed-use downtown that takes advantage of what is already there, rather than clearing it and starting over. "There are so many things you can do," he said. "Keep the high school downtown, even though state policy was against it." State policy called for regional mega-schools on the edge of town, like Brockton High. "You need community colleges downtown," he continued, "elderly housing downtown. Arrange public transportation to bring people downtown. Keep the post office and other vital services there, to get the margins into the center. A mixed-use downtown means live, work, school, culture, not just shopping. You need parks downtown. And heritage parks. Lowell had canals, but every city has its defining characteristics. Different cities come up with great things, physical embodiments, very often industrial-related or natural resources." These defining characteristics become the basis of "imageability," a quality of combined depth and sharpness in both a place's physical appearance and its cultural reputation. Visitors have to know how to get there, and they have to know they are *somewhere* once they do get there. Residents and businesses have to have a clear sense of what they are investing in, and why it matters. History helps, but so does fresh energy. New immigrants, for instance, are good, both replicating and rescripting the stories of previous immigrants. "The newcomers just extend the cultural richness and vitality of the community, and they in turn learn the history of the place, connect to the place through its history."[8]

Who had learned and applied the lessons of Lowell? "Worcester and Springfield are big cities"—by which Keefe meant they had more problems than most—"but their business communities really hung in there. Pittsfield. New Bedford will be a success. Fall River." My eyebrows must have gone up. "Yes, Fall River," he insisted. "Their downtown is vibrant and interesting. I think they're further along than Brockton." This would come as a blow to Brockton boosters, who made a habit of pointing to perennially depressed Fall River to remind me that things could be worse. "Lynn, even gritty Lynn," Keefe continued, "and Newburyport and Salem—not gritty cities, but successes on this model. And North Adams, of course." In North Adams, an old manufacturing town in the western part of the state, a converted mill-building complex houses Mass MoCA (the Massachusetts Museum of Contemporary Art, opened in 1999), a self-proclaimed "cultural factory for the twenty-first century" and a major center for visual arts, media, and performing arts. Keefe did not mention Providence's orchestration of a restored riverfront, mixed uses, and cultural attractions to revive downtown life, one of the most impressive examples of the recipe in action, but Providence is across the state line in Rhode Island and therefore out of bounds. Other foreigners had also emulated the Massachusetts model. "New York State's heritage parks are cribbed from us, and Europeans are asking about our model of public-private partnerships, mixed-use downtown, and reuse of downtown buildings." That left one notable laggard in the parade of postindustrial reinventions. "Brockton's really the last, and worst."

Why had Brockton's elites been so ineffectual in responding to change over the last half century? Keefe tried to be polite, but people all over the state will tell you that Brockton's self-inflicted wounds include a long history of incompetence, corruption, insularity, and paucity of imagination among its leadership class. The city has an especially weak tradition of planning that has alternated between doing almost nothing and toeing the party line of 1950s-style urban renewal and suburbanization, which for the most part meant leveling old buildings and breaking up downtown life. "And they were smug," said Keefe, "because the indicators of urban stress were muted by a unique development pattern.

Brockton is not a typical mill city in that the classic downtown is surrounded by sprawl development and new subdivisions, so Brockton didn't have typical indicators of urban stress, unlike Fall River, New Bedford, Lynn, Lowell, Lawrence. But it *had* the problems." Brockton's fill-in boom in the 1950s and 1960s produced about seven thousand ranch- and Cape-style houses, arranged in subdivisions that bracketed the old downtown and spawned mall-type commercial strips that helped draw business activity away from the center. This new construction raised standard census indicators enough to make Brockton appear to be less plagued by deindustrialization-driven poverty and disinvestment than its fellow mill cities. But, while the city's growing parasuburban sections padded the numbers, industrial Brockton continued through a decades-long bottoming-out occasioned by the long-term contraction of the regional shoe business.

Keefe, the former state planning director, could not forgive Brockton's ruling elites for wasting opportunities to help their city adjust. "Late in the game they started to use the finance mechanisms, but they missed the Dukakis administration entirely, missed the building boom. They didn't ask, they didn't get. I was giving it to everybody, any city that had a plan. We're project-driven in Massachusetts. A good mayor needs to have ten, fifteen plans ready to go, to get projects from the state." When he summed up by saying "Brockton is the pits," he did not mean the city itself—of which he is fond, having grown up near it. Rather, he meant the example set since World War II by its leaders.

But, he said, Brockton could still catch up. "One great thing is the regional transit, and the commuter rail gives hope." So did the current mayor, who once worked for Keefe in Lowell as an intern. "Jack Yunits is a firecracker of a guy, much better than what they've had." The list went on. "Live-work loft buildings around the rail station should happen. The central core and corridor has possibilities for low and high tech; not biotech, maybe, but the location is great. The schools are good. And the workforce; the hidden secret of Massachusetts is that the workforce is great." The city and its partners in the business community had hired Keefe as a consultant to study the feasibility of a minor league baseball stadium like Lowell's, but he convinced them that what they really needed from him was a downtown revitalization scheme. Equipped with Keefe's plan, the city could go to the state and federal government for help in creating the infrastructure required by his recipe.

Meanwhile, Steve Cruz was busy tearing down industrial Brockton. If Frank Keefe and his disciples are voices of a new-order boosterism guiding the transformation of Brockton, then Cruz, head of the Brock-

ton Redevelopment Authority, speaks the language of the old order—
and his words have had landscape-shaping authority, too. Just before
walking the Salisbury Brook with Chris Cooney of the chamber of commerce, I went to see Cruz in his office, which is a couple of blocks from
city hall. To get there, I walked across Montello Street, still lined with
factory and warehouse buildings, then through an underpass cut in the
railway's embankment. Cruz, a salty little fellow in shirtsleeves, received
me in his paneled office, which had the cut-rate, can-do feel of a moderately successful contractor's office circa 1972. He must be considerably
older than he looks, since he has been involved in the redevelopment of
Brockton for two generations.

"I started in 1964, '65, with urban renewal," he told me, thumping
down on his desktop a stack of aerial photographs of central Brockton,
taken over the last half century, with which he illustrated his story. "Total clearance, low-income housing, streets, we did all the downtown
lights." He worked through the pile of photos at great speed, discard-
ing each after a few seconds, stabbing a finger at one structure after
another as he itemized their destruction. "I demolished that. And I demolished *that*. Now let me get my bearings here. Oh, and that's the Old
Colony shoe factory. And there's a wood-frame outsole building I
demolished. Now, let me get my bearings. I wiped this all out. Jesus
Christ. All slums, three-decker houses, wood-frame, just junk. There
was a flophouse, there were bars here. Ninety-eight percent of black
people in the city lived here. We relocated them all over the city." A
shot of city hall from the 1950s came up next in the pile. "Jesus Christ,
look at that. Look at the congestion downtown. City hall had no vista."
Cruz had been at it for a long time, and not just in the distant past.
Chris Cooney ruefully estimated that four hundred buildings, most of
them derelict, had been demolished during the relatively history-
sensitive Yunits administration alone.

I asked Cruz if perhaps he felt now that he had been in too much of
a hurry to clear existing structures. He had heard variants of the question many times before, and he clearly considered the idea behind it a
misguided urban variant of tree hugging. "We saved the cream," he
said, "but the wood-frame crap with brick veneer, *that* we needed to get
rid of. But something historical you would not tear down." (This might
have been a nod to those who claim that Brockton's downtown has
never recovered from the demolition in 1954 of the City Theater, one of
Edison's triumphs, the first theater ever to be lighted with electrical
power drawn from a central station.) In defense of his aggressive clear-

ance practices, Cruz pointed out that there was a significant difference between industrial buildings in Brockton and those in textile centers like Lowell or Fall River. "The biggest machine in a shoe factory was for cutting the upper." He held his hands apart at bread box width to show how small the machine was. "I used to make shoes; I know there aren't any big machines in there. Go into a garment factory, they got big machines. Go down to Fall River, they're built out of granite blocks to deal with vibration. Solid. Not for shoes. A lot of those shoe buildings are crap." Here he launched into a taxonomy of the shoe business, which he illustrated by hauling up his own well-shod foot from behind his desk and pointing out a shoe's component elements. The point was that "more than half of the factories were wood-frame, plus most of the little satellite buildings around town that supplied them." Yankee industrialists and landlords had often built on the cheap—both factory buildings and three-deckers to house workers—and those buildings were not fit to renovate. "We remodel or get developers to remodel buildings downtown if we can, but some you can't keep. We do spot clearance." He threw up his hands to make a "that's life" gesture. "Look, buildings get obsolete. You can only fix a pair of shoes so many times, then you throw it away."

Cruz was not some cold-eyed technocrat imported to put the machine on Brockton. He had credentials as a regular Brockton guy from way back. "Before you were born," he reminisced, "downtown Brockton was a hub. We went downtown for everything—banks, lawyers, doctors." He got up, beckoned me to the window, and pointed out the shoe-industry buildings still standing and the sites of those he had torn down. "That's the last one left," he said, pointing. "FootJoy, best golf shoe in the world. The last of the Mohegans." Cruz had worked in those factories. "Not long, but I did it. I was going to high school, and college at night. When you re-tan leather, they use chemicals. Everything I touched, paper, books, everything turned yellow. I worked at Superior Polish—I tore that building down. I had the Cadillac job at FootJoy, I cut shoes. I cut alligator with a knife, pissing in my pants" because the material was so expensive. He also worked for a developer instrumental in Brockton's suburban-style construction boom of the 1950s. "I used to pick and shovel slabs for Campanelli when I was in high school. Dig down three feet, that's all. No cellar."

Despite his honestly come-by antipathy to the romanticizing of industrial work and infrastructure, Cruz had respect for his city's history. "Look," he said, "three or four important things happened in the city.

One, the shoe industry, it was an industrial city. Two, Edison was here. Three, firemen, we lost thirteen. What did they lose in Worcester? Six? Four, good sports. And hard workers. It took a shitload of three-deckers to house all the donkeys. That's why Brockton has an abundancy of three-deckers. You need a lot of donkeys to make shoes. You know how many hands touch a pair of shoes?" I asked what he thought of Marciano, figuring he would take the old-school line, but he surprised me. "They talk about Rocky Marciano, that's a lot of bullshit." He waved his arms. "This building right here"—he whacked an aerial photo of the old Edison power station that houses the chamber of commerce and the new switching station—"is the most important building in the city. Edison was a genius. He slept in that building in a sleeping bag." Cruz sketched Edison's idea for the power station's chimney system on a piece of scrap paper. He held up the finished product, all mad swirls and jabs, and considered it: "A genius." I expressed my surprise at his dismissal of Marciano, but he had already grown mellow on that score. "Oh, Rocky's great, but I think the focus should be on all of them. He's great. I went to his fights. I want the statues to all of them—Marciano, Edison, and the Strand Fire."

It appeared that even Steve Cruz—Brockton's own avatar of Shiva, lord of destruction—was willing, at least in principle, to seek a balance between the old and new in Brockton, to find a place for history and continuity in its landscape, and even to reserve places of honor for both Marciano and Edison. "I keep thinking of that book, the *I Ching*," he said, surprising me again. "Everything stays the same, but everything changes." Karmic musings aside, though, he had buildings to tear down. At the end of our conversation he sat back in his desk chair and said, "Ahh, it's a hell of a city, Carlo. But you gotta get rid of the crap."

What, then, is Rocky Marciano to contemporary Brockton? Is he part of the recipe for the city's adjustment to a changing world? I considered the question as I walked back from Cruz's office, under the railroad, toward city hall and the old Edison power station. Cruz had me thinking in his terms: Is Marciano's memory like a solid mill building that can be renovated and put to good use in postindustrial Brockton, or is it like an obsolete wood-frame building with brick veneer, better torn down and replaced, perhaps with the high-tech Edison? Is he a familiar, broken-in shoe the city can rely on, or a shoe that has been patched too many times? Cream or crap? Gerald Beals, of the historical society, had told me, "I'm Rockied out, myself." He said he had nothing against Marciano. The historical society maintained a Rocky Marciano exhibit, and Beals loved Marciano's story, especially for its ties to industrial urbanism. "I saw him regularly, as everybody did," Beals said, "running through the streets of Brockton, and I saw him train at the Y. It was obvious that if he hit somebody, he'd kill 'em. He was like the Italian workers you see—short, blocky, incredible endurance. You used to see more of them." And, Beals added, "He took a lot of crap. It was difficult to be Italian, especially with the Irish more established in politics and labor." But Beals sensed "a persistent bitterness toward the shoe industry in Brockton" that made it difficult to mobilize a broad popular interest in history through shoes, Rocky, and other totems of the old industrial working class. "In the self-appointed elite mind," too, "they're Marcianoed out. And they make a good case in a city overloaded with crime and violence. The boxing connection is ugly. What you have left is Edison. I mean, we got Rocky, we got shoes, but we got Edison, and people are starting to recognize that Edison"—as if he were electricity itself—"is clean and ubiquitous."

Rocky might be equally ubiquitous, but his hands were dirty. Being good with those hands might not be enough; in fact, it might be part of the problem. He had to be in shape to go the distance—bridging industrial and postindustrial, late nineteenth century and early twenty-first—in his role as an embodiment of Brockton.

THE ROCKY MARCIANO TRAIL

To Patricia Johanson, hired by the city in 1997, the answers to my questions about the continuing usefulness of Marciano's ghost to his hometown seemed obvious. She organized her master plan for Brockton's future around him. "From the beginning," she wrote in a description of the project published in a French journal, *Les Annales de la récherche urbaine*, "the major goal of my master plan for Brockton has been to unify the landscape visually and functionally, such that disparate neighborhoods and districts are connected, and ecological functioning is restored." Marciano's running route, formalized as the Rocky Marciano Trail, would serve as "the thread that unites every neighborhood of the city with nature" and with a physical and civic whole. Renovation of the "boarded-up and deteriorating home of Rocky Marciano" struck her as the ideal "metaphor that might resonate with Brockton's population, which still has a large percentage of recent immigrants and working-class poor." The very ordinariness of "the monuments of Rocky's humble Italian-American neighborhood—his church, home, playground, the shoe factory where his father worked, his neighborhood market and bar"—served to turn the urban village's mundane landmarks into elements of a living history featuring working people's enterprise and resolve. "It is clear," she wrote, "that 'Rocky's landscape'—the landscape of ordinary everyday life—could also become the impetus for multiple civic benefits, including physical fitness, recreational trails, youth programs, tourism, economic renewal, improved water quality and quantity, and wildlife corridors. Thus, the goal of 'The Rocky Marciano Trail' is not only a 'new image' but also a socially, culturally, and biologically reconnected city."[9]

Johanson's scheme calls to mind the process, reduced to cliché for all time in the training montage sequences of the *Rocky* movies, of a boxer getting into fighting trim. This time, though, it would be the city, not the man, getting into shape. Instead of sprints and sessions with the heavy bag, picture images of contractors taking the boards off the windows of the Marciano house on Dover Street, state and municipal workers putting up new signs on Route 24 and Main Street, National Park Service employees erecting historical markers along the Rocky Marciano Trail, citizen volunteers planting trees and cleaning up the banks of the Salisbury Brook—all culminating in a triumphal shot of lively streets crowded with proud Brocktonians and satisfied visitors. Johanson was inspired by a sort of rhyme between Marciano's body—shaped in the streets, in playgrounds, at the YMCA—and the city's physical form, for which she recommended a regimen of treatments that would improve circulation and flexibility, restore cultural energy and economic strength, and otherwise return Brockton not only to good health but to competitive vigor. The Marciano house on Dover Street, an embodiment of family life and a typical part of the city's landscape, made a perfect centerpiece because it served as a mediating term between Rocky and Brockton. Visiting the house in which he lived, or tracing his running route, or visiting the shoe factories he vowed to avoid at all costs, you could see how the city produced the fighter and infused his body and career with meaning. The house, embodying industrial urbanism in Brockton, was a machine for the production of Rocky Marciano; it would, in that sense, serve a function in Johanson's plan similar to that of the National Park Service's thunderous factory exhibit in Lowell, which displays machines for the production of textiles.

Although in time she would come to believe that she had made a mistake in centering her master plan on Rocky Marciano and the house, and although she would come to regret ever having had anything to do with Brockton, Johanson was initially enthusiastic in her conviction that Marciano's ghost could still do important work in his hometown. She was taken with him not only as a conceptual hook but also as a dedicated craftsman and as a man. "I also have to admit," she told me, "that I fell in love with Rocky, because how could you not?"

If you were to put stereotypical fight people at one pole of a sociocultural continuum and try to imagine what kind of person should go all the way at the other pole, Patricia Johanson would make a good candidate. She jokes that people in Brockton thought she was "a crazy artist lady," but there was nothing she could do about it, in part because she is in fact an incurably original artist. For the last forty-plus years, since her late teens, she has painted, sculpted, drawn, written, and otherwise created art at the intersections of human artifice and nature. She graduated in 1962 from Bennington, where she studied with the architect and minimalist sculptor Tony Smith, and she holds an M.A. in art history from Hunter College and a B.Arch. from New York's City College. She also served an apprenticeship as Georgia O'Keeffe's archivist. Although Johanson has always been an advocate of bringing art out of the museum and into the pluralist heavy weather of public life, and although she accurately describes herself as "an ecologist" (one might also call her a lay engineer, a landscape architect, or a green political operative), it is also true that her interests and most of her training have been in the fine arts.

"I started out as a traditional artist," she told me, "a painter and a sculptor. But I was never putting things on pedestals, or in a gallery." One of her first major works was a two-hundred-foot structural T—an I-beam cut in half—that she painted red and mounted horizontally, outdoors, in semirural Buskirk, New York, near her present home. "See, I always learn from projects. I think a lot of artists know what they want, and they do the project, and the project is finished, whereas to me my projects are all open-ended, and so there's always a lot of interaction between the user group, the community, and nature. What I learned from that first piece was that I began to see nature impinged on it." The sculpture developed what she called "spheres of influence of nature" as overhanging trees and shadows encouraged the growth of "microhabitats" of moss, insects, and other living things. "We began to get patterns of nature, the patterns of everything else around it, impinging on this very man-made, very industrial piece of steel." Impelled by lessons like this, she moved toward grand-scale landscape art that interacted with natural processes by design, rather than by happenstance, although she never did give up completely on her sculptural interests. She has made "tons of clay models" of her larger works; "that is something I do with my own hands."

Johanson gained a reputation as an innovative environmental artist in the 1960s and 1970s, in part on the strength of unbuilt projects. She wrote a series of illustrated essays about imaginary gardens on commission for *House and Garden,* but her meditations on the Line Garden, Illusory Gardens, Garden-Cities, and such were too far-out for that magazine to publish, even in 1969. The essays got into circulation by other means, and became known as manifestos for environmental art. Her drawings, which became art objects in themselves, typically suggested natural forms and functions as models for human architecture: a central sewage treatment facility in the shape of a giant flower, a storm water runoff network with channels and ponds patterned on the trailing stem and leaves of a plant, a park shaped like a butterfly, a house like a lizard. "People almost never know what they're looking at, initially," she once told me; she designs "total" artworks that people can inhabit, move around in, and come to understand over time by means more visceral than seeing from the standard distance that separates a spectator from art-on-a-pedestal. A visitor to a butterfly-shaped park or snake-shaped sewage treatment plant might never *see* the butterfly or snake shape but might, in time, come to *feel* it, and thus to absorb the principle of transformative renewal that informs the landscape design as well as the figures of the butterfly-that-emerges-from-a-chrysalis and the snake-that-sheds-its-skin. That was the idea, anyway, on the page. Her designs for landscapes that resembled plants, animals, or less identifiable biomorphic forms suggested that her mission was to reshape the man-made world to conform with nature's healthier, more sustainable intentions. "That's what *wants* to be here," she likes to say of her plans, or, "I'm trying to understand and use the strategy of this plant."

When Johanson began to complete large-scale design projects, she continued her tendency toward macroscopic use of nature's micropatterns and intentions. Her Fair Park Lagoon in Dallas renders the straggling shapes of two local plants, the delta duck-potato and the Texas fern, on a gigantic scale as a tangle of concrete bridges and paths that visitors can use to explore the swamplike five-block site. Her Endangered Garden built on the Sunnydale Facilities site on the edge of San Francisco Bay, a linear park atop a pump station and holding tank for water and sewage, features a walking path in the form of a garter snake a third of a mile long. The multicolored snake, culminating in a massive head-shaped mound and dimpled along its length with small depressions where rainwater can collect for birds to drink, is recognizable as such from a bird's-eye view, but not so readily from the ground. Other major projects—among them the Park for the Amazon Rainforest in Obidos, Brazil; Nairobi River Park in Kenya; and Ulsan Park in the smokestack city of Ulsan, South Korea—similarly adapt natural forms and processes to satisfy the demands of "art, ecology, landscaping, and functional infrastructure." [10]

Johanson's interdisciplinary, versatile work invites comparisons with a variety of other artists. Robert Smithson's entropy-minded landscape installations come to mind, especially Spiral Jetty, as do Christo's gigantic island- and cliff-wrapping projects. (She has opposed being grouped with Christo, though, on the grounds that his projects are "so ecologically irresponsible as to obviate any possible aesthetic merit.") [11] One commentator has grouped her with Claes Oldenburg because she blows up mundane objects to extraordinary proportions. [12] Lucy Lippard, one of the academy's strongest advocates of place-sensitive public art, has been a fan of Johanson's work for years. Lippard gives Johanson's Endangered Garden a place of honor in her discussion of new-order public art, in a chapter that also highlights Jane Greengold's sculpture on the site of Manhattan's obliterated Collect Pond, Viet Ngo's sixty-acre earthwork and wetlands project in North Dakota, Cliff Garten's Saint Paul Cultural Garden in Minnesota, and a variety of murals and public theater projects. [13]

But when I asked Johanson whose company she would like to keep, artistically, she reduced the list to one: Frederick Law Olmsted, late-nineteenth-century America's great designer of parks and other public spaces. "Olmsted is my hero," she told me. "He knew all about social factors, geology, landscape, plumbing, everything, and he had his troubles with Boss Tweed. He made landscapes for people, *citizens*, to use." Olmsted championed the reformist impulse to ensure that industrial cities on the make remained physically humane places, and to reconnect their citizens with nature through manipulation of the landscape. "Every place, even Brockton, has nature in it," Johanson reminded me from time to time; and every place has its local bosses and entanglements, as Brockton often reminded her. Like Olmsted, she has chosen the city, messy politics and all, as the ground on which to make her stand. Not only are cities and city people powerfully in need of reconnection with nature, but, she told me, "Cities are where we connect with others." Messy politics and competing communities of interest are integral parts of a total artwork that a citizen-spectator-participant inhabits over time. So are constraints imposed by limited funds and the dynamics of popular opinion. "I've worked with rich clients, but I never learned anything when I did. Working in places like this"—she meant Brockton—"I learn things."

In Brockton she learned, among other things, to love Rocky Marciano. Until she began working there, Johanson knew and cared nothing about Marciano or boxing. "And if I did have to choose a sports hero," she told me, "I wouldn't have chosen Rocky. He took the money and ran; he didn't do any good with it. Skeeter McClure is more of a hero; he got a Ph.D. and gave back to society." So how did Marciano win her over?

It began with the pendulum. When she was new to Brockton, she toured the semiderelict Marciano house with Peter, the youngest of Rocky's siblings. "He was pointing out all these little things. We went into Rocky's bedroom, and he said, 'This is where he had the pendulum.' I said, 'Pendulum?' And he said, 'Yes, when he was lying in bed at night he would watch the pendulum to build up his eyes so he could follow things more quickly.' I said to myself, 'This is a man after my own heart. He's very good, he thinks about all the details of how he can gain an advantage in some really very creative ways, like the punching underwater.' It's that he couldn't fail. And we came from the same kind of background. When I went to college, I knew that I was the flagship *Enterprise*. I was not going to fall on my ass."

She was inspired, above all, by Rocky Marciano's quality of indomitability, made up of equal parts diligence and will. "I totally believe in what he did," she said, "the training, knowing that you can do it, and then relaxing and just doing it, not listening to all the people who say you can't for all the reasons." She was especially taken with Marciano's obsessive running. "I understand that," she said. "I like to do it too. It's a mental thing: 'I can do it.'" I asked if she went on long runs; she laughed and said, "Not anymore, but I do go much farther than people know—for an old bag. I love it, and I'll go out when it's raining. My kids think it's crazy; I'll be out on the road at midnight. It's almost an act of faith. Sometimes I'll be cruising down the highway, when the fog is so thick I can just feel the road under my feet, and hope that no car comes along. But I do it, and I always learn something from it. When there's no visibility, you really hear the animals, the rustling." Johanson, who prides herself on fighting for her projects against long odds and powerful naysayers, has also had to fight a physical battle against an intimidating opponent. She was diagnosed with "terminal" cancer in 1989, and beat it. I suspect that experience, and the resulting sense of having pitted will against the limits of the body and the skepticism of others, informed her passion for Marciano's indomitability.

The resonances of working-class family life in the Marciano house also spoke to her. There were factory workers in her own background, including a grandmother who made airplane parts on the line. "She worked with big machinery," Johanson said. "People had their fingers cut off routinely. She was well versed in the horrors of the factory, and she was really very clear about that, that we need to get education and never go into a factory. She told me, 'Patricia, I don't care what you do with your life, but you must never work in a factory.'" Johanson's grandparents on the other side of the family had a house in Bay Ridge, Brooklyn, "just like" the Marciano house on Dover Street. "It even faced a park just like that. And when I saw the photographs of his mom receiving the call that said Rocky was okay, that he had won and that he hadn't been injured, I looked at that cabinet [in the photo]; we had a cabinet just like that. And I looked at that wallpaper, and I thought, 'What beautiful wallpaper, I love this wallpaper.' Then a couple of weeks later my mother said, 'You know, I'm throwing these old photographs out, do you want any? Here's your grandparents' house in Brooklyn.' Of course, they died long ago. And she throws down on the table this picture of the living room, and it's the same wallpaper!" Johanson laughed happily. "There are things that just resonate, and you don't even know why, and that's what I'm reaching for."

The wallpaper episode epitomizes Johanson's approach to making meaning. The wallpaper did not necessarily and inherently express an entire way of life, but it was just the right wallpaper for that kind of house, and as such it was available to a visitor who could use it to call up the way of life typified by the house where it intersected with his or her own experience. "My projects are frameworks," she said, "and the important parts are not the parts I design. The important part is everything around the parts I design, and people are able to find their own world because the whole world is there. If you do a design that leaves a lot of infill intact, you can't miss." The infill, in this case, was the domestic detail of industrial urbanism.

The initial seed grant that brought Patricia Johanson to Brockton came from the Cultural Economic Development Program of the Massachusetts Cultural Council (MCC), a state agency. Beate Becker, who was then in charge of the program, told me, "It was one of our first cultural economic development grants. The idea was to clean up, revitalize, and do a major art piece, all focused on the river. It was all related to the mayor's 21-Point Plan, which was a document he had put together when he was running for office. And the project got funded because of Patricia Johanson. She was known." Caroline Grayboys, head of Brockton's Fuller Art Museum, extended the invitation to Johanson, but the mayor and a broad cross section of civic leaders and boosters also seemed to be excited about working with a famous artist to improve Brockton. Johanson remembers, "So I went down there, to great fanfare. They had everybody, they probably had fifty people assembled at city hall, all the heads, of the water department, everybody, all the players. We're all sitting around an enormous table, and they were introducing me to everybody." Johanson lost her best local advocate when cancer forced Grayboys to withdraw from active participation in the project, and there were unpleasantly surprising adjustments in her contract with the city, but she was committed, she was excited, and she figured it would all work out in a climate of good faith and enthusiasm. "This is my life," she told the *Brockton Enterprise* in 1998.[14]

She began visiting Brockton regularly, making the 180-mile drive down from Buskirk, New York. She toured the city, talking to everyone she could find who knew something about Brockton's past, digging into the archives at the library and the historical society, stopping strangers on the street to ask them questions. "She's a real nightbird," said Beate Becker of the MCC. "She would be up at all hours, walking around the city, talking to people who were out." Johanson, who claims that she walked on every street in Brockton during her research, began filling up the notebooks in which she records a blow-by-blow account of all her work on each of her projects. Once she found out about Marciano, and especially about the long, looping routes of his runs through the city—which intersected the river, knitted the neighborhoods to one another and to parks and monuments, and gave the project an identity recognizable beyond the city's boundaries—she felt she had a workable unifying theme. The abandoned Marciano house was in danger of being torn down, and Mayor Yunits informed her that the city could not afford to buy it from the Brockton Community Corporation, the public housing agency that owned it. So Johanson bought the house for $45,000 plus back taxes, more than she would be paid in the project's first year. She figured the house was so important to the project that she had to do something right away.

The house was important because Johanson made Marciano an essential ingredient in her prescribed cure for what she diagnosed as a bad case of urban fragmentation. She saw Brockton as a brooding, fearful, physically and psychologically chopped-up city. Bisected by the raised railway embankment that bottlenecked east-west traffic, burdened with a forbiddingly "medieval" street layout that discouraged exploration, the city was cut off from the rest of the region and broken into a series of insular ethnic and racial enclaves. It was also economically depressed, suffering from a bad reputation, and dangerously estranged from its own natural resources. "The key to Brockton, to me," she told me, "is the fragmentation, the social separation of the ethnic groups, the separation of nature, the kind of disruption of the stream. You'll see a stream, and all of sudden, where's it going? What happened to it?"

Water provided a fitting example and metaphor of the city's condition. Looking at eighteenth-century maps made before the village of North Bridgewater was even renamed Brockton, she found the stream network intact. It had been disrupted by industrialization and urbanization, especially by construction of the railroad embankment that had been hailed as such an advance in urban design in the late nineteenth century. Not only had the long-standing water shortage held back economic growth, but the suburban-style development that had been accomplished in the last half century only added to the city's water problems. The siting of tract houses and the Westgate Mall on floodplains, for instance, had further damaged the watershed, exacerbating flooding in certain neighborhoods. Water was everywhere, and yet the city was dying of thirst; an ecologist's hand was needed to restore the original balance. "This is not my design," she maintained, directing my attention to a map that showed how she planned to restore the functioning network of streams. "This is the design that wants to be there. This is the watershed. Seeing what it looked like before all that industrialization went in, one of the things I tried to do with the green plan was to reconnect." She meant the literal reconnection of streams broken by railways and other development, but she also meant the flow of connections that accrue into the image of a city. Brockton needed the landscape artist's equivalent of acupuncture and Rolfing to readjust its blocked flow. "Basically," she said, "what I've done is change the image of Brockton, primarily through connecting links. And then I've just said, This is the Rocky Marciano Trail. And it is, because let's face it, he wasn't stupid, he ran along the nice streets."

She told me this one day at the end of July in 2000, while we were sitting in a gallery at the Massachusetts College of Art (known as MassArt), in Boston. While we talked, art students behind us raised echoes in the long gallery as they put the finishing touches on a collection of large, painted fiberglass cod that would soon be exhibited throughout Boston—part of a craze for collaborative, fiberglass-animal-based public art projects designed to play with a community's self-image and raise money for charity by bringing together artists, private sponsors, and popular interest.[15] Johanson was at MassArt to turn over copies of the drawings, maps, and written descriptions that made up her master plan for Brockton to curators who would be putting them in an exhibition. The papers were piled on the table between us, where she could refer to them as she explained her plan to me.

She worked with what was already there. If Brockton was in bad shape, it was not without assets, of which Marciano was only the best known. As she described those assets in her article for *Les Annales de la récherche urbaine,*

The planning potential for Brockton lies in the fact that it has nearly two thousand acres of patchwork recreation areas, parks, and conservation holdings, and a depressed economy has insured another two thousand acres of perennially vacant land. Almost thirty miles of small disconnected brooks and rivers flow throughout the city, and five hundred acres of industrially zoned vacant land is either floodplain or wetlands. Brockton's urban form, which still remains today, developed around a north-south glacial outwash trough—now Main Street—which parallels the railroad and the major waterway.

So much for nature; then there was culture: "Around this central axis grew the various cohesive ethnic neighborhoods of the successive waves of immigrants who manned the shoe factories—Irish and Italians, Polish and Swedes."[16] Their industrial legacy constituted the city's other main asset. "George Washington didn't grow up in this town," she said to me, "but they have this industrial heritage, and they have this gritty thing." She held up her fists over the pile of papers and clenched them so hard they shook, to indicate grittiness. "I was trying to show Rocky running through all this history, and being aware of some, but not being aware of it all, because none of us are aware of everything. There's so much authenticity here. That's why I started layering in the black history, and the Irish history," in addition to the Italian American immigrant history embodied by Marciano. "It's already here," she concluded. "I'm not putting it there."

The "it," the layers of meaning and grit and history, would accrue along the Rocky Marciano Trail, which connected a network of lesser monuments, facilities, and attractions arranged around three principal sites—each designed, in Johanson's words, to link "tourism, community benefit, and infrastructure with ecological restoration." [17]

The centerpiece would be the Marciano house, restored to midcentury condition, a fistic Monticello that memorialized Rocky as a champion of the urban village and its typical ways of life. To lead visitors to the house and accentuate their sense of the Old Neighborhood as grand historical subject, Johanson also planned a pair of "green Roman triumphal arches" at the entrance of the neighborhood, where George's Cafe and the Petti family's Italian grocery faced one another across Brook Street. She also hoped to start a shoemaking demonstration site in the nearby Stacy-Adams factory building (in which Rocky's father worked), like the textile mill exhibit in Lowell. The Marciano house would crown the Old Neighborhood as public monument, welcome visitors, serve as a terminus for the Rocky Marciano Trail (since his runs began and ended at the house), and also provide facilities for an afterschool youth program designed and led by Skeeter McClure. Describing that program to me, McClure stressed its emphasis on "some time-tested rules these kids don't have: study, stay out of trouble, choose your friends, work hard, watch those proper subject-object agreements." The program would "build self-discipline, interpersonal skill, and self-confidence," the mix of virtues that young people entering twenty-first-century Brockton's workforce needed to develop. "Where's the damn hope in Brockton?" he said. "When you see all the excuses that kids are given by adults for failing, they're not getting a chance. Like who's that girl—woman—who won the marathon who got her period halfway through? That's what I mean. Champions kick it *out*."

The second major site on the Rocky Marciano Trail would be Father Thomas McNulty Park, situated downtown, on a block-sized lot along the banks of the Salisbury. The park, named for the priest who supervised the construction of Brockton's St. Patrick's Church by parishioners and volunteer laborers, would feature "traditional Irish structures" like beehive-shaped huts and a sod house, decorative details inspired by the Book of Kells, a wildflower meadow, a bird garden, perhaps a flock of sheep or a small farm, and a multipurpose "Industrial Revolution water playground." Children could use the playground's miniature system of sluice gates, dams, spillways, and waterwheels to manipulate the flow of water through the park and into a natural, shoeprint-shaped depression that could be used for wading in warm weather and ice-skating in winter. The children's program at this site would teach Irish-inflected ecological and historical lessons in human

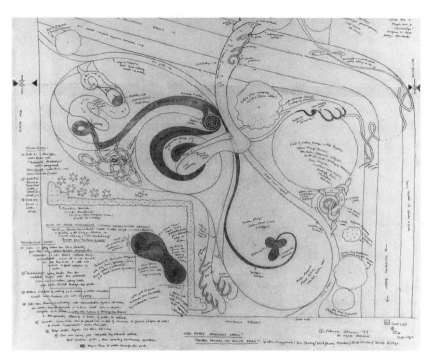

Detail of Patricia Johanson's plan for McNulty Park on the Rocky Marciano Trail, with shoeprint shape, Industrial Revolution water playground, shamrock shape, and other large-scale plantlike forms. Courtesy of Patricia Johanson.

interaction with nature. A block away from Main Street, McNulty Park would serve as the focus of the trail's downtown section, which also included city hall, the train station, a planned multiuse public space for performances and ethnic food markets, the YMCA where Marciano punched underwater, the public library where Allie Colombo read up on boxing, and St. Patrick's, where Rocky's mother went when he fought, to light candles and pray he would not be hurt.

The Rocky Marciano Trail's third major site would be Battery Wagner, to be built in a riverside neighborhood locally famous for its periodic floods.[18] This would be a Civil War memorial to the 54th Massachusetts, the black regiment led by white officers that has become the multiculturalist's Light Brigade, thanks in great part to works of art like the painting of the assault on Fort Wagner in Brockton's city hall, the Robert Gould Shaw memorial on the Boston Common, and the movie *Glory*. Johanson planned to build in Brockton a scaled-down replica of

the fort on the coast of South Carolina that the men of the 54th at-
tacked against suicidal odds and at great loss of life. The replica, like the
original, would be built principally of gabions, wooden baskets filled
with dirt. Youth programs would teach not only nature lessons but also
basic building skills. Kids would assemble and move the gabions to
maintain and reconstruct the site in response to changing water levels.
Between the fort and the nearby Salisbury Brook, Johanson planned to
create the Lemuel A. Ashport Swamp Garden, named for a veteran of
the 54th who became Brockton's first black police officer. This retention
basin and adjoining "wet meadow" would have a flood-control function as well as a decorative one. Johanson based the visual scheme of the
swamp garden—with gold-colored artificial stepping-stones forming
a floating path over dark water—on the markings of the African ball
python. She hoped that similarly black-and-gold ribbon snakes would
also take up residence in the swamp garden. The site would, she wrote
in a description of it, "reveal the poetry of rising and falling water,"
as opposed to "the property-damaging floods that occur routinely"
there.[19]

Historical markers and other explanatory apparatus at each site
would constitute only one of several connective systems that wove the
Rocky Marciano Trail's three principal sites into a larger whole. The Salisbury Brook, Trout Brook, and other waterways would be greened,
"daylighted," and reconnected where necessary to restore the watershed as a continuous public landscape. A system of intensively planted
"green streets" would radiate out from downtown to the highways and
Brockton's margins, drawing traffic to the center while improving the
city's appearance, air quality, property values, and habitats for small
animals and birds. At the city's edges, Johanson drew links to long-
distance bike trails and state parks. In addition to making Brockton
more interesting and appealing to its residents, her plan would more
sharply define the city's place in a regional network of tourist attractions. She reminded me that between Boston, Plymouth, Cape Cod,
and Salem in the east, and Tanglewood, Mass MoCA, and other artistic centers in the west, "Massachusetts is so filled with monuments to
the founding fathers and with high culture that that would be the last
thing in the world" she would want to attempt in Brockton. Instead,
Brockton could be the salt-of-the-earth stop on that larger tour. "This
is the industrial piece, the more gritty stuff. What I want is a place where
working-class families could stop, see the Marciano house, let the kids
run around at McNulty Park and Battery Wagner."

As much as the network of physical interconnections, an overlapping field of logical and thematic resonances further united Johanson's plan. Her design was about the interpenetration of nature and industry, art and daily life, ecological well-being and the up-from-under movement of working-class heroes. Shoes and shoe shapes were pervasive. Rocky's father, and Rocky himself for a few weeks, worked in the shoe factories; the ill-shod Confederate soldiers who buried the casualties of the 54th Massachusetts in a mass grave first stripped them of their Brockton-made footwear; even the naturally shoeprint-shaped wading pool and skating rink in McNulty Park would extend the image of Shoe City into nature. And water, of course, flowed throughout the scheme. Rocky Marciano ran along the rivers and built up his strength in the pool at the YMCA; the Industrial Revolution fountain at McNulty Park taught the lessons of mills and rivers; the rising and falling waters at Battery Wagner would echo the ocean that covered the mass grave of the 54th Massachusetts, now underwater off the South Carolina coast; and, most important, Johanson crafted a number of creative ways to involve Brocktonians in ameliorating and aestheticizing their city's long-standing water problems.

The landscape, she said, would be "tightly woven" with meaning. I will gladly accept that the landscape she envisioned is infused with multiple and interrelated meanings, but I have to draw the line somewhere short of "tightly woven." The cultural naïveté of Johanson's frankly eccentric work—especially as opposed to its ecological sophistication—can be exasperating. Take, for instance, the matter of ethnic and racial heritage. There is something dubiously simplistic about crafting imagery for the Marciano house and its neighborhood on the principle that Marciano was a "Roman" gladiator, and the same goes for the "Celtic" quality of McNulty Park's planned architecture and potentially nutty decorative flourishes, and the "African" inspirations for the Lemuel Ashport–Battery Wagner site's color scheme and its fish-shaped bridge. "I was using forms from the three different sources," she said in explanation, and then launched into a roundabout riff on the tendency of escaping slaves to set out during thunderstorms to throw off tracking dogs, which led her to explain how the design of her Battery Wagner site had incorporated elements of quilt patterns supposedly associated with the Underground Railroad's secret system of signals, which, after a couple of intermediate stops, led her to draw parallels between the resilience of Battery Wagner and that of Rocky Marciano. It all had something to do with water and "identity," and eventually it got back to

Rocky Marciano, but at some point the web of thematic affinities begins to become an idiosyncratic artifact of the artist's fancy—rather than something immanent in the landscape design that can be recovered by even the most informed or creatively astute observer.

Still, even when Johanson's associative inspiration outstrips the capacity of her plan to orchestrate logical connections, her commitment to finding the extraordinary in the ordinary (and vice versa) saves the day. "Mundane is the foundation," she said. "I aim for the mundane, as a designer." To know and love a city like Brockton is to take notice of the ordinary and extraordinary meaning in shoes and work, floods and other processes of urban nature, the railroad, the river, neighborhoods, the histories of working people, the interconnection of parts and the whole. If Johanson sometimes strained to make everything seem tightly woven when she talked about it, to look at the plan on paper is to see how it could have worked well in execution, maximizing some of the city's assets and addressing some of its principal weaknesses. Her plan inventively argues, too, that the link between nature and metropolis might have been stronger in the immediate aftermath of the Industrial Revolution than it is now. Shoe City was organized around the human body and local natural resources in ways no longer true of even the greenest, most "New Urbanist" postindustrial city.[20]

Johanson's plan was also bracingly realistic about commerce and politics, especially in scripting a broad variety of collaborations that range from youth programs to partnerships with all the players she could find: city and state and federal governments, the Massachusetts Cultural Council, the National Park Service, the Audubon Society, the Fuller Art Museum, Skeeter McClure, the historical society, local businesses, civic groups, even volunteers from trade unions and graduate students from MassArt. "Look," she said, "I've worked with cities before. I am a veteran of the political process." Because she had to work with Mayor Yunits, she was careful to base her plan on his twenty-one-point outline for Brockton's future, but she distinguished between his document, "a pie-in-the-sky thing to get elected," and her own. "These things were not just pie in the sky, I'm not just a crazy woman suggesting things. We had partners. We would have had free trees from the utilities, we would have had ongoing funding, the National Park Service would have done the trail. I had letters from Ted Kennedy, Barney Frank, William Delahunt. I was talking to John McCain—he really believes in Marciano, he gave me lists of grants I could apply for, and federal funding. My work is not about T-shirts, posters, and banners, it's about connecting neighborhoods, the economic revitalization of Brockton. The partners were there, the money for many of the pieces was there."

THE ALBATROSS

"So why are we driving around," Johanson added, "and nothing's here?" We were in Brockton on August 1, 2000, the day after our conversation at MassArt, visiting the Marciano house and other sites she had hoped to have completed or at least under construction by then. But the McNulty Park site was still just a vacant lot by the river, and a row of flood-damaged houses still occupied the Battery Wagner site. The Marciano house stood empty, locked against her. There were no green streets, no greened and daylighted rivers; there was no downtown village, no Rocky Marciano Trail, no tangible sign that anything significant had been done to turn her plan into anything but another unbuilt project. The first year of her two-year engagement was supposed to be for planning, the second for implementation. Three years after she had commenced work, there was just a plan. What happened? "They just did nothing," she said. "They just didn't know or want to take advantage of any of this. I got them leads to funding, programs, and they didn't *do* anything. I don't know," she added sarcastically, "maybe they didn't want me to get the glory." She had been invited to speak about her Brockton plan in England, to write about it in a French journal, to discuss it with the French Ministry of Planning. People all over were interested in the plan, it seemed to her, but not in Brockton.

Looking back in the summer of 2000, a year after formally concluding her business with the city of Brockton, Johanson regarded the initial big meeting at city hall as the last show of concerted goodwill toward her work. She had prepared the plan, turned it in, and been paid, but she had increasingly found that nobody was rallying around to act on her ideas. When one considers that she spent almost all of her fee on the Marciano house and other up-front outlays (like hiring Skeeter Mc-Clure to plan a youth program), and when one figures in the "fifty or sixty times" she made the 360-mile, round-trip drive to Brockton and all the hours she spent working there, it is fair to say that she gave Brockton its money's worth and then some. And still she could not even get through to the once-enthusiastic mayor on the phone to save her life. The clients' cold-shoulder attitude and the climate of mutual distrust got so bad, she said, that "when I turned in my last piece of paper on

July 30, 1999, I drove to Brockton, made them sign for it. Because I knew if I FedExed it they would 'lose' it. That's the last time I was in Brockton until today."

During the course of 2000 and 2001, I had several conversations with Johanson about what went wrong in Brockton; it was, understandably, on her mind. She frequently returned to the notion that people in power there felt threatened by any change instigated by an outsider. She told me that a locally prominent historian refused to help her get the Marciano house on the National Historic Register because he was worried it would "draw away from the historical society, which is funded with memberships, which has gradually been dropping off. That's what he told me: 'It will draw away from us.'" (I got the impression that Charlie Tartaglia had a similar worry that a Marciano house museum would supplant George's Cafe as the neighborhood's Rocky shrine, which might explain why he wanted to see the house torn down and replaced with a bronze statue of Rocky. It also might explain why Mark Casieri lost his part-time job at George's Cafe, a surprise development that scuttled one of his mortgage agreements.) Johanson thought that the directors and benefactors of the YMCA feared that youth programs associated with Johanson's sites would threaten their authority. Beate Becker adds, "Even Patricia's connections to outside sources like Audubon and the National Park Service were threatening. They could come in and help her change the way things happened in Brockton." Johanson told me much the same thing, "I came to the mayor with all this, with all these connections you could make that would be good for Brockton, and he was just appalled. It was like here's this girl who was always putting her foot into things she should know enough to stay out of." Johanson concluded that the mayor and the rest of Brockton's major players wanted cosmetic changes—new signs, maybe some quaint light standards, a river walk—but feared any real change that involved powerful outsiders and a comprehensive rethinking of the city's past, present, and future. She felt that people in Brockton shied away, especially, from her ambition to unearth and treat the industrial city's traumas—ecological injuries to landscape and watershed, tribal divisions between neighborhoods and social classes.

Johanson felt that Jack Yunits had turned on her. "I think the mayor was the one person who could have subdued the entrenched interests, and he was certainly eager to make a name for himself and be seen as a kind of visionary." At first, he helped her, even "putting the guy from the Brockton Community Corporation who owned the house over a barrel to force him to sell to me," but "at some point, for reasons still not totally known to me, the mayor pulled out of this project." What she called "the moment of death" occurred early on in 1998, in her retrospective estimation, when Johanson—and not the mayor—posed in front of the Marciano house in a photograph on the front page of the *Boston Herald,* accompanying a story about how an out-of-town artist was going to save Rocky's house and Brockton.[21] The gentle *Globe* may come first in Boston, but the *Herald,* a crabbier tabloid, tends to serve as the metropolitan paper of record in Brockton. Patricia Johanson told me she would have preferred not to be on the *Herald*'s cover, or in any photographs at all. But the mayor never made it back to the Marciano house for a planned photo shoot, and, she said, "Finally the photographer said, 'Look, please, I can't wait any longer, would you mind if I just took your picture?' Next day, Peter Marciano called and said, 'Pat, you look great!' It was the beginning of the end." Soon, Johanson said, Mary Waldron was blocking her access to the mayor.

When I asked Yunits and Waldron about Patricia Johanson, they both spoke admiringly of her talent—they still liked the idea that a bigshot artist had come to Brockton to make it beautiful—but they suggested she was impractical in her expectation that everything be done right away. "I'm consulted out," said the mayor. "Both Patricia and Frank Keefe leave you and say, 'Now, you got to do it.' You need money and you need patience, and the will of the people." He meant to do Johanson honor by grouping her with Keefe, the postindustrial turnaround guru, but the imputation was that professional visionaries like Johanson and Keefe got paid to dream, not to govern. "Patricia was focused on her project," added Waldron, "but the mayor had a lot of things to work on. We know we can't afford to see the Marciano house torn down—it would be bad for our image, bad for our history—but the city can't come up with $70,000 for that right now. There are other priorities, other claims on the money. We'll do what we can, in bits and pieces, but not right this minute." The mayor agreed. They might put up some historical markers along the proposed Rocky Marciano Trail. "It's doable locally," he said. And they would green the Salisbury Brook soon, which would be "expensive, but not a killer." But they would not rush to create a Marciano museum in the Dover Street house. "That will be the will of the people, plus private investors," said the mayor, which made it sound unlikely. Waldron pointed out that a Marciano museum had not been what they thought they would get from Johanson in the first place. The mayor nodded. They both seemed to feel that the crazy ecological artist lady had bait-and-switched them by concentrating on Marciano. "We hired her to work on the river," Waldron said, "and she got more and more into Marciano and the house."

"In retrospect, maybe it was a mistake to concentrate on Marciano," Johanson told a graduate class in public art at MassArt in October 2000, and maybe it all came down to that. Perhaps more Rocky was exactly what Brocktonians did not want from Johanson. The city's new-order boosters, hot for Edison, high-tech, espresso bars, brew pubs, and the river, did not necessarily want a new civic image founded on more of the same old grit. The old-school hard-liners, for their part, had to confront Johanson's makeover of their familiar champion into a sort of white-ethnic urban Swamp Thing, a mutant eco-hero associated with all sorts of environmental and multicultural causes that did not set them ablaze with inspiration. More than one regular at George's Cafe objected that Johanson had chosen the "wrong" Marciano house (since as a small child Rocky lived at a nearby home on Brook Street) and that she had not mapped his running route exactly right. These objections were not particularly persuasive, since Marciano did live in the Dover Street house during his fighting years and since he varied his running routes, but they expressed a larger discomfort with an outsider's handling of a local icon. Johanson's emphasis on social reconnection and cultural pluralism also might have cost her support, coming up as it did against Brockton's traditional tendency toward enclaves and insularity —heightened in this age of pseudo-hermetic privacy, sprawl, and disinvestment from the principle of face-to-face community. In the final analysis, the Rocky Marciano hook did not overcome resistance to her ideas, and it did not mobilize a passionately committed constituency within the elite or among the public. That failure made it very difficult for Johanson's project to succeed. "All of my projects have a life of their own," she said. "If they don't, they're not a success. What happened in this project is it was kind of smothered, I think."

Without a big push from engaged locals, the plan could not overcome the lack of some important elements of the recipe for urban revitalization. An influx of federal grant money might have washed away concerns about tight resources, an overextended mayor, outside influences, and the dubious efficacy of Rocky Marciano as a civic totem, but Johanson did not get the local assistance she needed to tap her national connections. She never had a simultaneously connected and committed local go-between to guide her business with the city. "Caroline Grayboys might have been the go-between to the city," said Beate Becker, "but she was sick, and then the people who followed were either not powerful enough or not committed to the project." Brockton also lacked a strong, vocal lobby of historical preservationists or environmentalists, the kind of property owners and businesspeople who might have helped push to landmark buildings and protect the watershed. There was no college downtown to provide Johanson with faculty allies, student interns, and a friendly base camp. She succeeded in involving MassArt in the project, even though it is in Boston, but Patti Seitz, an architect and professor at MassArt who brought her students to Brockton, told me that they received a chilly reception. "The people we met with in Brockton acted interested at first, but then they wouldn't work with us. They were threatened. They thought we were after their grant money or something."

And, it bears noting, Johanson especially needed go-betweens and allies because she was not necessarily easy to work with. Headstrong, passionate, attuned to her own often idiosyncratic set of resonances, touched with the trace of social autism that allows some creative people to invest themselves so completely in objects or plants or animals, she does not always pay close attention to the subtleties of human response around her. She may be a veteran of political struggles over public art, but she can still seem weirdly naive. She was shocked, for instance, to discover that "most of the people I've met in Brockton were interested in their own gain, not the greater good." She would have benefited from having somebody local to tell her when to push and when to ease up, somebody who could work a roomful of Brocktonian players for her. As the city's elite cooled to her, she felt her plan ceasing to be a blueprint for concrete reality and turning into another unbuilt project. So she pressed harder, and those she pressed started avoiding her, and even pushing back.

Once communication broke down, both sides felt free to imagine the worst of the other. On the Brockton side, Chris Cooney of the chamber of commerce told me, some people started muttering that Johanson had "ripped them off," or that she was "after the house" in order to profit from its resale. Both are patently silly ideas. Even if she managed to sell the Marciano house at double the original price, she would have done no better than break even financially on her Brockton work, and only a pathologically local mind-set would imagine that Johanson schemed to own a terribly dilapidated two-family house in a depressed midsize city in a neighboring state. For her part, Johanson began to see signs of a far-reaching conspiracy against her, with the mayor and his minions scaring off or co-opting those who wanted to help her, manipulating the newspapers to make her look bad, using MCC seed-grant money to fund the city's cultural affairs officer, harassing her about back taxes and permits for the Marciano house, and perhaps even embarking on a campaign to mess with her peace of mind.

Once Johanson had received her last payment, her only remaining connection to Brockton was the Marciano house, which she came to refer to as "the albatross." She wanted to sell it, but she held out the hope that the buyer might still turn it into a Marciano museum. "Oh, I would be happy for them to do any piece" of the plan, she told me in a forgiving moment. "Any piece would benefit them. And if they wanted to know how to get the money, I could tell them how to." Because she still controlled the house, she thought the Marciano museum portion of her plan still might have a chance of getting completed. "I'm like Rocky," she told me more than once, "I haven't given up. I want results." Since her cancer diagnosis in 1989 reminded her how short life is, she had become increasingly impatient with unbuilt projects. She wanted to sell the house to Mark Casieri, but his offers kept running afoul of his mortgage broker. Other offers came in, usually low ones, from a variety of characters with no interest in creating a Marciano museum. Some were speculators angling to pick up a cheap property in the rapidly escalating Boston area real estate market, but Johanson thought that others might be fronts for interested Brockton parties. She thought she saw the mayor behind one offer, perhaps the Brockton Community Corporation behind another. The house increased in value, and the offers straggled upward, but they remained dubious. She complained that the city was harassing her. Tax assessments on the Marciano house shot up suspiciously; the city demanded that she board it up and then ordered her to take down the boards. She would e-mail me vaguely ominous reports about the ongoing drama—"The tenor of the house has changed, things are going on, but it's not clear what"—but nothing happened.

In her less forgiving moments, of which there were more as spring turned into summer in 2000, she referred to her erstwhile ideal of gritty authenticity as a sinkhole, a pit, a dump. She reminded me frequently that sometimes people had jeered at Marciano when he ran through Brockton—because he was Italian, because he was in the wrong neighborhood, because they were jealous of his ambitions. When we visited Brockton together in August 2000, Johanson took me for a ride through D. W. Field Park. Wheeling along, she gestured with one hand and said,

"This was given by Field over the city of Brockton's dead body. They didn't want it. Another thing about Brockton, they take away anything that an ordinary guy would like. So, in this park, the city took out benches and grilling setups for picnics, and they drained the swimming hole. Brockton is the kind of place threatened by any grand vision." Her final verdict echoed Skeeter McClure's theory that geography is destiny: "Unfortunately, Marciano's tied to this deadbeat town, but Battery Wagner is movable, so maybe I can do that somewhere else. Everybody told me to stay away from Brockton, but I didn't listen. I've even thought about moving the house to Providence, but the problem is it belongs exactly where it is."

Brockton's history—as opposed to, say, Chicago blues—is not very portable, a strength when manifested as rootedness in the city's land-scape and the lived experience of its people, but a weakness when man-ifested as localism that violently defends its right to gnaw and perhaps choke on the bones of its own past. Mark Casieri, a local guy with suit-able skills and his heart in the right place, was Johanson's best hope of seeing the centerpiece of her Brockton plan turned from idea into fact. It even seemed possible that, bit by bit, with the city building some pieces and Casieri another and perhaps other inspired citizens some others, a significant portion of her plan might someday become more than just another unbuilt project. But it was Brockton business now, and thus out of her hands.

(Johanson's lawyer eventually made her bar Casieri from the Mar-ciano house—because she could be liable if he got hurt while working on it—but she continued to support his efforts to buy it. Casieri's difficulties in securing financing ended abruptly when he took her advice to apply to a mortgage company outside Brockton. The house finally changed hands in February 2001, with surviving Marciano relatives kick-ing in a cash contribution on Casieri's behalf. Soon he was beset by bur-glars, arson threats, and more runarounds from city hall, but he was working on the house every day, which was all he had ever asked for.)

CLOSING RANKS

When I was out cruising in Brockton with Mark Casieri and his dogs, we stopped in at Goody Petronelli's gym, which is housed in a redbrick building on a side street off Main Street, a couple of blocks from city hall and across from the offices of the *Enterprise*. Casieri used to go over there to knock the bags around a little, but he never took up boxing with any seriousness. Still, he felt we ought to stop in and say hello to Goody, dean of the city's fight people, who runs the gym alone, having fallen out with his brother. So we turned down the stretch of Ward Street renamed Petronelli Way and parked. On the sidewalk in front of the gym, Casieri stopped to organize and leash the dogs. A hard-looking young man approached us from across the street, exclaiming over the dogs, and asked from a respectful distance if he could check them out. After they had sniffed the stranger's hand, they allowed him to inspect them while he and Casieri entered into a deeply knowledge-able discussion of the virtues of Colby pit bulls, the special breed to which Casieri's dogs belong. "What beauties," the stranger said, crouch-ing down among them. "Perfectly matched, look at the lines on 'em, look at those *heads*. Oh, you beauties." Casieri remarked that Petey, the Little Rascals' dog, had been played by Colby pit bulls; the other guy said he knew *that*.

Casieri led me into the old building, up a couple of flights of steep stairs with the dogs straining ahead on their leashes, through a wood-floored gym—two boxing rings, heavy bags, speed bags, plenty of open space to jump rope, fluorescent lights, buzzer and bell, exhortatory wall art—and into Goody Petronelli's office. High on one wall of the office were molded a blank, shield-shaped crest and the curving motto "Union Made." The office's windows overlooked the street, which allowed Casieri to check on his car from time to time. Petronelli, a trim, vocif-erous fellow of advanced years, sat in his desk chair, shooting the breeze with Vinnie Vecchione, a portly trainer famous for maneuvering a Bos-ton palooka named Peter McNeeley into a fight with Mike Tyson and then throwing in the towel in the first round to save his man from harm. Casieri's arrival occasioned a discussion of pit bulls, about which almost everybody I met in Brockton seemed to know something. Petronelli, watching the dogs surging around his office, said, "They have the same qualities as Rocky," and I could see what he meant: narrow waist, com-prehensively muscled body, a quality of relentlessness. Casieri, agreeing, made an eerily graceful gesture with cupped, loose-wristed hands, alter-nately swooping and dipping them in the air in imitation of his dogs' heads, and said, "They never give up. When they chase a ball, they try to get it away from each other, they try this angle and then another angle. They keep coming." That was the ideal: never giving up, con-stantly seeking angles, coming and coming no matter what they were hit with, stopping only in response to their own discipline and training.

Looking at the blank shield on Petronelli's wall between "Union" and "Made," I thought about designing a municipal heraldic device for Brockton featuring a pit bull rampant on a field of shoe leather against a low skyline of brick factory buildings and three-deckers. Petronelli was telling a cautionary tale about a guy they all knew who used to raise pit bulls and train them as fighting dogs. "And you know what happened to him, right? His dogs, they closed ranks on him. He had to get rid of them, got out of the business." Welcome to Brockton. Patricia Johanson could tell you about closed ranks; Casieri, too.

Casieri took his dogs to run some errands, and Vecchione excused himself to see to Peter McNeeley, who had arrived for a late afternoon workout, which gave Petronelli a chance to talk about Marciano, Hagler, and Brockton before his own fighters started showing up.

First, though, Petronelli told me a stone wall–building story of his own. "I helped my father put up a wall for the Marcianos at their house. Just on the side there. It was when Rocky was away, fighting Ezzard Charles, I think. Rocky's mother came out and saw me working, and she said 'Rock-ee! Rock-ee!' I looked up at her and she said, 'Oh, you look joosta like my Rocky.' I wasn't near as big as he was, but I was bending over, working, and she couldn't really see me." After a pause he added, "The wall's still there."

Then we got down to boxing. Petronelli, a contemporary of Marciano's, said he was at ringside when Rocky took the title from Walcott in Philadelphia. He got up to enact the knockout. "Walcott was doing this walkaway move, and Marciano throws the right." This memory happens in the perpetual present tense of mythological time. Walcott is always making his big mistake after twelve-plus rounds of masterful boxing, and Marciano is always making him pay for it, reaping the ultimate reward of resilience and constant punching. Petronelli ticked off on the fingers of one disproportionately large, knobby hand the reasons that fight people were skeptical of Marciano: "They said he was too old; he was twenty-five when he started. They said he was too small, 'cause he was about 183 pounds. They said he had no science; they missed seeing how his defense was his offense." He switched hands to enumerate the reasons they were all wrong: "But he had the ingredients that matter. One, a chin of iron, which is God-given; two, the heart, really the balls; three, dedication; and four, he thought big. And his long endurance." For Petronelli, as for Casieri, Marciano's rise was a parable of local virtues triumphant. "Brockton is strictly a blue-collar town, or it was until the shoe business went. You had to work for everything. You want something, you got to earn it."

Marvin Hagler, Petronelli's star middleweight of the 1980s, embodied the same virtues, which made him a latter-day throwback. "Rocky put Brockton on the map," said Petronelli. "Hagler kept it there. They never met, but they had the same ingredients. And they were both loyal, too"—by which he meant loyalty to trainers and old friends, but also to Brockton and its home truths. Petronelli hoped to see statues of the two local champions in front of city hall, and soon. "It's been brought up before," he noted, although he did not mention that Hagler's guilty plea to a girlfriend's charge of domestic abuse in 1991 had contributed to a cooling of interest in a Hagler statue.[22] For the time being, Petronelli's gym would have to serve as Hagler's Brockton memorial. Photos of the handsome, shaven-headed champion decorated the walls of the office, and on one wall of the gym, next to a large American flag and a banner that read WELCOME HOME! "CHAMP" MARVELOUS MARVIN, was a large portrait of Hagler behind a lectern with arms raised. Attired in yellow warm-ups, wearing shades, holding a small American flag in one hand, Hagler stands tall against the backdrop of silhouetted buildings. A thought balloon rises from his head and floats over the scene: "Wow! I love these people—this city!" Other signs on the walls of the gym reminded fighters in training of the eternal verities by which Hagler had so scrupulously lived: "Fit Body = Fit Mind," "When in Doubt Jab Out," "Head Down Hands Up," and "Remember the Key Word Is 'WORK.' "

I had been advised by people who knew Petronelli not to ask him about his age or his money—he is older and richer than he looks—but I had been encouraged to ask him about sex. He is a strict and vocal fundamentalist on the subject of abstinence before a fight. "No sex two months before a fight," he said, grimacing to indicate the seriousness of the matter when I raised it. "Or six weeks. Depends how big the fight is. Medically, it's a fact that sex before a fight is bad for you. I'm from the old school. I'm against women boxing, I'm against sex before a fight." He proceeded to tell me horror stories featuring wobbly-legged, punchless libertines and onanists who had dissipated their essence before a fight. (A few weeks later, when I was hanging around Petronelli's office on a return visit, a young amateur middleweight who worked as a plumber was complaining about a postponement. "*Next* week? Can't I fight *this* Friday? I been doing everything." Petronelli, who did not understand, said, "Just keep doing it, that's fine, you're in great shape," to which the plumber replied, blushing, "But, you know, the no sex and all." Later, he was jumping rope shirtless in front of a mirror in the gym, looking good, in gloriously prime shape. The young woman who had come in with him sat on a folding chair along the wall, her long sleeves pulled down over her hands, looking supremely cute and bored. The plumber, who had not yet broken the news of the postponement to her, had a look of furious concentration.)

Petronelli, an old navy guy and a Brockton fight guy formed in the age of Marciano, sees himself as a defender of tradition in a changed world. "There used to be a lot of gyms, more fighters, more local shows," he said, but times have changed. He still teaches the basics, although fewer and fewer fighters develop the technical boxing skills once inculcated as a matter of course. I asked if he had any slick boxers these days; he grimaced in the negative and said, "Bruisers," although not unkindly. Fresh blood would certainly help. A mysterious-sounding Russian had called to set up a meeting, which could be good news. Large numbers of tough guys were coming out of the former Soviet Union; perhaps the Russian had some hungry Ukrainians, Kazakhs, or laid-off steelworkers from Magnitogorsk for him. Brockton's Cape Verdeans might provide some new talent as well. "So far, we've only had a couple," he said, "but you never know." You never know, that is, when the next champion in the making will mount the steep stairs for a first look at the gym. For the moment, Petronelli taught the boxer-puncher style to a motley assortment of men—white and black and Hispanic and otherwise, serious and not so serious, ranging from novices to those like McNeeley who were overdue for retirement. There was a hairstylist named Joe "Pino" Scarcella in the gym whose build and fighting style resembled Marciano's closely enough that an ESPN crew had used him as a body double for Rocky when they came to Petronelli's to shoot footage for a Marciano biography. And Petronelli had a giant, slow, brave heavyweight, an Irish construction worker from Dorchester named Kevin McBride, who might yet amount to something if he could be coaxed into getting serious about boxing. Petronelli had plenty of work to do, even if the glory days were long gone.

Casieri came back to get me; we had one more stop to make. Stanley Bauman, the photographer whose pictures of Rocky's life constitute the most extensive Marciano archive, had agreed to talk with me. "I love Stanley," Casieri told me. "He's all business. A worker. He's the main guy supporting me."

Bauman, who had a long, successful career as a photographer for the *Enterprise* and as a freelancer (for *Life,* among other publications), received me in the basement studio of his house. The dogs could not come in, so Casieri had to wait outside with them. A dignified man well into his eighties, Bauman cultivated a forbidding manner reminiscent of Professor Kingsfield in *The Paper Chase*—although with a less patrician affect, as befits a son of Brockton who never went to college and who lives in the house his parents bought in 1918. He told me about life in Brockton back in the day while I leafed through four thick albums of Marciano pictures: Rocky playing baseball at the playground across the street from the Dover Street house, Rocky running in the park, Rocky at home with his parents, Rocky in a gigantic convertible waving to the crowds in overcoats and hats who filled Main Street in an impressively solid mass to celebrate one of his victories. "Rocky came in here after he would train," said Bauman, "and he would sit right where you are, in gym clothes and worn sweaters, and we would talk. He was very, very poor. In those days, everybody was poor. You don't understand the euphoria he caused. People gathered to pay tribute to him. Not just the parades downtown when he won, but people gathering just to get the news of how he's doing, people waiting to hear news on the radio. This was before people had TVs." For Bauman, the key to Marciano's significance was "the atmosphere of the era that bred Rocky. There was a tremendous desire to achieve, not necessarily to be heavyweight champion. Nobody devoted themselves to the grind like he did. He never went to the bars. Never fooled around with women." Bauman wanted me to understand the most important thing of all: "Work is central to Brockton, but also central to that era. Kids of sixteen were unable to get work, and they wanted to, because they needed the money. Now, sixteen-year-old kids don't want to work, don't need to."

Bauman was a recognizable type, a Crypt Keeper, the impeccably local man of insight and intellect who guards the official meaning of a local memory with extralocal resonance. He therefore supported Mark Casieri's efforts to restore the Marciano house, but he pronounced Patricia Johanson "an interloper, a johnny-come-lately." He had at first been cooperative, loaning her prints and giving her advice, but later he closed ranks with others who ceased having anything to do with her. He told the story of Johanson's encounter with Brockton as a cautionary tale in which a flighty artist meets the hard facts of life on the streets of Tough Town, U.S.A. "She came up against the nitty-gritty. She was on a different level, she thought she was going to be the goddess who just came down here and did it all." He seemed satisfied, or perhaps just relieved, that she had been successfully encouraged to exit the scene.

When I left Bauman's basement studio, evening had fallen. Casieri's pit bulls did not know me anymore in the dark and barked furiously, throwing themselves against the windows of the Grand Marquis, which were now open only halfway. The dogs would not let me get in the car. Casieri had to calm them down by bringing them out one by one on a short leash to reintroduce me. Finally, they relented. We drove back to Dover Street, the dogs sullenly sniffing at the back of my head. I reclaimed my own car in front of the Marciano house and drove up Brook Street, renamed Marciano Way where it intersects with Dover, to George's Cafe. There I digested the day's events over a beer and inspected the Rockiana on the walls; then, finally, I pulled onto Route 24 northbound, heading back to Boston in the dark with the windows down.

I was thinking of Marciano's victory parades in downtown Brockton, which drew crowds larger than the city's population, and comparing that spectacle to Mark Casieri's lonely crusade to save an empty house. Marciano's ghost cannot bring together Brockton's fragmented constituencies in a solid mass as the living fighter once did, but he still has the power to inspire a closing of ranks, and to shape people's imaginations, their days, their labors.

CONCLUSION

GETTING THERE

ONCE, ON THE WAY to Erie from Boston to see a card of fights, I got caught in a December storm on I-90. I had been driving faster and faster, trying to make time before encountering the lake-effect snow prophesied by voices on the radio. Just before I reached Buffalo, though, I entered without preamble into a heavy snowfall. Big flakes blew hard out of the west, sailing on the wind like leaves and hitting my car with wet little thuds. Traffic slowed, ragged columns of cars crawling and sliding in the accumulating snow. Checking the rearview mirror for tailgaters and other potential menaces, I saw the car behind me, a Talon, which was coming on too fast, suddenly skid, swerve to the right, then overcorrect to the left and spin out, crashing solidly into a concrete abutment off the highway's left shoulder. The car sat for a moment, like a fighter taking a count, then backed up a few feet, spun its wheels as it got under way going forward, and fishtailed back onto the road again. Its right front end had been staved in, and a piece of metal hung crookedly off to the side. The driver—foolish, pigheaded, in shock, or determined to get right back on the horse that threw him— stepped on the gas and passed me, disappearing into the late afternoon gloom at an unwise speed. A few minutes later, I passed the damaged Talon. It was on the shoulder, no doubt having spun out once more, but its driver was angling to slip back into traffic and try his luck again. I did not see the Talon after that, though I checked my rearview mirror from time to time, worried. The car's travails and resilience had seemed like a Rust Belt portent of some kind.

The radio contributed to the afternoon's portentous feel. On a Christian talk station, somebody told a story about a Chicago couple

231

who ran over a piece of metal in the road, igniting a freakish car fire that killed six of their nine children—but, the point was, they still believe that God is sufficient. The big subject on Christian radio that afternoon, as is so often the case, was the Book of Revelation. The horned beast, the opening of multiple seals, and other elements of the coded arrival of the End of Days inspire creatively dire applications to the contemporary world: the horned beast is Iraq; no, it's North Korea; no, it's the World Bank, or the British royal family, or Hillary Clinton. On a sports talk station, a host who calls himself The Coach was leading callers in heaping abuse on Marv Levy, the aging, unfailingly decent, highly competent coach of the Buffalo Bills, who were 6–8 at the time after reaching (but losing) the Super Bowl repeatedly in the not-too-distant past. Everyone agreed that Levy was "too old," and that it would be "selfish" of him to stay on. Callers had only bad things to say about Todd Collins, the team's quarterback, too—"the worst QB in the NFC, ever," according to one caller heartily endorsed by The Coach. The discussion evolved into a macrohistorical debate over whether the rise and fall of football teams' fortunes is natural. Callers variously endorsed the notion of a structurally inevitable decline after a golden age and the notion that incompetent or perhaps even malign individuals like Levy and Collins were responsible for ruining a perfectly good team. Nobody suggested that Levy and Collins might individually or collectively be the horned beast, but they were clearly handmaidens of doom. Later, on an Erie station, a Mister Fletcher explained that shadowy conspirators were manipulating the climate, as freak storms in Malaysia and the Dakotas clearly proved. He cited corroborative facts from the Iron Mountain report (a notorious hoax, actually) and suggested the conspirators' identities in an excursus on North Korea's heroic resistance against the New World Order and its black helicopters. A caller, confirming Mister Fletcher's linkage of bad weather to darker forces marshaled on the world-historical scale by a train of villains stretching from the Illuminati to the Trilateral Commission, reported that his "research shows" that "we're being controlled" in ways most of us can neither understand nor resist.[1]

There is a particular ominous buzz in the air on this kind of afternoon in the upper Midwest and Northeast. The overcast sky seems heavy with more than snow; the way ahead seems occluded by more than slush and evening's early arrival. It seemed to me that the people on the radio felt it, too, as they talked of end times and current events, golden age and decline, bad weather, dark forces, crashing and burning.

When this particular order of entropic chill native to the Rust Belt starts to get to me, I want to be in somebody else's kitchen, or a bar, a bookstore, a pool hall, a gym—a place where it is warm and there is company. Instead, I was trying to get to Erie in time to watch some fights and perhaps have a follow-up chat with Liz McGonigal, if she showed up after all on what promised to be a bad night for going anywhere. It had something to do with an article I planned to write, which had something to do with a book I wanted to write, and at that moment it all seemed like a feebly insubstantial reason to be sliding all over the road so far from home. I was approaching an industrial city on a gray day—which is normally my idea of a good time—but even the most familiar sort of place can feel thin and cold, for want of better words, on this kind of afternoon.

There is nothing like work to warm and thicken the world right back up again. I did have a book to write, at least in theory, and on a Buffalo talk station I found a lay seminar on form and meaning in the Rust Belt that had me wishing I could risk pulling over to take notes. (I had both hands on the wheel, removing one from time to time only to find another radio station; when I got to Erie, I wrote down everything I could remember.) A host and his guest, a city councilman, were encouraging callers to suggest solutions to the problem of what to do with the Memorial Auditorium, known as the Aud, on Main Street in downtown Buffalo. For more than half a century, it had been the city's principal arena, home to the Buffalo Sabres hockey team and site of concerts, circuses, and political rallies, but it had been rendered obsolete by the opening of the new Marine Midland Arena. The vacant Aud, boarded up in 1996 and regularly abused by graffitists since then, now housed pigeons and bats. Everybody in town seems to have voiced an opinion about what to do with the Aud: some have urged its demolition; others have suggested turning it into a military or architectural or maritime or historical or children's museum, a convention center, a cultural center, an entertainment complex, an aquarium, an intermodal transit hub, a sports superstore, a film production studio, a giant indoor parking lot. Callers that day had a narrower range of options in mind. Turning the Aud into a casino headed the list. One caller suggested that "we get an Indian tribe in here right away," then "when it's legal, we can have the state take over." Others advocated refitting the Aud as a prison; the building "is literally bombproof," one of them pointed out. The host and his guest rejected this option not because it would be an evil, cretinous thing to do to a public gathering place on Main Street but because it would be "bad for tourism." (On the other hand, a prison might be turned into a strong draw, as the talk-radio crew might have realized had they considered the success of the cable television show *Oz*, which had completed its first season and already made a name for itself as hard-hitting drama by showing eager viewers the spectacularly awful things that can happen in prison. An ant-farm prison in the Aud, with glass walls and guaranteed violence, might well draw visitors in droves on their way to and from Niagara Falls.) Attracting tourists, the hosts agreed, was the given in this discussion. The caller who proposed turning the Aud into a golf driving range got a hearing because, after all, tourists do like to play golf.

They were talking about what to do with industrial Buffalo, the transport hub that attracted immigrants from Europe, migrants from the South, steel mills, grain elevators, the auto industry, the Pan-American Exposition of 1901, and an honor roll of major architects who designed important buildings there: H. H. Richardson; McKim, Mead, and White; Louis Sullivan and Dankmar Adler; Frank Lloyd Wright; Eliel and Eero Saarinen. That city boomed in the nineteenth century, but the development of the St. Lawrence Seaway in the 1950s and the steel industry's contraction in the 1970s marked the middle and late stages of its passing. The Aud, a Great Depression–era project approved by FDR, was built relatively late in Buffalo's high-industrial heyday, but it occupied a site with a longer history. It stood near what was the Erie Canal's western terminus, on the edge of one of the city's oldest sections, a stretch of waterfront that bore the marks of nineteenth-century urbanism in its cobblestones, docking slips, and railroad infrastructure. "The wealth that built the mansions on Delaware Avenue and our classic downtown buildings had its source in and around these twelve acres," wrote Donn Esmonde in the *Buffalo News* in 2000, urging his fellow citizens not to allow any more demolition or redevelopment in the vicinity of the Aud. "Experts say we have a historic cultural landscape— a physical record that can be used to tell the evolving story of a key site in American history. This is our Alamo, our Fort Sumter. The cobblestone streets and Commercial Slip and 1880s concrete railroad bridge tell the story of the canal trade and how it was later displaced by railways." Esmonde pointed out that cultural tourism was booming across America—"Philadelphia even includes the pit where Ben Franklin emptied his chamber pot on its historic trail"—and hoped that Buffalo would have the good sense to create a heritage park to exploit and preserve its history.[2]

Something had to be done because, as Esmonde reminded his readers, "Buffalo is desperate for any economic boost." The usual signs and portents told the story: a moribund downtown, an exodus of young people, a shift to a service economy anchored by health care and banking that had yet to pay off, a municipal reputation reduced to the banal stigma of Snow City, U.S.A.

South of Buffalo, the going got worse, then better. Despite the weather delay, I made it just in time for the fights, which were held before an excitable crowd in the ballroom of the Avalon Hotel in downtown Erie. It turned out to be an evening of well-contested bouts between competent regional tough guys. Johnny Bizzarro, a technically accomplished local welterweight who had developed a tendency to fight a bit too far from his opponent, lost the featured attraction to a persistent ham-and-egger from Cleveland named Henry Hughes. The class of the evening's field was Paul Spadafora, a lightweight out of Pittsburgh, who beat a guy from Buffalo named Roger Brown in the preceding bout. Spadafora got hit with some hard punches, but he had the makings of a champion (and later became one). He had classically elegant footwork and defensive form, he controlled his opponent's aggression by turning him in the clinches and "taking a walk" to reset the range when pressed, he had terrific hand speed and a gift for body punching, and he mixed his punches with an artist's touch. Spadafora made curious "ush-ush" sounds when he threw punches, as if speaking the secret names of the various blows. (The ring girls had the look of seasoned pros in the exotic dance trade. One of them, who went straight-backed through the ropes with a limber dip-and-step motion, rather than the usual bend-and-wriggle, distinguished herself by doing a handspring in high heels.)

After the fights were over, having had my chat with Liz McGonigal—who was looking forward to her next bout and thinking about applying to MIT's doctoral program in philosophy—I walked up State Street to Perry Square, where I had heard a blues band in a bar on a previous visit. It had stopped snowing, and the temperature had dropped. The wind came straight down State Street off the lake, sculpting snowdrifts and frozen slush into shapes one used to see on the covers of paperback science fiction novels. I found the bar, which appeared to have exactly the same people in it who had been there the last time, nine months before. They even appeared to be wearing the same sweaters. The blues was recorded rather than live this night, but the room was cozy, and I found a spot along the rail to hoist one in peace. I had found my way to the fights, blues, the close atmosphere of a bar on State Street on a cold windy night: expressions of the ordinary and extraordinary ways in which work and play—that is, life—accrue to a complex thickness in places like Erie, Pennsylvania. I had found my way through the landscape to some truth and beauty, Rust Belt style.

I did the same thing when I walked through the Trump Marina to hear Buddy Guy play, and I do the same thing when I go out to hear live blues in Chicago. Whether headed to the Checkerboard on the South Side, Legends downtown, or a North Side club like B.L.U.E.S., you must negotiate accrued layers of social, economic, and cultural history to get to the music. And often enough, once you get there, you find yourself mentally peeling back some of the accrued layers of musical form and performance in which that history has wrapped the blues—the guitar-heavy mix, the crowd that wants to hear "Sweet Home Chicago" again and roars at the mention of the Rolling Stones or Stevie Ray Vaughan, the twenty-seventh request to "Let me hear you say, 'Hell, yeah!'" and the audience happy to oblige. You can peel back those layers, but you cannot dispense with them. The movements of people and capital and ideas that produced those layers also condition the form of the music and your experience of it. How you get through the landscape to the music is not separate from the music itself; each is part of the other.

You can stretch the point to include what happens when, flipping through the channels, you come upon Popeye and Cloudy at work (or Shaft, or Priest), chasing somebody down the street in the grainy twilight of early 1970s cinematography. You have to negotiate many layers of electronic landscape—everything showing on all the other channels, the noise and smoke of advertising, the standardized plot and stock characters of the movie itself—but you can find your way to the inner city after the urban crisis, and to a moment at the start of the 1970s when the histories of city life and popular storytelling converged in a burst of stylistic creativity. The latter-day context in which you see a movie from that moment shapes the meanings you derive from it; conversely, the movie and its moment influenced what came after—as evidenced by the action movie on one channel, the 1970s-nostalgia rap video on another, the panic-stricken local news report on another, the shaky-cam "reality show" on another, the rerun of *Hill Street Blues* or *Homicide* or *NYPD Blue* or *Law and Order* or a Grosso-Jacobson production on another. So, again, the electronic "landscape" through which you travel and the world of the movie in which you finally arrive contain and condition one another.

The layering of history and meaning in the landscape produces the satisfying thickness that makes you feel you are *somewhere*, but it also produces tensions. The strong feelings motivating Patricia Johanson's and Mark Casieri's efforts to create a Rocky Marciano museum in the house at 168 Dover Street in Brockton—and the strong feelings inspired in others by that project—attest to the potency of the meanings layered into the landscape. The struggles touched off by those efforts suggest how much can be at stake in determining the proper relation of past to future in a changing city. Imagine for a moment that both the dream of a Marciano museum and the mayor's plans for downtown Brockton are realized. Picture arriving at the Marciano house after stopping downtown to stroll along the riverway, check out the stores and other new businesses housed in converted industrial buildings, and visit a redbrick brew pub or a coffeehouse. How would you put together the experience of the museum and the downtown? A history of Brockton inheres in the relationship between them, a tangle of stories fraught with strong feelings about what has been gained and lost in the city's long transformation. As a monument to a particular fraction of the industrial working class, the Marciano museum would be both of a piece with the converted downtown and in some ways a refutation of it.

You would expect to feel such tensions in Brockton, a quintessential "gritty city" in which you always feel that you are *somewhere*. It is perhaps more surprising to feel them even when you walk through a casino—a place designed to help you imagine yourself *nowhere*, outside of time and unconnected to the workaday social landscape to get to the fights. I do this frequently because, except for a few big bouts held at Madison Square Garden and similar venues, the upper end of the boxing business has largely migrated from the industrial cities that once served as fight capitals to gambling centers such as Las Vegas, Atlantic City, and Foxwoods. Even the prospective return of marquee bouts to old-school fight capitals, like Detroit, has been pegged to the establishment of legalized gambling in casinos. Boxing attracts players by generating excitement and television exposure, which is good for the gambling business, and it also allows a casino to offer a sort of triumphalist history lesson in suitably spectacular form: a performance under glass by antediluvians who work hard with their bodies and live by principles of self-denial. Casino culture affects to regard boxers in the same way it regards racehorses, as magnificent atavisms to be celebrated and patronized, survivals of an era (remotely antecedent to our current golden age of leisure and gaming) when people rode horses to get around and worked with their bodies to pay the bills. This conceit gestures back to the emergence of modern pugilism in late-eighteenth-century England, when aristocratic swells mixed with fistfighters, bearbaiters, touts, gin vendors, and others of low station to shape Regency sporting life. Contemporary casinos offer Americans, especially those of the working and middle classes who make up gambling's principal customer base, a chance to playact at being swells. The juxtaposition of boxing with gambling reinforces casino patrons' sense of swellness by offering them the spectacle of low types toiling—half-naked boxers fighting, half-naked women dancing and waiting tables, liveried servitors dealing cards, and so on.

But the presence of boxing in a casino also signifies against the grain of playing at leisure-class idleness. The fights, after all, offer an account of the history and meaning of the body at work. Leisure and luck, which are supposed to matter most in a casino, are heretical notions in the fight world. Work and skill, the keywords of boxing, might mean something to the casino employees who deal the cards or provide entertainment or bounce the unruly, but not to the overwhelming majority of gamblers who lose their hard-earned money on unlikely bets and go home hysterically satisfied. Almost everything about a casino's self-presentation, other than boxing, has been designed to make a visitor forget about work. You are intended to feel as if the money in your pocket has been magically devalued—made into something filthy to be shed as fast as possible—by the fact that you earned it. What you need to do is launder that tainted money by cycling it through slot machines or by turning it into chips, gaming with them, and then cashing them in for better money that has been magically supervalued because you won it through lucky play. When you walk into a casino, especially the large sections of it dominated by cacophonous banks of slot machines, you enter a parody of a factory straight out of *Modern Times* or *Metropolis*—an atrium filled with machines feverishly tended by people who make repetitive motions for hours at a stretch.[3] But nobody who gambles in a casino has to be good with his or her hands, and nothing is produced, other than profit and loss. I think part of the meaning, and perhaps the attraction, of boxing for casino patrons lies exactly in the reminder it offers of work, limits, material consequences, and other subjects rendered taboo or exotic by the logic of institutionalized "gaming."

I have always been reminded of this uneasy relationship between boxing and one of its chief patrons of the postindustrial age (television is the other) when I attend a fight at the Boardwalk Hall, the old convention center in Atlantic City. The building's facade, a modest sweep of arched stone bracketed and dwarfed by the steel-and-glass box of the (now defunct) Trump World's Fair on one side and the two-tone tower of the Trump Plaza on the other, has a headstone quality accentuated by the legend inscribed on it: "A permanent monument conceived as a tribute to the ideals of Atlantic City. Built by its citizens and dedicated to recreation, social progress, and industrial achievements." Like the figure of the citizen from whom power proceeds to duly elected officials, the notion of "industrial achievements" has become an archaic and indeed a subversive principle in a city comprehensively refashioned according to the logic of the gambling business—a brittle crust of promise and amusement stretching over a deep, dark sea of bad luck, bad jobs, and odds prohibitively stacked in the house's favor. Whatever the inscribers of the convention center's facade meant by "social progress" has been redefined as a matter of moving up from the five-dollar minimum blackjack tables to the ten-dollar tables. People visit Atlantic City because it is a place synonymous with goofing off, and with action. Yet very few people come to Atlantic City anymore to swim, sunbathe, breathe ocean air, move among crowds on the boardwalk, or otherwise engage in "recreation" as it used to be defined when the city functioned as a riviera for the urban villages of New York and Philadelphia. Those crowds are for the most part indoors, hunched over slot machines and tables, ignoring one another while sweating bullets in the deskilled pursuit of leisure. Atlantic City's principal economic achievement has always been separating visitors from their hard-earned money; the gambling industry's innovative contribution to civic ideology has been to encourage a kind of contemptuous blindness to work that makes "industry" a dirty word.

But when you pass under the old convention center's inscribed facade and find your way to ringside, you encounter two boxers, good with their hands, applying themselves to a problem that luck and leisure can never help solve. The ring occupies a landscape alive with meaning and with convergent stories, but the combatants are not symbols, and they are not history; they are working.

ACKNOWLEDGMENTS

Working on this book entailed hanging around and prying in places to which I had not always been expressly invited. I owe an unpayable debt of gratitude to the patient, forthright people on whose workdays and inner lives I trespassed. Their names are in the book, often just before or after the word "said." In particular, for extraordinary generosity with their time and insights, I am indebted to Liz McGonigal, Buddy Guy, Sonny Grosso, Patricia Johanson, and Mark Casieri.

The faculty, administrations, and students of Boston College, Harvard University, Lafayette College, and the University of Massachusetts, Boston, helped me write this book by providing time, money, information, good ideas, and goodwill. I owe special thanks to Henry Louis Gates Jr. and Richard Newman of Harvard's W. E. B. Du Bois Institute for a Du Bois Fellowship and continuing friendly support. The *Erie Times-News,* Marc PoKempner, the Museum of Modern Art's Film Stills Archive, the *New York Daily News,* the *Boston Herald,* the *Brockton Enterprise,* Stanley Bauman, and Patricia Johanson contributed illustrations; Boston College helped pay for them. Patient, expert people too numerous to list here helped me find my way to written sources: they include librarians at Boston College, Harvard, Lafayette, and Yale University's Beinecke Library; and archivists at the Municipal Archives of New York and the historical societies and public libraries of Erie, Chicago, New York, and Brockton.

Writing this book, I have come to appreciate the ways in which institutions can give form to individual inspiration. On this, my second go-round with the University of California Press, I have had the good fortune to work with Monica McCormick, Randy Heyman, Caralyn Bialo,

Susan Ecklund (an exacting and soulful copyeditor), two astute anonymous readers for the press, and many others with whom it has been my pleasure to collaborate. Linda Norton, editor and friend, guided the book's progress with a sure but light touch and a Dorchester-rooted feel for truth and beauty in the Rust Belt. I was in good hands.

Many more people than I can thank here have commented on pieces of this book, explained things to me, sent me useful information, put me up on the road, or got me in to see somebody I needed to see. Among them are Chris Erikson and Charles Cherington, trusted readers and discussants; Mike Ezra, Gary Moser, and Larry Holmes, my three wise men of boxing; Bruce Iglauer, Rocco Caponigri, and Bill Savage, exemplary Chicago guys; Jeanine Basinger, who whisked me past the barriers that keep people like me away from actors and directors; William Friedkin, who made time to talk to me and made sure that others did, too; Sean McCann and Chris Wilson, who abetted me in the study of crime stories; James Woolley, Lynn Van Dyke, and Neil McElroy, who helped me get started; Benjamin Filene and Carl S. Smith, discerning readers; Thomas J. Humphrey, Barry Bluestone, and Charlie Lord, who answered last-minute questions; and Jay Williams, at *Critical Inquiry,* whose editing of the article that became chapter 1 included a two-word substitution—"bolted onto" for "tucked under"—that still makes my day.

My parents, Salvatore and Pilar Rotella, and my brothers, Sebastian and Sal, have taught me all about work—especially that it is good for you—without having to say a word. They have also volunteered more than a few words on subjects addressed in the book (and on my work habits, which feature more couch time and loitering than theirs), for which I thank them. My in-laws, the many Kleins of Massachusetts and points south, have welcomed me to their part of the world with kindness. Beate Becker, my in-the-know sister-in-law in the cultural economic development business, tipped me off to what was happening in Brockton and introduced me to Patricia Johanson. H. Peter Klein provided clippings and shelter, both appreciated.

This book is dedicated to Tina Klein, possibly the finest natural flyweight ever to come out of Huron Village, because (1) she would get seriously bent out of shape if it were not; (2) I have been carried along on the surge of her inspirational thinking, editorial rigor, and encouragement; and (3) she taught me a secret about curiosity: exploring the world around you and taking an interest in what people do can be a form of gratitude.

NOTES

Quotations unaccompanied by footnoted citations are drawn from interviews I conducted or from conversations held in my presence.

INTRODUCTION. TRUTH AND BEAUTY IN THE RUST BELT

1. Jennifer Steinhauer, "7 Are Killed and 7 Injured in Car Crashes as Year Begins," *New York Times,* January 2, 1999, B1.

2. James Dao, "Bradley Wants More Spending to Ease Stresses on Families," *New York Times,* October 8, 1999, A24.

3. For the broadest argument I know about the implications of manual dexterity, see Frank R. Wilson, *The Hand: How Its Use Shapes the Brain, Language, and Human Culture* (New York: Pantheon, 1998). Arguing on the evolutionary scale, Wilson posits being good with our hands as that which has made us human.

4. I have told parts of this larger historical story, covering in particular the 1950s and 1960s, and I have considered its literary consequences in *October Cities: The Redevelopment of Urban Literature* (Berkeley and Los Angeles: University of California Press, 1998).

5. Robert Palmer, *Deep Blues* (New York: Viking Penguin, 1981), 277.

1. THE CULTURE OF THE HANDS

Larry Holmes is quoted from his book with Phil Berger, *Larry Holmes: Against the Odds* (New York: St. Martin's, 1998), 275. Kate Sekules is quoted in Nancy Hass, "When Women Step into the Ring," *New York Times,* October 1, 2000, sec. 9, 1, 7.

1. See "Town Built on Steel Industry Resigns Itself to End of an Era," *New York Times,* November 19, 1995, A27.

2. Peter T. Kilborn, "A City Prepares for Life after Steel," *New York Times,* December 6, 1994, A12.

3. See William P. Garvey, "Erie: The Anatomy of a City III" (Erie, Pa.: Erie County Historical Society, 1993), 9–10, 16–18. See also two papers (both released in March 1998) prepared for and disseminated by the Regional Government Opportunities Task Force of the Erie Conference on Community Development, an organization of chief executives and allied progrowth boosters: "How Do We Compare? Rating the Erie Region in a National Context" and "A Snapshot of the Community: Regional Baseline and Trend Indicators for Understanding and Improving the Greater Erie Area and Its Economic Future."

4. See John G. Carney, *Saga of Erie Sports* (Erie, Pa.: John G. Carney, 1957), 193–215.

5. In *Muscletown, USA: Bob Hoffman and the Manly Culture of York Barbell* (University Park: Pennsylvania State University Press, 1999), John D. Fair tells a similar story about bodybuilding in York, Pennsylvania, a city "known for the manufacture of air conditioners, chains, motorcycles, stoneware, caskets, and dentures" (1). The city is also known for York barbells and other weight-lifting equipment. That business grew out of an oil-burner factory, to which Bob Hoffman recruited men interested in bodybuilding. "That the training platform was situated in the middle of the oil-burner factory aptly characterized the relationship of lifting to the business," which was gradually "converted for use in underwriting and promoting American weightlifting" (3) and associated masculine ideals. Fair's account wraps physical culture around manufacturing in a tight, mutually shaping fit.

6. "Jim Donnelly Trains G.E.A.A. Boxers in Well Equipped Gym," *Erie Works News,* July 17, 1936, 7; "Herbie Phillips Kayos Tom Stanley in Main Bout of G.E.A.A. Show," *Erie Works News,* August 28, 1936, 6.

7. See Kathryn Marie Dudley, *The End of the Line: Lost Jobs, New Lives in Post-industrial America* (Chicago: University of Chicago Press, 1994), 59–61, 71–74, 107–108, 126–134. Dudley explores the nuances of her distinction between the cultures of the hands and of the mind in the cited passages, which provide useful background to my discussion of Liz McGonigal's place in both cultures.

8. The club moved again at century's end, displaced by a drugstore. This time it came to rest in a larger space above a restaurant. DeForce added more weight-training equipment and set about incorporating the club so he could qualify for grants that would allow him to buy a building.

9. Matt DeForce, quoted in Dave Richards, "Ready and Waiting: McGonigal Will Defend U.S. Title Next Week," *Erie Daily Times,* May 18, 1998, 8C.

10. Women's movement into boxing and the military combat arms has occasioned a good deal of public discussion and press coverage. Their movement into hunting, less prominently publicized, has also been noted. See, for example, James Barron, "A-Hunting She Will Go," *New York Times,* November 26, 1997, B1. Barron notes that women "have become the fastest-growing group among hunters, reviving an industry that was in danger of stagnating as fewer men signed up for hunting licenses." Many men remain ambivalent about the prospect of women saving hunting, though, as one female hunter suggests

in observing, "'Anytime women become associated with weapons, it's really problematic.'"

11. See Allen Guttmann, *Women's Sports: A History* (New York: Columbia University Press, 1991), 74–76, 99–100; and Jennifer Hargreaves, "Bruising Peg to Boxerobics: Gendered Boxing—Images and Meanings," in *Boxer: An Anthology of Writers on Boxing and Visual Culture*, ed. David Chandler, John Gill, Tania Guha, and Gilane Tawadros (Cambridge, Mass.: MIT Press, 1996), 125. It appears that women bent on mixing it up have always found their way into the fights. The recent discovery of a young woman buried with gladiatorial honors in a Roman cemetery in London, for instance, seems to confirm archaeologists' belief that fighting women carved out a place for themselves in the ancient world's bloodsport trades.

12. Jimmy Finn, quoted in Marion Lloyd, "Scores of Knockouts Later, Risks for Women Still a Mystery," AP wire story, May 4, 1997. The Women's International Boxing Federation is not the same organization as the International Women's Boxing Federation. Women's boxing, just like men's boxing, now has its own mess of competing sanctioning bodies.

13. Bruce Silverglade, quoted in John Powers, "Throwing a Combination," *Boston Globe*, November 15, 2000, A1, F3.

14. Hass, "When Women Step into the Ring," 7.

15. Finn, quoted in Lloyd, "Scores of Knockouts Later."

16. "Women's Boxing on the Rise," *The Onion* (www.theonion.com), 1999. I downloaded the chart, which bears a copyright by *The Onion*, in 1999; as of July 2001, I could no longer locate or retrieve it from *The Onion*'s archive.

17. Advertisement in *Weekly Journal: or, The British Gazetteer*, October 1, 1726. I am indebted to James Woolley for this citation. Moving forward almost two centuries and across the Atlantic, Madelon Powers's fine history of barroom culture (*Faces along the Bar: Lore and Order in the Workingman's Saloon, 1870–1920* [Chicago: University of Chicago Press, 1998]) finds a similar tension between skill and sex in women's boxing in American saloons. Powers cites a program for a card of fights at a saloon in 1899 that describes one participant, Bessie Raymond, as "Handy with Her Mitts." But foxy boxing, either between women or between foxy boxers and men who paid for the titillating privilege of laying hands on them, was already part of vaudeville's lower reaches. "In the same era," Powers notes, "a wealthy bon vivant in New York . . . reported witnessing a saloon boxing match 'between two ladies, with nothing but trunks on'" (158).

18. Finn, quoted in Lloyd, "Scores of Knockouts Later."

19. John Curran, "Women in the Ring: A Card of Their Own," AP wire story, January 11, 1998.

20. See John Sugden, *Boxing and Society: An International Analysis* (New York: Manchester University Press, 1996), 18; Hargreaves, "Bruising Peg to Boxerobics," 125.

21. S. Kirson Weinberg and Henry Arond, "The Occupational Culture of the Boxer," *American Journal of Sociology* 57 (March 1952): 460.

22. Loïc J. D. Wacquant, "The Pugilistic Point of View: How Boxers Think

and Feel about Their Trade," *Theory and Society* 24 (August 1995): 502. Wacquant has published his boxing work at book length in *Corps et âme: Carnets ethnographiques d'un apprenti boxeur* (Marseille, France: Agone, 2001). It will be published in English, translated by Christopher Rivers, as *Body and Soul: Reflections of an Amateur Boxer* (Berkeley and Los Angeles: University of California Press, forthcoming in 2003).

23. I have engaged with this argument at length elsewhere; see Carlo Rotella, "Three Views of the Fistic Summits from College Hill," *South Atlantic Quarterly* 95 (spring 1996): esp. 306–320.

24. Wacquant, "The Pugilistic Point of View," 519.

25. John Goodman and Pete Hamill, *The Times Square Gym* (New York: EVAN, 1996).

26. John Lahr, "Sinatra's Song," *New Yorker,* November 3, 1997, 78.

27. A. J. Liebling, introduction, *The Sweet Science* (New York: Penguin, 1982), 2.

28. A. J. Liebling, "A Blow for Austerity," in *A Neutral Corner: Boxing Essays,* ed. Fred Warner and James Barbour (San Francisco: North Point, 1990), 118.

2. TOO MANY NOTES

Bruce Iglauer is quoted in Laurence J. Hyman, introduction to *Going to Chicago: A Year on the Chicago Blues Scene,* photographs by Stephen Green, ed. Laurence J. Hyman (San Francisco: Woodford, 1990), 14.

1. The original version is Eddie Boyd, "Five Long Years," J.O.B. 1007, 1952 ("Five Long Years" [Eddie Boyd] © 1952 Music Sales Corp. [renewed]; all rights reserved). Guy's performance of the song on July 23, 1998, at Trump Marina in Atlantic City differed from Boyd's in a number of ways: it was slower, there was a great deal more soloing, and, as usual, Guy altered the lyrics where he pleased. Guy sings "chucking steel," for instance, while Boyd sang "trucking steel," and Guy habitually turns the line about his next wife bringing home some dough into a frantic finger-ticking litany of all the different forms of work she will have to do, a routine that usually culminates in a shriek before he stops counting on his fingers and lays them on his guitar once more.

2. Eddie Boyd, quoted in Jim O'Neal and Amy O'Neal, "Living Blues Interview: Eddie Boyd, Part Two," *Living Blues* 36 (January/February 1978): 20.

3. Peter Watrous, "A Veteran Bluesman Glides Past the Inevitable Necessities," *New York Times,* August 3, 1998, B7.

4. See Bill Dahl's versions of decline in "Stale Home Chicago," *Chicago Tribune,* March 15, 1996, Tempo p. 1; "Last of a Breed," *Chicago Tribune,* May 29, 1996, Tempo p. 1; and his liner notes for *The Golden Age of Blue Chicago* (Blue Chicago, BC 5003). See also Steven Sharp, "Billy Branch: Don't Start Me to Talkin'," *Living Blues* 139 (May/June 1998): 25. Among countless other decline stories, repeated especially in obituaries, one of the most comprehensive is

Stephen Braun, "A Fading Legacy for Chicago Blues," *Los Angeles Times*, February 28, 1998, A1, A16-A17, which opens with the funeral of Junior Wells, Buddy Guy's old running partner.

5. For examples of arguments that make such claims explicitly, see Sharp, "Billy Branch," 23-24; and Francis Davis, *The History of the Blues: The Roots, the Music, the People: From Charley Patton to Robert Cray* (New York: Hyperion, 1995), 238.

6. See Jesse McKinley, "On Stage and Off," *New York Times*, April 30, 1999, B2.

7. Jim O'Neal, "Pepper's Lounge," *Living Blues* 2, no. 5 (summer 1971): 32.

8. Buddy Guy, quoted in Donald E. Wilcock with Buddy Guy, *Damn Right I've Got the Blues: Buddy Guy and the Blues Roots of Rock-and-Roll* (San Francisco: Woodford, 1993), 27.

9. Willie Dixon, quoted in Wilcock with Guy, *Damn Right*, 33.

10. See extended versions of the cutting contest story in Wilcock with Guy, *Damn Right*, 35-37; and Timothy White, "A Portrait of the Artist," *Billboard*, December 4, 1993, 20.

11. In *Romancing the Folk: Public Memory and American Roots Music* (Chapel Hill: University of North Carolina Press, 2000), Benjamin Filene examines the brokering of roots music as authentic folk culture in the twentieth century. "Mastering the Cult of Authenticity," his chapter on Muddy Waters, Willie Dixon, and Leonard Chess, offers a superb case study of some of the conditions of blues production I have not emphasized, especially the often contradictory consequences of labeling the blues as roots music.

12. See, e.g., Barry Bluestone and Bennett Harrison, *The Deindustrialization of America: Plant Closings, Community Abandonment, and the Dismantling of Basic Industry* (New York: Basic Books, 1982); William Julius Wilson, *The Truly Disadvantaged: The Inner City, the Underclass, and Public Policy* (Chicago: University of Chicago Press, 1987); Wilson, *When Work Disappears: The World of the New Urban Poor* (New York: Knopf, 1996); Reynolds Farley and Walter Allen, *The Color Line and the Quality of Life in America* (New York: Russell Sage Foundation, 1987); and Reynolds Farley, ed., *State of the Union: America in the 1990s* (New York: Russell Sage Foundation, 1995).

13. "Live Chicago Blues," *Living Blues* 1, no. 3 (autumn 1970): 2; "Chicago Blues Today: In the Clubs," *Living Blues* 18 (autumn 1974): 4.

14. "Chicago Blues Club Guide," *Living Blues* 45/46 (spring 1980): 10-11.

15. O'Neal, "Pepper's Lounge," 34-35.

16. U.S. Travel Data Center, *The Economic Impact of Travelers on Chicago, 1997*, a report prepared in November 1998 for the Chicago Convention and Tourism Bureau and the Chicago Office of Tourism.

17. In *Fantasy City: Pleasure and Profit in the Postmodern Metropolis* (London: Routledge, 1998), John Hannigan examines the reconfiguration of inner cities to sell atmosphere and experiences.

18. John Huebner, "Whose Blues Will They Choose?" *Chicago Reader*, December 1, 2000, 1, 18-31. Huebner presents a thorough and well-informed ac-

count of the controversy over the planned blues strip and its larger implications for the South Side, Chicago, and postindustrial city life.

19. Bruce Iglauer, quoted in Bill Dedman, "Chicago: For Fans of the Blues, It's No Heartbreak Hotel," *New York Times,* December 6, 1998, 16.

20. Bruce Iglauer, quoted in Wilcock with Guy, *Damn Right,* 107.

21. Davis, *The History of the Blues,* 84.

22. Iglauer insisted that he was not proposing a crude racial essentialism. Later he made a list of white people who in his opinion can sing the blues. "Lonnie Mack, for instance. Grew up as a dirt farmer in southern Indiana, a hillbilly, and he would say he was a hillbilly. I kind of like the way Jonny Lang sings. A little overmelodramatic, but boy can he hold a pitch and he can bend a note. I grew to like the way Stevie sang, even though it's all ripped off from Doyle Bramhall Sr. I like the way Doyle Bramhall Sr. sings. I like the way a lot of country guys sing blues. I like the way Elvis sang blues; Carl Perkins too. Amongst people who grew up culturally like I am, though, almost no one can do it."

23. Steve Waksman's *Instruments of Desire: The Electric Guitar and the Shaping of Musical Experience* (Cambridge, Mass.: Harvard University Press, 2000) considers the rise of the electric guitar and its commanding role in rock.

24. Jas Obrecht, "Buddy Guy," in *Blues Guitar: The Men Who Made the Music,* ed. Jas Obrecht (San Francisco: Miller Freeman, 1993), 205.

3. GRITTINESS

Pauline Kael is quoted from her review "Urban Gothic," *New Yorker,* October 30, 1971, 113.

1. "The archetypal film of the period might well be *The French Connection;* it certainly was the most successful and imitated," asserts Carlos Clarens in *Crime Movies* (New York: Da Capo, 1997), 311. As early as 1974, Stephen Farber observed that "the phenomenally successful *Dirty Harry* and *The French Connection* have spawned a couple of dozen police movies" ("Violence and the Bitch Goddess," *Film Comment* 10, no. 6 [November–December 1974]: 8). When the DVD of *The French Connection* was released in 2001, the *New York Times* described the movie as having "largely set the standard for crime drama ever since" its original theatrical release thirty years earlier. Bruce Goldstein, repertory director of New York's Film Forum, called it "the best action film of the modern era" (Peter M. Nichols, "Super Tuesday of Big Hits," *New York Times,* September 14, 2001, D20). One testimony to the lasting influence of *The French Connection* can be found in Steven Soderbergh's assertions that he had Friedkin's movie firmly in mind, and watched it often, when making *Traffic* almost thirty years later. During an interview on the National Public Radio program *Fresh Air* (aired on WBUR, Boston on January 7, 2001), Soderbergh repeated these assertions and also mentioned the influence of *Z* and *The Battle of Algiers,* both of which shaped Friedkin's ambitions for *The French Connection.* Another, weirder instance of *The French Connection*'s continuing influence on

Hollywood's capacity to imagine cities and crime can be found in Oliver Stone's description of the movie he would like to make about the attacks on New York and Washington of September 11, 2001. Stone said he had in mind "a bullet of a film about terrorism, like *The Battle of Algiers*," that combined directorial sympathy for the perpetrators with satellite-tracking special effects and a post-1960s malaise theme, all delivered with "a *French Connection* urgency" (Stone quoted in Tad Friend, "Oliver Stone's Chaos Theory," *New Yorker*, October 22, 2001, 25–26).

2. James Monaco, "Why Is Kojak So Tough?" *More*, February 1977, 42.

3. Mark Kermode and Russell Leven shot many hours of interviews with people who worked on *The French Connection* for a one-hour BBC documentary, *Poughkeepsie Shuffle: Tracing the French Connection*. Kermode and Leven generously shared transcripts of this mostly unaired footage with me, and I quote from those transcripts with their gracious permission.

4. Pauline Kael ("Urban Gothic," 116) saw a "right-wing, left-wing, take-your-choice cynicism" in the movie, amounting to "total commercial opportunism passing itself off as an Existential view." Gary Arnold, in the *Washington Post* (November 12, 1971), argued that Popeye Doyle "outdoes the screen *Patton* at agitating on both sides of the socio-political street." Others sought to put the movie's politics on one side of the street or the other. Stephen Farber ("Violence and the Bitch Goddess," 8) lumped it with *Dirty Harry* as "implicitly fascist" in its "celebration of vigilante justice" and "respect for the 'order' provided by a billy club." Others took a similar line of approach: Garrett Epps asked, "Does Popeye Doyle Teach Us How to Be Fascist?" (*New York Times*, May 21, 1972, sec. II, 15); Michael Shedlin, in "Police Oscar: The French Connection," *Film Quarterly* 25, no. 4 (summer 1972): 2–3, called it "rightist propaganda" moving beneath the veneer of a liberal "social comment" film. (Those who took this view could also point to the sinister fact that G. David Schine, a onetime aide to Senator McCarthy, received an executive producer's credit, although he had little or nothing to do with making the movie.) Andrew Sarris, in the *Village Voice* (October 21, 1971), took the contrary position, finding instead that the movie naively intimates "an inevitable bloodbath between the personalized premises of capitalism (sell to the highest bidder for the highest profit and damn the social consequences) and puritanism (save people from their own vices even if you have to blow out their brains to do it)" (Arnold and Sarris are quoted in *Film Facts* 14, no. 14 [1971]: 331–333).

5. There was a car-train "chase" during the French Connection investigation, but it was an unremarkable event with very little cinematic promise: the cops hurried crosstown to catch up with a suspect on the Times Square–Grand Central subway shuttle (not an elevated train). The chase in the movie owes its existence entirely to the producer's and director's ambition to top the car chase in *Bullitt*.

6. The setting of *The French Connection*'s final shootout, the ruins of a large industrial bakery on Randall's Island, reasserts the outlines of that epic one last time: in this city they made bread; now they sell junk and kill each other.

7. Claude Brown, *Manchild in the Promised Land* (New York: Macmillan, 1965), 179, 253.

8. Sean McCann has helped me to see how central the status and maintenance of the liberal welfare state have been to the crime genres' political imagination. See, e.g., Sean McCann, *Gumshoe America: Hardboiled Crime Fiction and the Rise and Fall of New Deal Liberalism* (Durham, N.C.: Duke University Press, 2000); and Sean McCann, ed., *Crime and the State: Narratives of Violence, Government, and the Law* (Minneapolis: University of Minnesota Press, forthcoming).

9. In the last chapter of *Gunfighter Nation: The Myth of the Frontier in Twentieth-Century America* (New York: Atheneum, 1992), 624–660, Richard Slotkin offers a definitive account of what he calls the crisis and subsequent reconstitution of public myth during and after the 1960s. It bears noting that the movement of Western stars, characters, plots, and formulas to the postindustrial inner city in the 1970s was part of this crisis-and-reconstitution, and that this process recapitulated a similar urbanization of Western genre elements in response to the maturing *industrial* city in the latter part of the nineteenth century.

10. A Salvatore A. Grosso lived at 231 Hopkins Street in 1955, but Sonny Grosso says, "I never heard of any family around there. If he's a relation, I don't know about it. My father died, and I didn't know his side as well. I'll be straight with you, I don't know." He added, "Now, if Eddie was alive and you'd asked him the same kind of question about some guy named Egan, he would have said, 'Yeah, sure, that's my uncle!' Whatever would be a good story, whatever you wanted to hear—that's what he would have said."

11. This reconstruction was done using insurance maps, census maps, and telephone directories in the New York Public Library, supplemented by the extensive collection of block-by-block photographs at the Municipal Archives of New York.

12. The need for graininess and grittiness may not have survived the moment of the movie's making. Roizman told me that, watching a video of the movie recently, he was shocked to see how little of the force-developed grainy effect survived the video transfer. "It looks," he said, "like somebody gave it more vivid colors, rich blacks, to try to get a more 'normal' look." How post-1970s.

13. Kael's review was typical in linking the movie's stylistic qualities to its importance as a portrait of the contemporary city. There was much talk of "gritty realism" (*Time*, November 1, 1971, 109), "the palpable air of a tough city" (*Films and Filming* 18, no. 6 [March 1972]: 50), and the like, the point being that William Friedkin had come up with "a very good new kind of movie" uniquely suited to its subject and moment: "The central characters repeatedly appear as if out of the city's mass and then disappear into it again" (*New York Times*, October 8, 1971, 35). Richard Schickel, in *Life* (November 19, 1971, 13), called it "a very good street picture. You can taste the pollution in the air his characters breathe, smell the garbage that seems always to be overflowing its container. And the cold, that god-awful damp, biting cold of the place in midwinter. . . ." Schickel concluded that Hackman's Popeye Doyle comes "closer to the real thing . . . than any other movie detective I've ever seen."

14. I have explored this transformation of writing about cities in *October Cities: The Redevelopment of Urban Literature* (Berkeley and Los Angeles: University of California Press, 1998).

15. I found the story of Commissioner Valentine in Christopher Wilson's *Cop Knowledge: Police Power and Cultural Narrative in Twentieth-Century America* (Chicago: University of Chicago Press, 2000), 93, which examines from a variety of enlightening angles the relationship between policing and authoritative storytelling.

16. For greater detail about the economic importance of film production in postindustrial New York, see two reports: Port Authority of New York and New Jersey and Cultural Assistance Center, Inc., "The Arts as an Industry: Their Economic Importance to the New York–New Jersey Metropolitan Region" (New York: Cultural Assistance Center, 1983); Exploring the Metropolis, Inc., "The Entertainment Arts Industry in New York, Part 3: The Film and Video Industry—A Profile" (New York: Exploring the Metropolis, 1997).

17. "Mayor Lindsay Charms H'wood, But Did He Sell 'Em N.Y. as Location?" *Variety,* November 22, 1967, 1, 10. The mayoral papers collected at the Municipal Archives of New York show evidence that Lindsay's and, later, Ed Koch's efforts particularly benefited William Friedkin over the years. When Friedkin was shooting *The Night They Raided Minsky's,* Lindsay delayed the scheduled demolition of the north side of East Twenty-sixth Street between First and Second Avenues so that Friedkin's set designers could redo the block in 1920s style ("Making Films in New York," Lindsay Papers, Confidential Subjects, 1966–1973, Box 8, Folder 99). In 1979, Nancy Littlefield, director of the Office of Motion Pictures and Television, wrote a letter to Mayor Koch commending Lieutenant Paul Glanzman, who headed "our special movie Police Tactical Unit," for his work during the filming of Friedkin's *Cruising.* The movie's volatile subject matter whipped up considerable resentment, and "were it not for the personal efforts of Lt. Glanzman during the actual filming, a great deal more of the ugly confrontations and possibly even more violence would have taken place." Littlefield concluded that "the all-out effort to complete the filming of 'Cruising' without mishap demonstrated that there is no lack of cooperation on the City's part in assisting them in production in New York despite many obstacles" (Littlefield to Koch, September 25, 1979, Koch Papers, Departmental Correspondence, 1978–1989, Box 219, Folder 11). The Lindsay papers also suggest that the mayor enjoyed a cozy relationship with David Brown, one of the executives at Twentieth Century-Fox responsible for *The French Connection* (Lindsay-Brown letters of May 11, May 25, and November 10, 1971, Lindsay Papers, Confidential Subjects, 1966–1973, Box 8, Folder 99). Two other documents of note in those files are a request to the mayor from a subordinate, Christine Conrad, to set aside part of the old First Precinct for location shooting ("Precincts of a certain vintage are disappearing rapidly and we are often hard pressed to come up with precincts that have the right look") and Conrad's "Report on Filming in Harlem," which reeks of its historical moment. Shakedowns of film companies shooting *Shaft's Big Score, Across 110th Street,* and *Come Back, Charleston Blue* were undermining "the glorious promise of

lots of production in Harlem," and Conrad expressed serious doubt about the ability of the police "to insure trouble free filming in Harlem during the summer months without the possibility of a major conflict developing." She concluded that city government "cannot be in the position of recommending that a film company pay off to insure peace" (Conrad to Lindsay, January 18, 1973, and May 19, 1972, Lindsay Papers, Confidential Subjects, 1966–1973, Box 8, Folder 99).

18. See, e.g., Nat Segaloff, *Hurricane Billy: The Stormy Life and Films of William Friedkin* (New York: William Morrow, 1990), 110–113; and two biographies of Gene Hackman that make extensive use of collected magazine interviews: Michael Munn, *Gene Hackman* (London: Robert Hale, 1997), 50–54; Allan Hunter, *Gene Hackman* (London: W. H. Allen, 1987), 66–72.

19. See, e.g., Munn, *Gene Hackman,* 52–53; Hunter, *Gene Hackman,* 70–71.

20. Kael, "Urban Gothic," 114.

21. Clarens, *Crime Movies,* 293–294; David E. James, *Allegories of Cinema: American Film in the Sixties* (Princeton, N.J.: Princeton University Press, 1989), 25–28; Gerald Mast, *A Short History of the Movies,* 4th ed. (New York: Macmillan, 1986), 422–442.

22. Bill Ornstein, "Bill Friedkin Sees Plotted Picture on Way Out; Youth Wants Abstract," *Hollywood Reporter,* April 6, 1967, 3.

23. Segaloff, *Hurricane Billy,* 101.

24. As Friedkin himself will freely admit, it is not difficult to amass descriptions of his bad behavior in the 1970s. One might begin with Segaloff's *Hurricane Billy* and Thomas D. Clagett's *William Friedkin: Films of Aberration, Obsession, and Reality* (Jefferson, N.C.: MacFarland, 1990), but the definitive guide to the swinish behavior of Friedkin and his peers in the New Hollywood—many of whom seemed to believe that a real artist must act like an auxiliary member of Led Zeppelin on tour—is Peter Biskind's *Easy Riders and Raging Bulls: How the Sex-Drugs-and-Rock 'n' Roll Generation Saved Hollywood* (New York: Simon and Schuster, 1998).

25. In the course of our conversations, Friedkin claimed that Steven Spielberg, Stephen Bochco, and John Woo—to name three influential figures—had all told him how much his work had influenced them. Even if Friedkin made up or exaggerated such encounters, he may well be right to see *The French Connection*'s pacing (and Roy Scheider as a cop) in *Jaws* and its camera style in *Hill Street Blues,* and to see its overmatched ambiguous police heroes as well as its action-movie pattern of set pieces and stylish lulls in Woo's Hong Kong movies. In a perceptive article that described William Friedkin as "a man of the '70s," Larry Gross reminded readers, "It's tough to grasp how completely Friedkin's two early successes, *The French Connection* (1971) and *The Exorcist* (1973), helped create the idiom of serious/popular Hollywood filmmaking over the last 25 years." He especially underscores Friedkin's effect on Spielberg, who "borrowed Linda Blair's powers" from *The Exorcist* "for the funny aliens and monsters in *Close Encounters of the Third Kind, E.T. the Extra-Terrestrial,* and *Jurassic Park.* I'm not exactly saying Friedkin is owed royalties on Spielberg's billions of

dollars-worth of hits, but it's close" (Larry Gross, "Whatever Happened to William Friedkin?" *Sight and Sound* 5 [December 1995]: 14–15).

26. To say Friedkin has mellowed since the 1970s is not to say that he has lost interest in his own legend. Like others who worked on *The French Connection,* he lets himself get carried away by his enthusiasm for the film and its star-making consequences. Moviemakers, like cops, are so professionally and temperamentally programmed to produce a good story (moviemakers do it to make art and money, cops to make cases and to avoid getting in trouble for questionable behavior) that they tend to make a story good even if it means cutting corners around the facts—which, unlike what the movie industry and the courts regard as a good story, usually resist the imposition of neat, conclusive form. The filming of *The French Connection* has become particularly silted over with legend and exaggeration. Friedkin's account of the famous car chase, for instance, plays up how daring and uncompromising he was in pursuit of the perfect take. He maintains that most of the footage was shot in uncontrolled traffic without police escort or clearance or even a siren, that Bill Hickman often drove seventy to ninety miles per hour (exceeding ninety miles per hour in a twenty-six-block death run through crowded streets that became the scene's master shot), and that the camera was never undercranked to accentuate the audience's sense of the car's speed. (Friedkin has told this story more times than he can remember; he told it twice to me in one interview. Soon after making the movie, he told it most completely in "Anatomy of a Chase," *Action* 7, no. 2 [March/April 1972]: 8–19.) Grosso and Jurgensen say the top speed was more like sixty miles per hour; Owen Roizman says that, except for the one famous master-shot take that "might have gotten up to sixty" and was done on uncleared streets but with a siren (Jurgensen claims there was no siren), they shot the chase at much slower speeds on cleared streets in choreographed traffic, with the camera often undercranking at twenty frames per second instead of twenty-four. In Friedkin's account of his ride-alongs with the cops, they gave him a gun, a potent image of the maverick director as authentic cop; Grosso confirms that story, but Jurgensen says they just gave him a badge, which takes more than half of the charge out of the image. Friedkin says that when they first began shooting the movie, they did thirty-seven takes of the interrogation at the end of the Santa chase without getting it right—and that with each take Alan Weeks, playing the suspect, became more bruised and Gene Hackman became more unwilling to hit him—but that later in the shoot they returned to the scene and got it done on the first take. Perhaps. More likely, they did more than one take the second time and fewer than thirty-seven takes the first time. Friedkin himself told his biographer they did thirty-two (Segaloff, *Hurricane Billy,* 112); Hackman remembers only that they did "more than 27" (Munn, *Gene Hackman,* 53). Some hairs are not worth splitting. Even if the numbers thirty-seven and one are exaggerations, what Friedkin tried to impress upon me by telling the story still has validity: he, his crew, and the actors had to find their way into the movie's style; their emphasis on improvising from true-life examples raised real bruises on real bodies; and once they mastered that style, it became second

nature to them. More generally, the fact that Friedkin (among others) tends to embroider his memories does not invalidate his accounts of making the movie, but those accounts must be treated as well-made stories demanding interpretation in their own right.

27. Perhaps sensing my need to revisit childhood traumas associated with Garfield Goose, Friedkin went on to describe Frazier Thomas, Garfield's human costar, as "a terrible guy." This last confirmed an old suspicion. The fiendishly smug Thomas acted as if he understood Garfield, a hand puppet of rudimentary design who produced no other sound than the futile clacking of his beak when he tried to talk. As a child, I had suspected that Thomas only pretended to understand what Garfield was saying, or that he did understand but was cruelly misinterpreting the mute goose's desperate appeals for help in order to torment him. It always seemed to me that Thomas could not wait for the cameras to stop rolling so he could drain a pint and give the goose a knuckle sandwich. "The guy who did the puppet hated him," added Friedkin. "A stupid show."

28. On editing *The French Connection,* Friedkin told me: "I tell him where to put the frame. Very often I mark the frames. To take nothing away from Jerry Greenberg, it was his first editing job. He was an assistant on *The Boys in the Band* to Carl Lerner, who I learned a lot from in editing, but what I also learned was nobody can edit for me, nobody knows the pace I want. Jerry Greenberg did an assembly of *The French Connection*—I thought I'd kill myself. And I then went back, and we redid it frame for frame." On the screenplay: "There was no real script with that dialogue in it, ever. After the fact, the script was made up. Ernest Tidyman, may he rest in peace, did not write this script. It was mostly put together from tape-recorded stuff by me with Eddie and Sonny, and Jimmy Breslin's ad-libs, when he auditioned." (Both Grosso and Owen Roizman say that Tidyman wrote a workable skeleton script to which the various local experts added flesh.) To the extent that Friedkin describes a close, fluid working relationship with multiple collaborators, his account seems to have some validity. To the extent that he makes a belated grab for Greenberg's and Tidyman's Oscars by continuing his sustained effort to minimize their contributions, his account asks to be dismissed as too self-interested to be reliable.

29. See note 4.

30. Segaloff, *Hurricane Billy,* 23.

31. Jurgensen and Grosso were intimately involved in the investigation of the murder of Officer Phil Cardillo during a melee at the Harlem Mosque on April 14, 1972. During the riot that occurred outside the mosque as police converged on the crime scene, Jurgensen was badly injured when a thrown object hit him in the head. He and Grosso worked devotedly for months to make the case against their prime suspect, Louis 17X Dupree, and both felt that Dupree ultimately got away with killing a cop because their incompetent or politically motivated superiors impeded the case's progress.

32. Wilson, *Cop Knowledge,* 101.

33. Pete Hamill, interview with Gene Hackman, *Film Comment* 10, no. 5 (September–October 1974): 41.

4. ROCKY MARCIANO'S GHOST

Patricia Johanson, "Architecture as Landscape" (*The Princeton Journal: Thematic Studies in Architecture* 2 [1985]), is in Lucy Lippard's catalog essay "The Long View: Patricia Johanson's Projects, 1969–1986," in Debra Bricker Balken, *Patricia Johanson: Drawings and Models for Environmental Projects, 1969–1986* (Pittsfield, Mass.: Berkshire Museum, 1987), 9.

1. An obscure Danish heavyweight named Brian Nielsen reached the 49–0 mark in the 1990s by beating third- and fourth-rate competition. His only victory of note was an egregious hometown decision over the forty-seven-year-old Larry Holmes in Copenhagen in 1993—although Nielsen, his employees (a group to which the ringside judges could well be accused of belonging), and members of the Danish sporting press were nearly alone in failing to acknowledge that the superannuated Holmes had decisively outboxed and outscored Nielsen. Nevertheless, Nielsen sought to break Marciano's record in June 1999 when he entered the ring against a roadworn journeyman from Omaha named Dickie Ryan. But Nielsen's new trainer, hoping to reduce his fighter's suet-battened middle so he would look good on television in this audition for a chance to serve as a patsy for Mike Tyson, had ordered Nielsen to run around in a rubber suit to lose weight the day before the fight. Nielsen, who had little stamina to begin with, became dehydrated during the bout, and Ryan wore him out with body punches, scoring a tenth-round TKO. Nielsen's record fell to 49–1. Fight people reminded one another that somebody up there appeared to like Rocky Marciano.

2. Rocky Balboa is, among other things, a fantasy on the theme of Rocky Marciano. Sylvester Stallone fulfilled in fiction the prayerful wish arising in certain quarters for Marciano, or an avatar of him, to rise up from the urban village (Brockton's Ward 2 in Marciano's case, South Philly in Balboa's), returning to action to give Muhammad Ali a taste of old-school white-ethnic manhood. Casual observers probably make too much of race in boxing, and therefore of the intermittently recurring desire for a White Hope to give a black heavyweight champion his comeuppance, but that desire does have a long history reaching back at least to the first decade of the twentieth century, when Jack London and others voiced a hope that Jim Jeffries would return from retirement to give Jack Johnson a taste of Anglo-Saxon manhood. (A few years after *Rocky* was released in 1976, this desire took fresh form in the hope that Marciano would be reincarnated in Gerry Cooney, who was expected to give champion Larry Holmes a taste of Irish manhood.) *Rocky*, partaking of this tradition, identifies Rocky's opponent, Apollo Creed, as a fictional projection of Muhammad Ali. Creed, the champion, is a master showman, an astute businessman of the television age, much faster than Rocky with both his hands and his mouth, and given to pointing with gloved hand while delivering mock-poetic japes à la Ali. The movie identifies Rocky Balboa, similarly, as a fictional projection of Marciano—endearingly inarticulate, slow but indestructible. "You remind me of the Rock," says Balboa's trainer, Mick. "You move like him,

you got heart like he did." Mick tries to improve Balboa's footwork by making him train while hobbled at the ankles with a string: "Now Marciano had the same problem," he says, "and this string cured him." Balboa's other training techniques—running with bricks in his hands, punching sides of frozen beef hanging in a meat locker—reference Marciano's often improvised methods and their labor-related resonances. Balboa keeps his pet fish in a bowl next to a picture of Marciano in his apartment. When he says, "How you doin', Moby Dick," he seems to be talking not to the fish but to pugilism's undefeated, undisputed White Whale.

3. Everett Skehan, *Rocky Marciano* (London: Robson Books, 1983), 38.

4. City of Brockton, Massachusetts, "Comprehensive Policy Plan" (1998; updated April 15, 1999), 3.

5. Walter F. Carroll, *Brockton: From Rural Parish to Urban Center* (Northridge, Calif.: Windsor Publications, 1989), 57–64.

6. Armond Colombo, quoted in Frank Dell'Appa, "Football Takes the Field as High School Season Opens," *Boston Globe,* September 10, 1989, South Weekly, 1, 12.

7. For a full account of the incident and its aftermath, see Scott S. Greenberger, "Principal Says He Chose the Lesser Evil," *Boston Globe,* June 7, 2001, B1, B9.

8. Frank Keefe's recipe for urban comebacks is part of a larger turn toward urban planning inspired by Jane Jacobs and other critics of postwar planning orthodoxy. For formulas on the same model, see, e.g., Roberta Brandes Gratz with Norman Mintz, *Cities Back from the Edge: New Life for Downtown* (New York: Wiley, 1998); Roberta Brandes Gratz, *The Living City: How America's Cities Are Being Revitalized by Thinking Small in a Big Way* (New York: Simon and Schuster, 1989); Paul S. Grogan and Tony Proscio, *Comeback Cities: A Blueprint for Neighborhood Revival* (Boulder, Colo.: Westview, 2000).

9. Patricia Johanson, "La Ville comme forme d'art écologique," *Les Annales de la récherche urbaine* 85 (December 1999): 171–75. I have quoted from Johanson's original unpaginated English manuscript (in her private papers), which was then translated into French. Johanson has also described her strategic plan for Brockton in another article, "Brockton Reborn," *Sanctuary: The Journal of the Massachusetts Audubon Society* 38, no. 2 (November–December 1998): 1, 15–16.

10. Johanson, "La Ville," English original.

11. Johanson's private papers, cited by Debra Bricker Balken, "Patricia Johanson: The House and Garden Commissions, Before and After," in Balken, *Patricia Johanson: Drawings and Models,* 19.

12. William Zimmer, "The Viable Vision of Patricia Johanson," in Patricia Johanson, *Patricia Johanson: Public Landscapes* (Philadelphia: Painted Bride Arts Center, 1991), 3.

13. Lucy R. Lippard, *The Lure of the Local: Senses of Place in a Multicentered Society* (New York: Free Press, 1997), 273, 275. Susan Leibovitz Steinman includes Johanson in her "Compendium" of about a hundred artists doing "new genre public art"; see Suzanne Lacy, ed., *Mapping the Terrain: New Genre Public Art* (Seattle: Bay Press, 1995), 245–246.

14. Mary Julius, "City Gets Funds for Marciano Project," *Brockton Enterprise,* September 9, 1998, A1.

15. The decorated-fiberglass-animal public art craze started with cows in Switzerland, then the cow idea acquired a stockyard whiff of industrial nostalgia when Lois Weisberg imported it to Chicago. The phenomenon gathered momentum from there: copycat cows in New York, pigs in the old hog-killing mecca of Cincinnati, catfish in New Orleans, flamingos in Miami, ears of corn in Des Moines, moose in Toronto, horses in Rochester, and Mr. Potato Heads in Providence, courtesy of the Hasbro toy company, which is headquartered in nearby Pawtucket.

16. Johanson, "La Ville," English original.

17. Ibid.

18. Stanley Bauman, the Brockton photographer who took so many pictures of Rocky Marciano, also took a much-reproduced picture of a woman swimming across the intersection of Sycamore Avenue and Belmont Avenue during a major flood at this site. It is reproduced as it usually is, without context other than a mention of heavy rainfall, in Carroll, *Brockton,* 89. Johanson also reproduces the picture in "La Ville," 172, but she uses it to illustrate the effects of building unwisely on a floodplain.

19. Patricia Johanson, working site description in her private papers.

20. For more on the relationship between the industrial metropolis and nature, see William Cronon, *Nature's Metropolis: Chicago and the Great West* (New York: Norton, 1991).

21. See Jack Sullivan, "A Rocky Proposal," *Boston Herald,* May 28, 1998, 1, 18. The inside headline on page 18 was "Artist Saves Rock's Home from Hitting the Canvas."

22. Winthrop Farwell, who was mayor of Brockton in 1993, stirred up a debate by moving a painting of Marvin Hagler from a city hall meeting room to the building's basement. Farwell said that the city had "to send a clear message that domestic violence is unacceptable." But the Reverend Michael Wayne Walker and others accused Farwell of maintaining a racial double standard. "No one would dream of treating Rocky Marciano like this," said Walker; others pointed out that even though Brockton's nonwhite population had reached 22.3 percent by 1990 (and 43 percent of the public schools' rolls), the city council and the school committee were both all white. A Brockton official requesting anonymity pointed out to a reporter that Hagler's image in the painting was "still the only prominent black face in City Hall." See Michael Grunwald, "Shifting Site of Hagler Painting Stirs a Fight," *Boston Globe,* July 17, 1993, 1, 38.

CONCLUSION. GETTING THERE

1. Bob Fletcher, a fulminator against the New World Order who refers to himself as "Mister Fletcher," has enjoyed intermittent prominence on AM talk radio in recent years. According to Fletcher, he was an innocent toy manufacturer in Georgia until a shady business partner, who turned out to be a high-ranking

covert intelligence agent, dragged him into the margins of the Iran-Contra affair. This experience opened his eyes to the existence of a fantastically far-reaching, centuries-old conspiracy to rule the world involving the Illuminati, the Rothschilds, the Rockefellers, the Bolsheviks, the Nazis, the United Nations, the Council on Foreign Relations, the Trilateral Commission, and almost every world leader. The conspirators exert near-total control with a variety of secret technologies—weather-making machines, plasma weapons, injectable transponders—but Mr. Fletcher and his associates in the militia movement continue to defy them.

2. Donn Esmonde, "It's a No-Brainer: The Erie Canal Site Is a Piece of History and Must Be Preserved," *Buffalo News,* June 11, 2000, H1, H4.

3. George Packer argued a similar point about the resemblance of the casino floor to an assembly line in a great essay on casino gambling, "Read 'Em and Weep," *Dissent* 42 (summer 1995): 393–396.

INDEX

Indexer:	Carol Roberts
Compositor:	G & S Typesetters, Inc.
Text:	10/13 Galliard
Display:	Helvetica and Galliard
Printer and Binder:	Sheridan Books